TRAVELS IN ATOMIC SUNSHINE

Robin Gerster is a professor in the School of Languages, Literatures, Cultures and Linguistics at Monash University. He is the author of several books, including the award-winning study *Big-noting: the heroic theme in Australian war writing* (1987); the travel book *Legless in Ginza: orientating Japan* (1999); the critical anthologies *Hotel Asia* (1995) and *On the Warpath* (2004), and *Pacific Exposures: photography and the Australia-Japan relationship* (2018), co-authored with Melissa Miles.

His articles have been published extensively in scholarly journals in both Australia and abroad, and he has been a frequent writer of travel pieces for newspapers and magazines.

TRAVELS IN ATOMIC SUNSHINE

AUSTRALIA AND THE OCCUPATION OF JAPAN

ROBIN GERSTER

SCRIBE

Melbourne • London

Scribe Publications
18–20 Edward St, Brunswick, Victoria 3056, Australia
2 John St, Clerkenwell, London, WC1N 2ES, United Kingdom
3754 Pleasant Ave, Suite 100, Minneapolis, Minnesota 55409, USA

First published by Scribe 2008
This edition published 2019

Typeset in 12/15.6 pt Adobe Garamond by the publishers

Printed and bound in Australia by Griffin Press, part of Ovato

Scribe Publications is committed to the sustainable use of natural
resources and the use of paper products made responsibly from
those resources.

9781925849370 (Australian edition)
9781912854448 (UK edition)
9781950354030 (US edition)
9781925113204 (e-book)

Catalogue records for this book are available from the National Library of Australia
and the British Library.

scribepublications.com.au
scribepublications.co.uk
scribepublications.com

To Bill Gater and Teruaki Fujishiro

an old soldier
lodged in our house
tells a war story
that says nothing
about killing an enemy
Zenmaro Toki

What else is there in Japan? Old men making pots
moulded of ash from the bomb,
bearing MacArthur's thumbprint.
Elizabeth Riddell

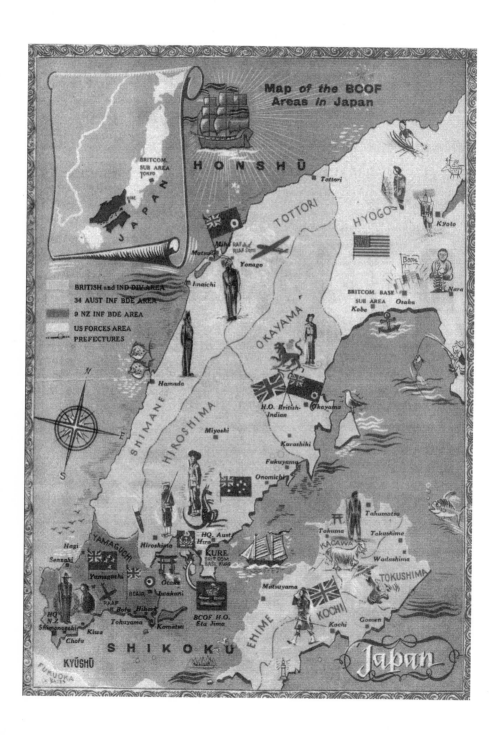

Contents

Part IV
Embracing Japan: conquest and contact

Occupying Japan

I n Hiroshima, they say that the best view of the fabled isles of Japan's Inland Sea is to be had downtown, from the 'Sky Lounge' on the 33rd floor of the Rhiga Royal Hotel. It seems a tactless thing to call something in Hiroshima, of all places – oblivious to the bolt from the blue that struck just after 8.00 a.m. on 6 August 1945, when the *Enola Gay* flew across the sky of a perfect summer's morning and dropped a 4000-kilogram atomic bomb called 'Little Boy', incinerating the city and much of its population. Nevertheless, the bar attracts tourists as well as drinkers. The panorama is indeed spectacular, although on a day of dazzling sunshine the distant islands appear to sit on the sheen of water like lumps of molten and solidified metal.

The spectator's gaze settles first on Miyajima, lying just off the mainland in Hiroshima Bay. Armies of sightseers are ferried there daily, paying their respects to the ancient Shinto shrine Itsukushima, with its photogenic vermillion *torii*, which, seeming to float out at sea, provides an idealised image of Japan as familiar

1

as snow-capped Mt Fuji. At low tide, visitors are disappointed to find the enormous structure rooted in a field of wet mud. The island itself has been venerated for centuries. Once, neither birth nor burial were permitted to defile its sacred ground. Expectant mothers were shunted off to the mainland and remained there for weeks, for 'purification' after delivery. Even today, burial and cremation are prohibited; they bury or burn their dead on the opposite shore. Adjacent to Miyajima, tiny Ninoshima is as associated with death as the other island is with life. During the chaotic aftermath of the atomic bombing, thousands of the grievously suffering made their way to the island to die. They perished in caves, or on open ground; the corpses were so numerous that the customary cremation rites were dispensed with and bodies were piled into vast burial plots. Mass graves were excavated as late as the 1970s. A little further east lies Etajima, the home of the Imperial Naval Academy and a short boat trip from the naval base at Kure, Japan's most important since the 1880s. Etajima miraculously survived the American aerial attacks that gutted the Chugoku region of southwestern Honshu during the weeks leading up to that cataclysmic moment when 'Little Boy' both wiped out Hiroshima and forever placed it, notoriously, on the world map.

The 'new and terrible weapon' – as the Japanese emperor Hirohito described it in mid-August 1945, when accepting the Allies' demand for an unconditional surrender – did the job for which it was intended. Six months later, the men of the British Commonwealth Occupation Force (BCOF) were handed the task of 'demilitarising and democratising' the remote and ravaged Hiroshima region. The omnipotent ruler of post-war Japan, the United States, had gifted it to its wartime allies, none of whom was more enthusiastically committed to the occupation of its recent and still deeply despised enemy than Australia. BCOF entered a literally explosive environment for, when the war ended, the islands of the Inland Sea were honeycombed with tunnels containing thousands of tonnes of sequestered ammunition, armaments, and deadly chemicals, some of which had not yet been located and destroyed. On the mainland, the ruin and despair were pervasive. Orphans had made homes in wreckage; people were living on their wits, or however they could. The only thing to thrive was prostitution. After their wartime travails, the Occupationnaires, most of them veterans of the bloody conflict that had just been brought to such an abrupt conclusion, appeared to have arrived at the end of the world.

The first convoy of the Australian contingent of BCOF disembarked at Kure in early February 1946. Volunteers in the national military tradition, they had come from the tropical swelter of the battle theatres of the South-West Pacific into the fag end of one of the bitterest Japanese winters in history. The 'nip in the air', as some of the men were amused to call it, seemed to be matched by the cool indifference of the Japanese welcome. To a young West Australian soldier, T.A.G. Hungerford, the arrival was one of pure tourist bathos. The day-long journey up the Inland Sea aboard the SS *Stamford Victory* had seemed like a voyage though an illustrated brochure called 'Beautiful Japan: a day in the Thousand Islands': the seas sparkled, the gulls wheeled, little fishing vessels bobbed in the wake of the troopship. But Kure was a letdown: young Australians who had dreamt of a noisy, triumphal conqueror's welcome arrived at a city that had taken a terrific pounding by Allied incendiary bombing. Dry-docks and warehouses had been reduced to rubble; the harbour was a shipping graveyard, a morass of twisted metal. They marched into a silent city. Sidewalks and roads were deserted; winter temperatures had plummeted to record lows. Nonplussed soldiers trudged to their billet through a 'Dali landscape of solids blasted and melted and seared into eerie plastic shapes of petrified flame', and bedded down in a plaster-and-lath former office block whose doors had been blown out and windows blown in.[1]

Distant Hiroshima and its desolate surrounds were a world away from Occupation General Headquarters (GHQ) in central

Tokyo. Much of the wooden-built capital had been obliterated by the ruthless American firebombing of 9–10 March 1945, an urban holocaust that consumed 100,000 lives and left more than a million homeless. But the fashionable uptown areas of pre-war Tokyo, around Ginza and Marunouchi, were surprisingly intact. From here, the US set about reconstructing and redeeming the Japanese with a missionary zeal – 'democratising the hell out of them', as one cynic observed. The epicentre of American power was the suite of offices of SCAP, the Supreme Commander for the Allied Powers, General Douglas MacArthur. These were situated on the top floor of the neo-classical Dai-Ichi Mutual Life Insurance building, pointedly overlooking the moat of the Imperial Palace, in an enclave dubbed 'Little America'. The Americans redrew the very cartography of Tokyo to make themselves feel at home, after their arrival in September 1945. Soon, the old military parade grounds in Yoyogi would be taken over for family housing and renamed 'Washington Heights'. Senior officers resided in Frank Lloyd Wright's Imperial Hotel, located on a boulevard redesignated First Avenue, just along the way from MacArthur's HQ. At the famous, endlessly photographed intersection in Ginza, the elegant Hattori building was converted into a 'PX', the Eighth Army Post Exchange, selling tax-free consumer goods to the cashed-up GI, from cameras to diamond rings. At the PX grill, he could feast on Coke, milkshakes, hot dogs, French fries, and (in a nice touch) 'B-29 burgers'.[2]

Meanwhile, nearly 900 kilometres to the west, the Australians had started settling in to their atom-bombed backwater in their thousands. They were mobilised in what was technically a non-combat environment, though it was not one of peace, either, at least until the Treaty of Peace with Japan (signed in San Francisco in September 1951) came into force in April 1952. The Occupation was a major military commitment lasting nearly seven years – longer than the conflict that preceded it.

Composed of the 34th Australian Infantry Brigade, a British-

Indian division, a brigade of New Zealanders, substantial air and naval components, along with various support and administrative units, BCOF totalled nearly 40,000 men at its maximum strength, at the end of 1946 – just over one-quarter the size of the US force. At that time, around 12,000 of these were Australians, though the overall total swelled to at least 17,000 (official numbers are perplexingly inexact). The death toll was small, but not insignificant: 77 deaths were recorded among the Australian contingent. Additionally, nearly 500 wives of Australian servicemen, with over 600 children in tow, travelled to Japan in 1947 and 1948, and more than 150 children were born into service families in Japan during the Occupation itself. From its base in Hiroshima Prefecture, the Commonwealth garrison controlled approximately 20 million Japanese inhabitants in nine prefectures of southern and western Japan, a region covering about 50,000 square kilometres. For the first time, Australia assumed the leadership of a combined Commonwealth force. A trio of Australian lieutenant generals – firstly John Northcott, then Horace Robertson and, finally, William Bridgeford – commanded the force, and JCOSA, the Joint Chiefs of Staff, which implemented policy, met in Melbourne. From 1948 until April 1952, when in the context of the peace treaty and the conflict in Korea the force was renamed British Commonwealth Forces Korea, the Commonwealth was virtually solely represented by Australians.[3]

These impressive facts are matched by the event's formidable historical significance. Australia invested enormous political as well as military capital in the Occupation of Japan. The venture was the expression of the Chifley Labor government's determination to make Australia's presence felt in post-war Asia-Pacific affairs. The forerunner of the peacekeeping missions that have come to mark contemporary Australian armed activity, the Occupation was a pivotal moment in the nation's military history and its international relations. BCOF was the penultimate armed endeavour of a moribund empire.[4] Australia's proactive leadership of the force further distanced the emerging nation from Britain, while heralding its post-war enmeshment in American geopolitics. Now, when Australia has again obligingly participated in a US-led military occupation of a 'renegade' non-Western nation defeated in war, the nation's role in Japan more than half a century ago suddenly resonates with contemporary relevance.[5]

For all its rich political and military import, however, the Occupation of Japan speaks most compellingly as a *cultural* experience. Donald Richie, one of the most influential Western commentators on Japan – who arrived in Tokyo fresh from Lima, Ohio on New Year's Day 1947 and never returned home – has boldly proclaimed that this was 'the greatest head-on cultural collision of modern times'.[6] Occupying Japan was more a moral test than a physical one, an exercise in the use and abuse of power given a special tension because it involved Westerners in a position of domination over an Asian people. In terms of the specific Japanese–Australian relationship, it was an unprecedented domestic encounter between the individuals of two nations that had very recently been at each other's throats, peoples with apparently incompatible traditions and temperaments. As a human event, involving ordinary people having to get on together rather than routinely trying to destroy one another, the Occupation was rather more complex than the murderous, and somewhat maniacal, conflict that preceded it – and much more salutary.

IN THE JAPANESE spring of 2006, I am sitting in the Rhiga Royal's Sky Lounge admiring the view while waiting to meet an elderly Japanese man named Shizuo Inoue. I learned of Inoue-san a year earlier, in an interview with a former veteran of the Occupation, Gordon Edwards, at his house in Guildford, a working-class suburb in western Sydney. Gordon had met Shizuo, or 'Sam', as he calls him, in 1947, while serving in a radar unit in Hiroshima. Gordon was 22 years of age, Shizuo just 18. Like many young local men at the time, Shizuo had been employed by the Occupation as a day labourer, and the two of them struck up a friendship that has lasted more than 60 years. Shizuo's mother and two sisters treated Gordon like family. 'Sam's mother made a fuss of me,' he recalled. 'I became number-one son.' Flicking through his photograph album, he showed me a faded snapshot of a picnic on Miyajima with Shizuo and one of his sisters, young faces smiling confidently at the camera. Gordon threw himself lustily into the life of Japan. 'I took the attitude that I was young, I'm in a strange country, and I'll spend the rest of my days back in Australia, so why not enjoy the experience?' Since Japan, Gordon has spent his working life in a variety of jobs – mostly on his home turf in Sydney's west – making furniture, driving, and welding. He is now well over 80, has had a triple heart-bypass and, for many years, endured sporadic bouts of 'feeling crook', a mysterious malady that he tentatively attributes to intimate exposure to residual radiation in Hiroshima. But he speaks of his sojourn in Japan with unalloyed affection, albeit in a reticent Australian workingman's sort of way.[7]

Struck by their story, I sent Shizuo a copy of a questionnaire I had circulated to Australian participants in the Occupation. His response came back straight away, suffused with simple but eloquent nostalgia. The Occupation had been the most memorable time of his life, and Gordon had been his 'big brother'. His Australian friend 'kindly taught me not only English but many other things, which were all new knowledge to me'. From the time Gordon returned home in 1950, Shizuo wrote, 'we have been corresponding about everything: marriage, children, house building, work and exchanging photos occasionally so we knew every mutual situation very well even if we did not see each other for years'. In 1992, Gordon visited Japan for several months, residing with Shizuo and his family; and in 1998, Shizuo and his wife returned the compliment, staying in the Guildford house and travelling, in the indefatigable Japanese way, around Australia. Though his excellent English hardly required elaboration, he drew on an impeccable literary source 'to speak for' his regard for his old friend:

> When to the sessions of sweet silent thought
> I summon up remembrance of things past ...
> ... I think on thee (Gordon), dear friend,
> All losses are restored and sorrows end.[8]

Shakespearean sonnets did not feature strongly in the responses from BCOF veterans. I knew I had to meet Shizuo.

I recognise him the moment he enters the bar. The handsome young man I had seen in Gordon's photograph album is, at over 80, awesomely fit. He still climbs mountains – of which there is no shortage in Japan – every summer, and he is mentally nimble to boot. Shizuo's is an exemplary 20th-century Japanese story. He was born in Chinnampo in Japanese-Occupied (now North) Korea, where his father, a newspaper reporter, died young of a stroke, in 1935. Aged seven, young Shizuo returned to Japan with his family, settling in Hiroshima. Like his mother and sisters, he survived the atomic bombing, emerging unscathed from the rubble of collapsed buildings and a storm of dust to see 'a mushroom cloud soaring high up in the sky'. After working for BCOF in a variety of jobs, he studied hard, and secured a job at the Atomic Bomb Casualty Commission (ABCC), located in wooded parkland above Hiroshima. At the ABCC, he graduated from the motor pool to a variety of posts of increasing responsibility, including chief of the director's office and, eventually, the assistant chief of secretariat. All up, he worked there for nearly half a century, only retiring in 1997.

Shizuo speaks as warmly about Gordon in person as he did in the questionnaire. When I compliment him on his English, he remarks, 'Gordon was my best teacher.' Inspired by their friendship, he even contemplated migrating to Australia. He did not act on this ambition, vain as it would have been, given the country's intransigent anti-Asian migration policy at the time. Eyeing me directly, but with a hint of sorrow and embarrassment, he said, 'We heard that Australia hated us and didn't want us there.'[9]

IT HAD NOT been difficult for citizens of Occupied Japan, like Shizuo Inoue, to detect an Australian animus that continued to fester beyond the battlefields of war. The Australians went to some lengths to advertise their dislike. Shizuo did not personally attend the Hiroshima Peace Festival, held on 6 August 1948 to commemorate the third anniversary of the bombing of the city, but he may well have heard about it, for what transpired that day became an urban legend of the Occupation era. At the time, Hiroshima was an emerging shantytown rising from the rubble, in which survivors of the catastrophe peddled atomic souvenirs (a melted bottle, a twisted tile, a broken cup) to curious tourists. Many of these were Australians, for whom the city was the first sightseeing port of call.

The city elders were determined to preserve the painful memory of what happened in August 1945, and to establish Hiroshima's status as a hub of international anti-nuclear activism, a 'Mecca of world peace', as it now styles itself. According to the solemn ritual of the Peace Festival, doves had just been sent fluttering into the summer sky. Bells had tolled. Poets had earnestly recited commemorative odes. And then, BCOF's commander-in-chief, Lieutenant General H.C.H. Robertson, descendant of an officer at Waterloo and himself a veteran of two world wars, strode to the microphone. Behind him on the podium sat members of a visiting Australian parliamentary delegation. Looking down on a bedraggled cross-section of Hiroshima citizenry that included women, children, and the aged, some suffering the vicious effects of radiation and many of whom had lost loved ones in the blast, Robertson had an uncompromising message to deliver:

I must remind you that you caused this disaster yourselves ...
The punishment given to Hiroshima was only part of the
retribution of the Japanese people as a whole for pursuing the
doctrine of war.[10]

The Japanese could take a leaf out of BCOF's book, according
to its commander, for the Commonwealth force's mission in Japan
was not one of aggression but 'a mission of peace'. To emphasise
the sincerity of this pacific enterprise, Robertson had detailed a
squadron of Mustang fighters to fly ear-shatteringly low over the
ceremony. In an interview published in the US service newspaper
Pacific Stars and Stripes, Robertson justified this brazen display by
saying:

I always have a squadron or two of aircraft wherever I go. At any
meeting, on any occasion, there is always the aircraft and usually,
a group of armoured cars. I have them there as a reminder, a
constant reminder ...[11]

This was the mouse roaring, the little big man flexing his muscles and berating a belittled former foe who was never to be
allowed to forget that it had started, and lost, the war.

Like his predecessor as BCOF commander, John Northcott,
Robertson was given to expostulating airily on democracy, albeit
without the proselytising fervour of Douglas MacArthur. In
September 1948, he told the visiting Australian journalist Frank
Clune that he saw it as 'a philosophy of life, not a political theory'.
This laudable sentiment was rendered ridiculous, however, by the
unbending BCOF rule of non-fraternisation with the Japanese,
which forbade all but formal contacts with the population.
Dismayed by press reports that large numbers of women had
greeted the vanguard of the Australian contingent when it landed
in Kure on 13 February 1946, Northcott issued a non-fraternisation
order within days, which reminded servicemen that they were

'representative' of the British Commonwealth 'and all that it stands for in the world'. Relations with the 'conquered enemy' should be 'formal and correct'; 'unofficial dealings' with the Japanese were to be 'kept to a minimum'. Japanese homes were not to be entered, nor were the troops to participate in their family life.[12] The Occupationnaires, most of whom were ignorant of Japan other than what the propagandists had told them, were placed in a bind. To assist them in their encounter, an official guidebook for the forces was issued. Called *Know Japan* (1946), it contained detailed factual information about the country's natural features and customs, and was prefaced by Northcott's 'personal instruction' forbidding fraternisation. The men of BCOF, in other words, were to 'know' Japan by having nothing to do with its people.

Predictably, the policy was an abject failure. For a start, it offended and alienated the Japanese, who unfavourably compared the Australian attitude with that of the more relaxed Americans who originally occupied the Hiroshima area. The rule reinforced the Japanese feeling that they were being ostracised for what their troops had done in the war, and made BCOF look simply and instinctively vindictive. 'We cannot understand why your British soldiers are so standoffish,' one local resident complained. 'When the Americans were here they behaved quite differently.' The depth and pervasiveness of Australian antagonism found its way into the Japanese press and penetrated the very highest levels of Japanese society. In May 1946, the Melbourne academic and diplomat W. Macmahon Ball was invited to dinner by no less a figure than Prince Takamatsu, the emperor's younger brother, who was then living in a house near the palace. The previous month, Ball had arrived in Tokyo to begin his duties as the Commonwealth member on the Occupation's principal multinational advisory body, the Allied Council for Japan. The prince and his wife were perfect hosts; guests dined on luxuries such as asparagus, strawberries, and French wine. At the table, Ball's only moment of discomfort came when, raising his glass of claret, the princess raised hers as well, and yelled, 'Bottoms up!' After dinner, Takamatsu and Ball retired to the drawing room, where the prince peppered his guest with some searching political questions, culminating in the shattering comment, 'I understand that Australians hate the Japanese. That is true, is it not?'[13]

The non-fraternisation edict was like waving a red rag to a bull. Making it illicit to form social contacts with the local people, particularly its women, served only to increase their attraction. The closed life of the camps heightened the urge to cut loose. Especially in the early, bitterly cold days of the Occupation, the quarters provided for the arrivals were abysmally equipped. Amenities, in a dreary area of Japan, were virtually non-existent. The men were cold, and they went looking for comfort. That, anyway, was the excuse. 'Hell, the only way we can keep warm is to shack up with a Jap sheila,' one soldier told a visiting journalist. In truth, they would have sought out carnal encounters whatever the standard of their accommodation. Half a century later, the BCOF veteran John Collins looks back at the time in language free of humbug: 'We were young and fit and horny and far from home,' he writes.[14] Victory had handed the men in Japan carte blanche. A large group of men had found themselves controlling the people of a defeated and humbled country, with easy access to grog, guns, and girls. Many of them behaved in the time-honoured fashion of young male military travellers abroad – badly.

Rampant boozing and brawling, intimidation and unprovoked violence, and venality and rapacity were symptomatic of contempt for Japan. Allan S. Clifton, an Australian interpreter and Intelligence officer who made sensational allegations of pack rape in Hiroshima in his memoir *Time of Fallen Blossoms* (1950), wrote that the Australians 'reacted as if they were still at war and Japan and its inhabitants a vast village in overrun territory, subject to the whims and passions of battle-inflamed soldiery'. Douglas Mancktelow had joined the army in Australia in May 1942 and had seen action all through the New Guinea islands; he was on parade in Wewack for the formal surrender of the local Japanese forces. Initially, he had rejected the idea of joining the Occupation – Japan was 'just as rotten as the jungle'. But the tantalising antici-pation of the spoils of war soon intruded. 'After all,' he wondered, 'we were the conquerors, the victorious; why not go to Japan and march through the streets of Tokyo? We could do as we liked and the Japanese would not dare stop us.'[15]

The entire country was up for grabs. Many Occupationnaires were ruthless exploiters of the black market – or 'wogging', as the practice was known. The artist Clifton Pugh, then a 22-year-old who volunteered for BCOF from New Guinea, wrote letters home to his mother that are replete with references to his involvement in running rackets in sugar and other commodities desired by the needy local population. Pugh's burgeoning artistic talent drew inspiration from exposure to Japanese culture and the beauty of the countryside, but he loathed the people, especially the men. 'I've just about had this stinking mess they call Japan – to think that these purile [sic] stinking bastards … thought they could rule the world, the small weak objects'.[16]

Some of the unruliest and most cynical Australian military travellers had in fact been too young to fight in the war itself. They had been drafted to reinforce BCOF only after original volunteers changed their minds during their protracted wait to get to Japan, or as the Occupation progressed and men of the original force were discharged, having completed their tour of duty. Many of the reinforcements had little experience of anywhere, let alone a world as removed from their own as Japan. They did not see themselves as ambassadors of Anglo-Saxon virtue for the edification of the Japanese. Noble motives of democratic reconstruction didn't register on their mental map; wanderlust was a much more potent motivation. In T.A.G. Hungerford's Occupation novel *Sowers of the Wind* (1954), the young Sydney tearaway Andy Waller 'hadn't the foggiest notion of what the Force was doing, or of what it hoped to accomplish'. Japan was a 'sweet cop', a chance to see the world with 'no chance of gettin' your head knocked off' while having a 'damn good time'. This was a characteristic attitude. Experienced soldiers didn't need to be reminded what men were capable of doing to one another, and many took the anti-Japanese propaganda with a grain of salt. But the younger men who went to Japan were susceptible to inflammatory race-hatred and, hence, to the impulse to run amok. Some Australians sought revenge for wartime crimes committed against their countrymen and women, bullying the population and revelling in the role of Occupier. 'It was our turn to return some of the favours,' recalls a veteran who had been one of the young reinforcements.[17]

The prevailing attitude toward Japan was possessive as well as antagonistic. BCOF was collectively happy to engage in the habits of the conqueror. Like the Americans, the Australians fostered the practice of bringing out families to join their menfolk, in order to 'civilise' the force, employing Japanese servants in commodious, newly built, Western-style housing. This was a military circumstance 'without parallel in Australia's annals', as Frank Clune observed in the record of his tour of the BCOF areas, *Ashes of Hiroshima* (1950).[18]

Residential complexes such as the Nijimura, situated at Hiro, a few kilometres from Kure, on what had been an abandoned airstrip jutting out into the Inland Sea, epitomised a post-war suburban nirvana that could still only be dreamt about back in Australia. But the cantonments reminded Clune of something much older: the English regiments stationed in Imperial India. He wasn't the only Australian to make this connection. In his writings describing his year in Japan teaching the children of BCOF personnel, Hal Porter constructs a picture of privilege that calls to mind *A Passage to India* (1924), E.M. Forster's satire of the vulgarity of the British Raj. Porter's portrait of Nijimura as a 'burlesque suburban reservation' in which 'the dispossessed toiled for the trustees' contains a harsh truth about the unnatural divisions created by Occupation – an enclave mentality bred contempt for the hosts. Barry Demmler, an officer's son who lived in both the Nijimura community and in the dependants' village on Etajima, looks back in horror at his insolence towards the family house girls: 'I was really rather bad, an appalling little shit. It is to their credit that they managed so well.'[19] People from remote Australia found themselves in the position of lording it over the 'little Nips', and it took a singular individual not to succumb to the temptation to indulge such an historic opportunity.

FOR ALL ITS neocolonial excesses, the Occupation had its noble as well as its ugly side. The Australian story to emerge from postwar Japan contains contradictory, if complementary, aspects that make it facile to deride it as a simple exercise in conquest and hegemony. It has been observed that, in a startling paradox, the experience of the prisoners of war enslaved by the Japanese signalled a positive development in Australian relationships with Asia. In the most oppressive circumstances, the POWs had to come to terms with people who had long been viewed from a comfortable distance. These were the earliest Australians to venture en masse into the alien neighbourhoods to their north – and into an abject situation that was rankly devoid of prestige, which was unusual for European peoples in the oriental context. As such, they were the trailblazers of an era of Australian engagement with the region, later signified by reorientated travel itineraries and the embrace of Asian cultures.[20]

Perhaps it was the Occupation of Japan, however, that provided a better example of this paradigm. Certainly, BCOF was an anachronism, its members empowered in a way that was reminiscent of the great age of white rule in Asia. But if the Occupation caused some collateral human damage, it also produced surprisingly constructive results within the ruling community, over and above the reconstruction of Japan. 'Travelling is victory,' according to an Arab proverb that impressed Joseph Conrad; it teaches wisdom and tolerance. It is a motto that could be fixed to the BCOF community in Japan. This was a kind of cultural reconnaissance; the first time large numbers of Australians were able to explore an Asian culture and landscape in any depth and detail.[21]

'War leads the men of Terra Australis into many strange places, but surely never into a stranger than this', Clune remarks in *Ashes of Hiroshima*. On the contrary, the Occupation record suggests that a substantial number of the Australian cohort came to find Japan and its people not as 'strange', or 'alien', or 'weird', or any of the usual epithets that had been associated with the country, over time. Outside the degrading context of prostitution (and sometimes within it), men and women fell in love. In 1946, Gordon Parker had been part of a cohort of young BCOF reinforcements who were 'aggressive, cocky and hungry for adventure'. They had also been acculturated to hate the Japanese, and then indoctrinated by the army to despise them too. As volunteers, they were lectured on the Japanese, as well as their cultures and customs, learning that 'they were riddled with disease, disgusting and unAustralian [sic]'.[22] Six years later, after a long public campaign, Parker was the first to marry a Japanese bride – several hundred of whom would literally change the face of white Australia.

Disregarding the non-fraternisation edict as nonsensical, Australians mixed with Japanese men and women employed by BCOF as clerks, interpreters, kitchen staff, servants, and labourers, through police and intelligence networks, and even the black-market trade. Shizuo Inoue's bond with Gordon Edwards was replicated many times over.

Living and working in Japan at an impressionable age had an enlarging effect on men from a provincial country. George Martin, who spent three years in Japan from March 1946, recalls 'children skating on a frozen lake at twilight, seen from a train window'. He experienced 'the slow, and almost reluctant, dawning of the fact that these people, with all their recent history, were a remarkable race'.[23]

Soldiers who had fought the Japanese and who had good reason to hate them found themselves seduced in ways other than sexual. Tom Hungerford had served as a commando in the jungles of the Solomons, mired in a struggle that seemed as if it would go on forever. The Occupation changed everything. The friendship Hungerford enjoys with a Japanese schoolteacher heralds a reorientation of affinities, the discovery of an Eastern mentor figure of the kind that has become familiar in Australian cultural life in recent decades. The Japanese teacher had read Joseph Furphy's classic *Such is Life*; he in turn inspires the Australian soldier (and budding novelist) with examples of *haiku*. In Occupied Japan, a mutual future is prepared: 'Sometimes I wondered what I, the Occupation soldier, was doing to Japan,' Hungerford remarks. 'Very soon I was to wonder what Japan was doing to me'.[24]

Resistant at first, many Australians, in the popular phrase, turned Japanese. They made valiant attempts to tackle the language, and they visited shrines; some even tried their hand at such unsoldierly pursuits as *ikebana*. The BCOF autobiographer Murray Elliott writes of being exposed to a 'new and great culture', which altered his 'way of seeing' and gave him 'a new perception of the world'. Exploitation and churlishness were undeniably prevalent in the extended BCOF community, but many of the Occupation wives behaved with goodwill to the Japanese, involving themselves with the host community, or simply watching, listening, and learning. After a social engagement at the home of a Japanese dignitary, Betty Page, the wife of a warrant officer in the RAAF, writes in her diary of her embarrassment at the manners of 'our women and their offspring' in a context of 'extreme hospitality'. 'Why we should set ourselves up as paragons of virtue to the Japanese, I do not know,' Page ponders. 'As far as the cultural aspect of life is concerned … they are way ahead of us.' BCOF children and teenagers made exciting discoveries of their own: they walked in the Japanese forests, swam in the Inland Sea, and played games (when allowed) with local children. One of them, Bruce

Fisher, recalls sharing an illicit cigarette – 'Peace' was the popular local brand at the time – with affable local fishermen. The symbolism is raw, but indicative of a new generation of Australians making their own private treaty with the old enemy.[25]

Coming to terms with Japan drove a wedge between the men, women, and children of BCOF and the folks back home. Indignant at Japanese brutality towards its prisoners, as horrifying stories of the pestilential POW camps of South-East Asia continued to surface, the general public believed the Occupation was too easy on the Japanese. In April 1946, Macmahon Ball was paid a visit by two leading Sydney journalists, Massey Stanley of the *Daily Telegraph* and Jack Percival of the *Sydney Morning Herald*, who told him that they believed the American regime was 'ridiculously soft', and that the Japanese 'were laughing up their sleeves'. Rapprochement was for weakies (and Yanks). This was a view to which the public held tenaciously. In March 1950, the former Labor immigration minister Arthur Calwell, an implacable Jap-hater, 'voiced the views of many' by bemoaning the fact that 'more and more people' are coming back from Japan 'to surprise and disappoint their friends and relatives with their favourable views of the Japanese'.[26]

People couldn't grasp the idea that the wartime enemy might be likeable – even admirable. It was a rare experience for Australian soldiers on a tour of duty not to enjoy the indulgence of the public at home; it has been paralleled only by civilian animosity toward those fighting the controversial war in Vietnam in the late 1960s and early 1970s. Australians had traditionally forgiven the Digger for his hard drinking, womanising, and general rowdiness, taking it as evidence of his cheerful native larrikinism. The Occupationnaires did not fare so well. Shocking suggestions of their flagrant black marketeering and whoring were manna from heaven to a public that thought only bad things could come from mixing with the Japanese. In particular, the vaulting rates of venereal disease in the Australian contingent scandalised a conservative society, and fuelled suspicions that the men of BCOF were debauched malingerers and miscreants on a paid holiday.

Commander-in-chief Robertson's harangue in Hiroshima was therefore music to the ears of many Australians. The Japanese had had it coming; they needed to be put in their place – in *their* place. A Gallup poll taken in September 1945 revealed that 83 per cent of people thought the atomic bombings were justified. They had ended the war; that was what mattered. The great news was greeted with unadulterated joy by the Australian combatants still battling away in the South-West Pacific. Peter Ryan, then a commando in New Guinea, remembers feeling a 'vast, upswelling surge of relief, of gratitude, of deep joy'. [27] With the dire prospect of invading the Japanese mainland looming, the bombs had possibly saved his life and that of thousands of others. Such is war's brutal arithmetic.

Yet the memories of the BCOF men are suffused with disquiet at Hiroshima's nuclear destruction; seeing firsthand what was left of the city usually turned hatred into sympathy. To Bill Towers, who had fought the Japanese in New Guinea and New Britain, the bombing was 'cold-blooded murder'. Jim Grover, who went through the city on his second day in Japan, remembers feelings of 'deep remorse, sorrow, and some disgust at our action'. The damage was confronting and morally disorienting. After disembarking at Kure in that frigid February of 1946, the airman Gerry Walshe caught a train to the RAAF base in Yamaguchi Prefecture. The journey took him through the wasteland of Hiroshima, and the sight of it shook him to his core: 'I felt lost, and for the first time I felt for the Japanese people.'[28]

Many of the Australians in Occupied Japan saw helping the Japanese reconstruct Hiroshima as being the noblest outcome of their service. They could not but be impressed by the will of the residents to rebuild as a metaphor for post-war Japan itself. It was also impossible not to be moved by the plight of the grieving, the ailing, and the bereft – and particularly, by the plight of Hiroshima's children. Some units acquired local kids as mascots, feeding them, mucking around with them, and teaching them some English, including a few songs. A favourite was the popular melody of the day, 'You are My Sunshine'. No doubt this was an insensitive selection as one of the Occupation's signature tunes – after all, the sun is Japan's national emblem; the very identity of the Japanese people is bound up with it, through the emperor's mythic relationship to the sun goddess Amaterasu. Hal Porter recalls his cringing embarrassment at being present at a bombed-out school while an Australian schoolmistress, 'fat and forceful, hung with blackmarket cultured pearls', cajoled a class of bemused Japanese teenagers to sing along with the song.[29] But the men themselves thought they were just being friendly, communicating as best they could. They knew as well as anyone, and much better than the bigwigs back at GHQ in Tokyo, what had been done to Japan in the name of its liberation from a militarist tyranny.

If the BCOF veterans nostalgically recall their Japanese sojourn as a golden time of their youth, they also know that their pleasures and personal conquests took place under an atomic sun.

PART ONE

Gulliver in Lilliput: Japanese Travails

CHAPTER ONE

The Long Road

Travellers of a certain vintage still visit Japan with 'the war' on their minds. The novelist Peter Carey, who was born in 1943, remembers, as a child, playing with Occupation money that must have been brought back to Australia as a souvenir. Visiting Japan with his son, he searched 'in every cultural artefact for echoes of the atomic bomb, the firebombing of Tokyo, the American occupation'. But war tourists do not find much concrete evidence in Japan's constantly mutating capital to satisfy their curiosity. What nature and American bombers have not achieved, Tokyo has done to itself. Things get knocked down and put up again, destroyed, replaced, remade. The city, it has been remarked, 'has as much permanence as a Bedouin encampment'.[1]

Overt reminders of the Occupation era are few, and you won't see them advertised in official tourist literature. General MacArthur's spartan offices in the Dai-Ichi building have been carefully preserved, and can be viewed (if you can get past the concierge), though they attract few visitors. Security is heavy at the vast Japan Defence Agency complex at Ichigaya – a couple of kilometres away, by the river – but tours can be arranged. The chief attraction is the Memorial Hall, constructed in 1937, in which Hirohito had once received each fresh batch of graduating military cadets on an elevated platform, to which two sets of stairs had been constructed: one for the dainty feet of the divine emperor, the other to handle common human traffic. From May 1946 to November 1948, this was the venue for the Tokyo war trials, the International Military Tribunal for the Far East, presided over by a Queenslander, Justice Sir William Webb. Visitors are ushered to one side of the hall to view display cases showing some innocuous historical material relating to the building. In solitary splendour on the other side, in a cabinet of its own, lies the manuscript of the 'Dissentient Judgment' of Justice Pal, the Indian jurist who refused to go along with the guilty verdicts handed out to General Tojo and his ilk, arguing that the proceedings were victor's justice and that the list of war crimes that were considered neglected to include, for example, the atomic bombings.

But most visitors are more interested in the grisly events that took place in a room upstairs, on 25 November 1970. There, after one last 'banzai!' for the emperor, the celebrated writer and arch nationalist Yukio Mishima committed *hara-kiri*, choosing as his location a symbolic site of Japanese post-war humiliation. More is made of how Mishima literally lost his head (it being clumsily dispatched according to the ritual) than of the madness of his bungled coup d'état aimed at restoring Japanese military strength.

IN MAY 1946, almost a quarter of a century before Mishima's fatuous performance of emperor worship, a battalion of Australian soldiers marched onto the streets of Tokyo to mount the first BCOF guard on the Imperial Palace. The Tokyo trials had opened just a week earlier. The war's ordeal had seemed to come to a satisfactory end; at last, the Australians could preen. That they were mounting guard on the palace of a figure they wanted brought to justice lent the moment a special pleasure. Even the Americans were impressed. The *Pacific Stars and Stripes* ran a photograph of 'smart-stepping, arm-swinging' Diggers on its front page, calling them 'top-notch troops' who gave the Japanese yet another glimpse of 'Allied military might' – as if that was necessary after Hiroshima and Nagasaki.[2] John Northcott, the first BCOF commander-in-chief – soon to be rewarded with the honour of being appointed the first Australian-born governor of New South Wales – telegraphed the national government. He had a simple but climactic message to pass on: 'Australian troops took over duties in Tokyo today and mounted guard on the emperor's palace. The end of a long road.'[3]

As one long road ended for Australia, another opened up for Japan. Perhaps Northcott was reading from Hirohito's 'rescript' announcing the termination of the war, broadcast on the radio at high noon on 15 August 1945. The emperor had used the same image while imploring his 'good and loyal subjects' to abstain from 'outbursts of emotion that may engender needless complications' in the wake of their defeat. Hirohito spoke in a shrill singsong to a stupefied national audience that had never heard his voice before, using such a florid and arcane court style that a radio announcer then re-read the entire speech in common language. The message was doleful but determined. The emperor directed the nation to keep its faith in itself, 'ever mindful of its heavy burden of responsibilities, and of the long road before it'.[4]

The trope of 'the road' to signify the war's long travail appears time and time again in the language of the footsloggers on their tours of duty, and in that of the rarefied military leaders who design and direct their itineraries. American GIs photographed in Bougainville in 1944 rest on a large sign bearing the legend, 'Last Stop on Road to Japan', with a large arrow pointed toward 'Main Street Tokyo'. True to form, Supreme Commander MacArthur had personalised the course of the conflict by tracing its trajectory according to his wartime career. Its nadir had been fleeing from Japanese surrounded Corregidor in the Philippines in March 1942, followed by the perilous journey south to Australia, first by boat, and then by decrepit aircraft across the captured enemy islands of the South-West Pacific, with an entourage that included his wife Jean and four-year-old son Arthur. Soon after his arrival in Melbourne, he was appointed Supreme Commander of the South-West Pacific area, after which he famously told the Australian prime minister, John Curtin, 'You take care of the rear and I will handle the front'.[5]

The war's high point, from MacArthur's point of view, was descending upon a vanquished Japan from on high as its unchallenged conqueror, on 30 August 1945. MacArthur had flown from Manila to Atsugi air base, 48 kilometres southwest of Tokyo, into a Japan in which the advance American occupying force was outnumbered 1000 to 1 by trained Japanese troops in the Tokyo vicinity alone. Kamikaze pilots with clipped wings were billeted in the area – Atsugi had been their training base. Stepping briskly from the plane, wielding nothing more dangerous than his corncob pipe, the conqueror returned the salute from General Robert L. Eichelberger, the commander of the US Eighth Army – which was to comprise the bulk of the American occupying force – shook his hand and remarked casually: 'Bob, from Melbourne to Tokyo is a long way, but this seems to be the end of the road.'[6]

The Americans relished both the happy conclusion to the war's proceedings and its aftermath. From the first days, weeks, and months of the Occupation, they mastered post-war Japan with the insouciance that comes when ideological certainty is backed up by absolute military domination. The story of the genesis of the post-war Japanese constitution, as smugly related by the head of SCAP's powerful government section, General Courtney Whitney, is instructive. Early in the new year of 1946, the section was ordered to create a new constitution in secret haste, in order to present the Japanese with a fait accompli before the forthcoming general election. MacArthur sought Japan's renunciation of war and the abolition of its armed forces, and wanted to see the constitutional investment of sovereignty in the people, with the emperor reduced to a figurehead; he sought also the abolition of the peerage system and all forms of feudalism. 'Here,' Whitney wrote, 'was an opportunity to help an entire nation throw off the virus of militarism.'

The team worked in a frenzy for six days to draft the document to meet the deadline of 12 February – Lincoln's birthday. American and European constitutions were studied along with the old Meiji constitution that was to be discarded. At the private residence of the Japanese foreign minister Yoshida (soon to be prime minister), and in company with two senior American officers, Whitney sprang the constitution on members of the Japanese cabinet, who had gathered to debate another draft that they had prepared themselves. Whitney put the document, written in English, on the table, stressing to the Japanese that it had the strong support of the SCAP himself. The Americans then repaired to the gardens of the foreign minister's residence, basking in their serenity. It was a glorious day. After about an hour, one of the flustered Japanese appeared in the garden, apologising for keeping the visitors waiting. 'Not at all,' Whitney replied with a smile. 'We have been enjoying your atomic sunshine.'[7] At that very moment, a B-29 roared overhead; it was as if the *Enola Gay* was flying a lap of honour.

'For the Japanese', as General Eichelberger cockily ended his memoir *Our Jungle Road to Tokyo* (1950), 'the Americans are still the giants in the earth'.[8] Douglas MacArthur, as the Occupation's Supreme Commander, was the most gigantic American of them all. The general's first encounter with Hirohito had established the new hierarchy in Japan. The meeting took place not at the Imperial Palace but in the US embassy, on 27 September 1945. To make this circumstance even more humbling for the emperor, whose routes through the capital had always been cleared to facilitate his easy passage, his Daimler was stopped by a red traffic light at the crossroads near the embassy, up the hill in Toranomon, on the northern side of his palace moat. This was no longer his city, let alone his country.

Upon his arrival in the embassy compound, MacArthur's aide, Major Faubion Bowers, thought Hirohito looked 'frightened to death'. His hands were trembling. Meeting MacArthur on the threshold of the drawing room, 'he bowed low, very low, a servant's bow'; his hands were still trembling when he accepted the offer of an American cigarette. The pair met for about 40 minutes. What transpired went unreported; but, on 29 September, GHQ had the Japanese newspapers run an official photograph of the pair, taken by an army photographer. It was a picture that spoke several thousand words. The small, stiff emperor stood frozen in frock coat, cravat, and striped pants. Beside him, less than two feet away and a good foot taller, the unsmiling but disarmingly relaxed MacArthur, a couple of decades his senior, eyeballed the camera. Dressed casually in khaki, with no insignia of rank, hands in pockets, collar open, and hands on hips, he is the at-home host giving his precious time to an ill-at-ease, absurdly overdressed visitor. It was the first of five visits Hirohito made to the general; MacArthur never reciprocated. The demeaning image appalled Japanese police censors, who ordered that the newspapers be confiscated and sought to invoke a national law of 'Crimes Against the Imperial Household'. With totalitarian logic, GHQ quickly rescinded the ban, and ordered the government to cease all efforts to censor or control the media.[9]

The Japanese authorities were right to be concerned about the humiliating impact of the photograph. A pun circulating in Tokyo referred to MacArthur's vast height advantage over the Lilliputian emperor to make a satirical aside about the new place of Hirohito in the Japanese body politic: 'Why is General MacArthur like a navel?' 'Because he is above the *chin*'.[10] *Chin* is a first-person pronoun used exclusively by the emperor; Hirohito had employed it, confusingly to many of his subjects, in his momentous broadcast on 15 August. It also happens to be Japanese slang for 'penis'. Hirohito was a pragmatist, and knew that the American interloper had saved his skin by resisting pressure, much of it stemming from the Australians, to have him tried as a war criminal.

Another running Occupation joke was that the once-divine emperor 'stopped claiming to be God when he discovered MacArthur was'. The general was on a pedestal; his towering presence put Hirohito in the shade. In January 1947, an old high-school friend of MacArthur's, Ed T. Coleman, wrote to Hirohito from Plainsville Texas, advising the emperor to honour 'the great man' to whom the Japanese 'owe much', by making his birthday, 26 January, a public holiday to be called 'MacArthur Day'. At 'High Noon', Coleman suggested, all Japanese should face east, a salute should be given, and these words uttered: 'May the spirit of Douglas MacArthur live and endure forever'.[11] There is no evidence that Hirohito dashed off a reply.

The Americans never deviated from their view that their mission in Japan was an act of benevolent redemption. In his study of post-war Japan, *Embracing Defeat* (1999), John Dower dredges up one of the defining tags of the age of empire in describing the Occupation as 'the last immodest exercise in the colonial conceit known as "the white man's burden"'. Kipling's famous euphemism is even more germane than Dower thinks. In 'The White Man's Burden', first published in 1899, Kipling urged the US to take up the challenge of empire ('to serve your captives' need') previously borne by Britain and other European nations. The poem was written to coincide with the American conquest of the Philippines and acquisition of other former Spanish colonies, such as Puerto Rico and Cuba. What makes the reference so pertinent to Japan is that the first military governor of the newly American-occupied Philippines was none other than Douglas MacArthur's own father and greatest influence, General Arthur MacArthur, who thought it the duty of the 'magnificent Aryan races' to create 'progressive social evolution' in Asia. [12]

Whether the Occupation of Japan was the *last* American assumption of the white man's burden is debatable; Dower was writing before the 2001 terrorist attacks on the World Trade Center, and before the invasion and occupation of Iraq in 2003. Whereas the US started talking of spreading Anglo-Saxon civilisation in the early 20th century, Max Boot writes in *The Savage Wars of Peace* (2003), 'today they talk of spreading democracy and defending human rights'. The trend started in post-war Japan. Edwin O. Reischauer, the Tokyo-born son of Presbyterian missionaries, who was deeply involved in Occupation policy while working at the state department, wrote in 1950 that – in words that ring a distinctly contemporary bell – 'We are anxious to prove that democracy is an article for export'. [13]

Japan was a wreck when the Americans moved in. Of the more than two million of its people killed in the war, nearly 600,000 were civilians killed outright or fatally injured in the air raids, the atomic bombings, and the fight-to-the-death struggle in Okinawa, in which one-third of the local population perished. Sixty of its cities had been pulverised, napalmed, nuked. The homeless numbered more than eight million; the unemployed, even more. People were displaced and dying of malnutrition. The aftermath of the war almost seemed worse than the war itself, especially in the ruined cities. The humiliation of defeat was ameliorated by an overwhelming sense of relief at the prospect of deliverance.

Exhausted, the country wanted to make a fresh start. It was thus a perfect 'laboratory', as MacArthur himself envisaged, in which to conduct an experiment in national reconstruction. [14] Until the obsession with rooting out 'the Reds' in the liberated Japanese political landscape took hold of American policy, this was a *mission civilisatrice* of the old-fashioned kind. A 'feudalistic', backward, heathen, inferior Oriental nation was to be recast in the image of the 'free', progressive, Christian, superior West, as most powerfully exemplified by the US.

The Occupation was a military dictatorship informed by an autocratic insistence on 'Democracy'. This was conjoined with Christianity, as the great ideological coupling. While MacArthur talked vaguely about 'the Anglo-Saxon idea', it was specifically America, because of its 'advanced spirituality', which had assumed the mantle as the propagator of Christian virtue in the Far East. MacArthur wanted to augment the reconstructive work of the troops by filling Japan with American missionaries to encourage Japan's 'spiritual regeneration'. The Occupation ordered that ten million Bibles translated into Japanese be issued to the populace. This was an opportunity, through the 'practical demonstration of Christian ideals', to lift up a race 'long stunted' by 'ancient concepts of mythological teaching'. The 'little Japanese', indeed. MacArthur's personification in 1951 of the Japanese as 'a boy of twelve' ('compared with our development of forty-five years') who is ripe for re-education reveals the overweening paternalism of the Occupation.[15]

With the arrogance of moral certainty came an incapacity for self-criticism, which revealed itself very early on. The biggest self-deception of all was that the US was in Japan solely on an errand of mercy. In a speech made to World War I veterans in Washington DC in 1935, MacArthur had described America as a 'pre-eminently Christian' nation that is 'far less militaristic than most nations' and, hence, 'not especially open to the charge of imperialism'. During the Occupation itself, he had remarked that Christianity was imbued with 'a spiritual repugnance of war'.[16] These are disarming observations, coming from a man whose whole life and career were associated with combat.

That America hated war must have come as a surprise to Japanese Christians, as American bombs destroyed many hundreds of their churches. It would assuredly have come as news to the residents of Nagasaki who survived the plutonium bomb dubbed 'Fat Man' that was unleashed over the city three days after Hiroshima, on 9 August 1945. The bomber's target was the enormous Mitsubishi shipyards, down by the harbour. Miscalculating in overcast weather, the American crew instead released 'Fat Man' a few kilometres to the north, over Urakami, the neighbourhood of the country's biggest and long beleaguered Roman Catholic congregation, virtually wiping out Japanese Christianity in one fell swoop. One US-made bomb had achieved in a diabolical flash what the Shogunate could not do in more than 200 years of trying.

Not that the Japanese people as a whole ever really got to know much about the atomic bombings: SCAP threw a rigid blanket of censorship over them. At the official signing of the surrender, aboard the USS *Missouri* in Tokyo Bay, on 2 September 1945, MacArthur had made an analogy of the impending Occupation with Commodore Perry's arrival in Japan in 1853, in ushering in 'an era of enlightenment and progress' by lifting 'the veil of isolation' from the country. 'Freedom of expression, freedom of action, even freedom of thought,' MacArthur asserted, had been denied the Japanese 'through the suppression of liberal education, through appeal to superstition, and through the application of force'. So how did SCAP go about lifting the 'veil'? Within days, a complex bureaucracy had begun to enforce a press code, whose ten-point guidelines contained an Orwellian paradox. Point one stated, 'News must adhere strictly to the truth'; yet point two said, 'Nothing shall be printed which might, directly or by inference, disturb the public tranquillity'. Tell the truth, then, unless it is upsetting. Evidently, it did not occur to the Press, Pictorial, and Broadcast division of the Civil Censorship Detachment (which was a department of the Civil Intelligence Section) that the guidelines were riddled with contradictions. SCAP's purpose, however, was unequivocal: points three and four both concern 'false or destructive criticism' of the Allied powers and forces that might invite 'mistrust and resentment'.[17]

The 'public tranquillity' clause of the press code could be invoked to censor just about anything the Americans disliked. In fact, it was SCAP's own tranquillity that was most fragile. In the early months of the Occupation, GHQ was acutely averse to the

Japanese people hearing about what had happened in Hiroshima and Nagasaki. An Australian, the journalist Wilfred Burchett, was the first Western observer to venture into Hiroshima, which was officially out of bounds to inquiring foreign eyes. In late August 1945, hordes of foreign newsmen had invaded Japan, along with the Occupation forces. Burchett was one of them, having reported on the campaign in Okinawa. An estimated 600 Allied journalists covered the great occasion of the official Japanese surrender on 2 September.

Wilfred Burchett had other plans. Feigning illness, he went instead to Tokyo station, and boarded an overcrowded train bound for Hiroshima. It was filled with hostile demobilised Japanese troops, the officers still bearing their swords and 'looking daggers' at him all the way. After a tense 20-hour train journey, he entered the atomic desolation. What he saw and smelled shocked him: a miasma of dust and mists rising from the fissured soil, and an odour that was 'dank, acrid and sulphurous'; dead fish were floating belly up in the river; in filthy improvised hospitals, people were dying horribly of mysterious illnesses. Published in the London *Daily Express* on 5 September and relayed around the world, Burchett's vivid dispatch was profoundly shocking. Headlined 'The Atomic Plague', it was unapologetically didactic – 'a warning to the world'. MacArthur was displeased. Upon his return to Tokyo, on 7 September, Burchett had his press accreditation withdrawn, and he was immediately expelled from Japan – an order later rescinded. A similarly frank eyewitness account of Nagasaki penned by George Weller of the *Chicago Daily News* never even made it to print. Other than those specifically approved by SCAP, all reports on Hiroshima and Nagasaki were banned within two weeks of Burchett's dispatch.[18]

The Americans systematically silenced the *hibakusha,* the survivors of Hiroshima and Nagasaki who lived to tell the tale. Reading the survivors' horror stories was not merely potentially upsetting; it might also stoke latent Japanese resentment. As the

Hiroshima poet Sadako Kurihara commented: 'We were not allowed to write about the atomic bomb during the Occupation. We were not even allowed to say that we were not allowed to write about the atomic bomb.'[19] In fact, some literary works did escape the censors, but it was not until the Occupation was over that the explosive literary record created by the twin calamities was fully brought to the public's notice.

It was Japanese anger that the Occupation wanted to contain, but the suppression of the imagery of nuclear destruction was motivated by another political impulse – the protection of the prestige of the US as a beacon of humanity. From images of grotesquely burned individual corpses to massed skeletal remains, documentary evidence of the dead bore an unsettling resemblance to the shocking scenes from the Nazi death camps. The secretary of war Henry Stimson had foreseen a problem looming on the geopolitical horizon, in June 1945. In the light of the pitiless destruction of Japanese cities throughout 1945, and the plans on the drawing board for using a nuclear weapon, Stimson was worried that the US would gain 'the reputation for outdoing Hitler in atrocities'. Accordingly, the Occupation authorities withheld intimate ground-level shots of Hiroshima and Nagasaki. Instead, the bombings came to be represented by the uncensored sight of the mushroom cloud, a quasi-mystical icon of atomic fission far removed from the horror down below.[20]

THE AUSTRALIANS JOURNEYED to Japan just as earnestly as the Americans, if less complacently. But they found it difficult to give their ambitions proper expression. As Donald Richie quipped, the 'A' for 'Allied' in SCAP stood for 'American'.[21] For all Australia's keen political ambition and military pretension, the Occupation was primarily an American affair, run to suit its interests. If the Americans, in Eichelberger's description, liked to see themselves as 'giants' who bestrode Japan as if they owned the place, the

Australians, with an essentially subsidiary operational role – and virtually none at all in the military governance of Japan – were six-inch pipsqueaks from a minor nation. And the Americans never let them forget it.

In Australia, as in the US, the fallout from the war was cultural as well as military and political. During the dark days of Japanese terror, those fraught early months of 1942, the Australian Department of Information conducted a hate campaign against the Japanese aimed at stiffening determination to repel the invader. Radio broadcasts, press articles, and posters denigrating the Japanese were reproduced as advertisements in major daily newspapers. Each of the advertisements ended with the words, 'We've always despised them – now we must smash them!' Dehumanising the enemy is as old as war itself, of course. 'Strong hatred, defender of peoples,' writes Homer of the fierce antagonism between the Greeks and the Trojans, a mutual loathing whipped up by the gods themselves.[22]

In fact, Australians had not 'always despised' the Japanese. In the latter decades of the 19th century, newly expansive, open Japan was quite the object of fascination and admiration. In 1889, the traveller, teacher and, later, distinguished scholar James Murdoch had reported that 'Australian popular opinion is wonderfully favourably inclined towards Japan and the Japanese'.[23] A country hidden from the foreign gaze for so long had started revealing a seductive image of itself to the world, albeit one largely limited to the decorative vases, screens, and fans that had become modish in Australia, as in Europe. The Japanese were popularly regarded as picturesque and harmless, a people both 'queer and quaint', as the chorus of nobles sing in the opening song of Gilbert and Sullivan's *The Mikado* (1885), the opera that did so much to stereotype the Japanese in the Western mind. The Victorian illustrated children's book *My Very First Little Book about Other Countries*, published in London early in the 20th century and widely available in Australia, describes 'quaint Japan' thus:

The Japanese is an odd little fellow,
His hair is black and his face is yellow
But he's very clever and very brave
And how very politely he does behave![24]

By the latter half of the 1940s, this belittling but relatively affec-
tionate caricature was replaced by the personae of the simian buf-
foon, the pitiless fanatic, the maniacally cruel captor. While the
drastic devolution of the Japanese in Australian opinion owed much
to shuddering reaction to the Imperial Army's criminality during
the late war, it was also the culmination of a gradual historical
process whose cultural roots lay deep in Australia's anxieties about
its vulnerable place in a region teeming with Orientals. The war
was the traumatic realisation of a national dread.

In the latter years of the 19th century, newspaper cartoonists
used images of pigtailed 'Mongols' invading the space – a large
room, or a comfy armchair – inhabited by the contemporary personification of innocent white Australia, the 'Little Boy from
Manly'. In 1886, the *Bulletin* cartoonist Phil May drew the
emblem of an oriental octopus throttling the life out of Australia,
to denote the horrors of large-scale Asian migration. It was to
endure as a potent image of threat: Murray Elliott, who served as a
medical officer in the Occupation of Japan, remembers, as a child
in Adelaide during the late 1920s, being scared by a calendar in
his grandmother's parlour, which portrayed a slant-eyed octopus
with eight tentacles caressing the northwest coastline of Australia.[25]
Increasingly, in the first decades of the new century, the octopus
unmistakably and scarily hailed from Japan.

This former comic opera of a country was on the march, flexing
its military muscle in a series of triumphant campaigns that began
as early as the 1890s, with the defeat of the Chinese in the first
Sino–Japanese War in 1895. A key historical moment came a
decade later, when the Japanese navy smashed the Russian fleet at
Tsushima, near where Kublai Khan's invading force was destroyed

by a providential typhoon seven centuries earlier. This was an amazing Asian defeat of a European power. Frank Clune, then a Sydney paperboy, remembers making four times his usual profit from the sales of the *Evening News* and the *Star* that memorable day when the destruction of the Tsarist armada became news. Clusters of people gathered in Sydney's streets, reading of a 'new figure of world fame', Admiral Togo.[26] Australians didn't mind an expansionary Japan, as long as its plans didn't include them. The annexation of Korea in 1910 and the invasion of Manchuria (and its conversion into the vassal state of Manchukuo) in 1931 could be viewed benignly, as the Japanese octopus was spreading its tentacles north and west, rather than south.

The escalation of aggression in China in 1937 sharply reinvigorated Australian fears. Trade interests jostled with security concerns. Australia was anxious not to offend its growing commercial partner, but Japan was looking unstoppable. Clune read the public mood: in May 1938, he had returned from a tour of North Asia, reporting for the Australian Broadcasting Corporation with the objective of nurturing 'a better understanding between nations of the Pacific'. Instead, he presented readers of the *Sydney Morning Herald* with the disturbing news that maps of the burgeoning Japanese empire on sale in Japan included Australia, along with the East Indies and New Zealand. 'The East' – the inherited geographical signifier that Australians ascribed their Asian neighbours – had become the Near North.[27]

When war did finally come, it was explicitly envisioned in racial terms. After the fall of Singapore left the region bereft of British power, the Melbourne newspaper the *Argus,* in February 1942, editorialised that Australia had assumed the mantle of 'the real bastion of the white race'. Some months earlier, when prime minister John Curtin sought parliamentary approval for his government's declaration of war against Japan, he invoked the national need to defend the 'principle of a White Australia'.[28] The ensuing struggle in the Asia-Pacific region was charged with an uncompromisingly vicious mutual racism. If the Japanese convinced themselves that they were going into battle as Asia's champion in a fight to the death against white supremacists, the Allies saw themselves pitted against a monstrous enemy whose animal cunning was amply suited to the principal theatre in the South-West Pacific – the dark, tangled wilderness of New Guinea. 'Fighting Japs is not like fighting normal human beings,' the Australian commander General Sir Thomas Blamey commented, in an interview published in the *New York Times* on 9 January 1943. 'We are dealing with something primitive. Our troops have the right view of the Japs. They regard them as vermin.'[29]

Blamey was not misrepresenting his men's opinion of the Japanese. The American Faubion Bowers was posted to Australia in 1943 as a member of ATIS, the Allied Translator and Interpreter Section, and accompanied the Second AIF to the New Guinea front to translate Japanese documents and interrogate prisoners. In a slightly precious rebuke, given the dog-eat-dog slog of jungle warfare, Bowers ticked off the Australians for distributing a leaflet which read, 'Remember, you are not fighting men, you are fighting beasts, you are fighting yellow-bellied beasts.'[30] Violation of slain Japanese was one expression of this remorseless race hatred. This was a case of an eye for an eye, sometimes literally, given the infamous Japanese desecration of Australian dead. Like the Americans, the Australians were assiduous souvenir hunters, plundering enemy corpses for gold teeth. Body parts were highly sought-after items, with skulls and bones particularly prized. Captured Japanese were sometimes dispatched before they were interrogated – shot on the spot. More elaborate means of disposal were also enacted. In *War Without Mercy* (1986), John Dower quotes the wartime journals of Charles Lindbergh, who flew as a civilian observer with the US forces in New Guinea in 1944, in which he claims that 'the Australians often threw Japanese out of airplanes on their way to prison compounds and then reported that they had committed hara-kiri'.[31]

As rumours of Japanese ill treatment of its POWs started circulating, any grudging respect for the capabilities of Japan's soldiery was lost in recrimination. For the sake of public morale, explicitly documented details of Japanese atrocities were largely suppressed, although the massacre of Australian prisoners at Tol plantation in New Britain in February 1942 had received widespread publicity in newspapers and Cinesound newsreels. In June 1943, the government appointed the Queensland Supreme Court judge Sir William Webb to report on Japanese war crimes. Webb's investigations were kept quiet while the fighting raged, though several atrocity stories were released in the US. When Webb's report was finally released, soon after the official surrender in September 1945, it contained a litany of shocking revelations including the casual slaughter of prisoners by bayonet or machine-gun, the rape and mutilation of native and white women, the infamous beheading of the Australian airman Bill Newton at Salamaua in March 1943 and, most appalling of all, indisputable documentary and forensic evidence that starving Japanese soldiers had resorted to butchering unburied Australian and American cadavers and even to 'eating one another'.[32]

Consuming human meat in order to survive has a long and grisly military history: the Crusaders are known to have fed on their dead Arab opponents on their march to Jerusalem. But the attribution of cannibalism has always been a potent cultural libel. Early observations of native peoples by European travellers are so abundant with references to its practice that it is a wonder there were indigenes left to observe at all. They sated the prejudice of a metropolitan audience – the gullible readers famously targeted by Jonathan Swift – who would swallow any lie told about the peoples inhabiting remote corners of the world as 'evidence' that they were populated by arrant savages. The reputation of the Japanese has never quite recovered from this shocking aspect of the conflict. Rather than the nuclear annihilation of two cities, it remains for Australians the ultimate horror story of the Pacific War.

It is impossible to downplay Japan's mistreatment of its prisoners. The statistics bear repeating: around 8000, more than one-third of the 22,300 Australians captured and incarcerated by the Japanese, died or were murdered in captivity – a figure tragically inflated by the approximately 1500 POWs lost at sea, as a result of Allied submarine attacks on the Japanese 'hellships' that transported men like doomed cattle across the Pacific. The death rate was ten times that of the German and Italian internees. Many of the rest survived by the skin of their teeth, and never recovered their health.

Yet the press and the personal accounts of what took place in the camps of South-East Asia, especially those along the Burma Railway, contain an undeniable racial element. That it was the Japanese dishing out such treatment made it even worse. Much of the outrage stemmed from the fact that Orientals had forced Australians into slave labour. The image of 'white coolies' was an appalling one that transgressed nature and belief. Writing in 1946 in *Behind Bamboo*, Rohan Rivett, a career journalist originally seconded from the AIF to work for the Malaya Broadcasting Commission (MBC), recognised that 'the whole gigantic project of mass murder' undertaken by the Japanese was 'a tremendous story' which, upon his release, he proceeded to tell posthaste, after more than three years in captivity. Among the worst crimes perpetrated by the Japanese was that 'white men' were forced to perform 'coolie' labour, along with 'Asiatics' such as Malays, Tamils, and Burmese. When Rivett composed a list of 20 indictments against Japanese authorities, in a report published in Australian newspapers in September 1945, he put the sight of white men working in loin cloths and wooden clogs 'under the eyes of the local Asiatics' right near the top of the list. Submitting to an enemy regarded as racially inferior compounded the humiliation of incarceration. Norman Carter, who was working with Rivett at the MBC when Singapore fell, recalls how it had been especially galling to surrender to a 'simple-minded people', 'a nation of geishas and house-boys'. The 'Honourable Houseboy had become dishonourable conqueror'.[33]

The Occupation would fix that. To turn the 'dishonourable conqueror' back into an 'honourable houseboy', and in his own country, was not merely a matter of squaring the historical ledger. It was the proper expression of precedence; a reassertion of the natural order of things. But vengeance is not necessarily a simple matter. The Australians arrived at the end of the war's long road suffering from what the Anglican priest Frank Coaldrake, the first Australian civilian to enter Occupied Japan, called 'the subtle elated exhaustion of victors'.[34] Getting even was one thing; making effective use of their power was another.

But first, the Australians had to get to Japan.

CHAPTER TWO

Approaching Japan

Public anger towards Japan in the immediate post-war period was seasoned by lingering fear. In part, government policy reflected that mood. 'The overriding aim was security; to ensure that Japan would not again be able to return to the paths of aggression,' reflected Macmahon Ball. But there was also a constructive, and even visionary, aspect to the Chifley government's plans for Japan. Anti-Japanese talk, as Christine de Matos has observed in her detailed investigations into Australian post-war diplomacy, was 'partially designed for public consumption'; 'rebuilding, not solely retribution' was an abiding concern. Australian policy sought to neuter Japan as a future military threat, but it also aspired to facilitate the process of its social, political, and economic reform. This was not mere grandstanding. Australia promoted education and land reform, and the dismantling of the *zaibatsu* (the leviathans of Japanese business so implicated in the country's militarism). It also advocated the creation of genuine political freedoms for men and women, including a strong, organised labour movement. The objective was to attack the social and economic discontent that feeds nationalist aggression.[1] Ben Chifley's vision of the 'light on the hill' – the benevolent objective of 'working for the betterment of mankind not only here but anywhere we may give a helping hand' – even applied to the benighted Japanese.

Australia had been handed an historic opportunity to be acknowledged as an international player. Through its ambitious minister for external affairs, Dr H.V. Evatt, the Chifley government asserted a national determination to exert an influence on regional affairs. Australia sought a status that recognised its military contribution to the Pacific conflict and the suffering Japan's aggression had wrought. In the aftermath of the Japanese surrender, observes T.B. Millar (an Occupationnaire who went on to a distinguished academic career in international relations), Australian diplomacy was 'vigorous and somewhat chip-on-the-shoulder'. British assumptions of Commonwealth leadership were pointedly disregarded. Australia initially wanted to go it alone in Japan, by sending a separate, independent Occupation force, directly under SCAP. After testy negotiations between the British prime minister Clement Attlee and Chifley, it was only persuaded to join a unified British Commonwealth force when Britain proposed that an Australian be appointed commander-in-chief – eventually nominated as John Northcott.[2]

Australian alacrity was alarming to the US as well as Britain, a challenge to its prerogative to exercise sole control of Japan. Initially, MacArthur had been resistant to the idea of any form of force separately identified as 'British', instead wanting it seamlessly integrated into the US military. Agreement for a combined Commonwealth force was achieved by late September, but the US, which was worried that the Soviets might also want to be involved, remained ambivalent about its role. Finally the MacArthur–Northcott Agreement was signed in Tokyo on December 1945 and ratified more than a month later, after haggling over logistical issues and the size of the force. BCOF was to be responsible for 'military control' and 'demilitarisation and disposition of Japanese installations and armaments' within Hiroshima Prefecture (later extended to the incorporation of adjacent prefectures); however, its land, sea, and air components were to be operationally subordinate to US commanders, a humiliating stipulation that led Lieutenant General Robertson to regard the agreement made by his predecessor as an 'iniquitous document'. BCOF was under the supreme command of the Americans and had no military government function, though the force's commander would have 'the right of direct access' to MacArthur on matters of policy affecting BCOF.[3]

Finally, on 31 January, on behalf of the Americans already ensconced in Occupied Japan, MacArthur offered the 'heartiest possible welcome' to the British Commonwealth forces. He singled out the Australians for a special mention:

> The Australian contingent served under my command with brilliant honour during the long and arduous campaigns on the road back and I take special personal pride in again being associated with it.[4]

MacArthur's reference to the Australians he commanded 'on the road back' is telling. Quite apart from its independent policy imperatives, the fact that the Occupation was to be led, and indeed personified, by the former Supreme Commander for the South-West Pacific area, the individual most identified with saving the nation from a near-death experience, made Australia's participation seem especially fitting. The story of the inkstand illustrates MacArthur's wartime standing in Australia. In June 1943, prime minister Curtin wrote to the general asking if he would accept a gift from a Melbourne craftsman, a 'lasting memento' as 'a token of his esteem'. It was an inkstand set made of native Victorian timbers, which included a pen, a ruler, a paper knife, a cigar stand,

and a boomerang. This was not a present to send the pulse racing, but a sincere gesture nonetheless. The letter initiated a flurry of correspondence between Curtin and MacArthur. Finally, the latter accepted what he described as an 'artistic and representative' item, which Curtin, acting as delivery boy as well as go-between, handed over personally. MacArthur inspired loyalty not merely among his personal staff and military associates, who followed him around the Pacific like faithful retainers and ended up peopling his court in Tokyo; he also held the ongoing gratitude of the Australian government. On the day of Hirohito's surrender broadcast, Ben Chifley telegraphed the general, offering him the Australian people's 'heartfelt thanks'. The nation, he remarked, was 'deeply indebted' to MacArthur's 'wonderful courage and devotion'.[5] MacArthur's command of the Occupation did not compel Australia's determination to occupy Japan, but it made its participation a logical extension of the war.

IN THE WEEKS after MacArthur's dramatic arrival at Atsugi air base, outside Tokyo, on 30 August, American soldiers flooded Japan. Over 4000 airborne troops landed that day alone, deposited onto Japanese soil by troop transport planes that touched down at Atsugi every few minutes from 6.00 a.m. Some of the first American arrivals, recalled Herbert Passin, who worked for SCAP as the head of the Public Opinion and Sociological Research Division, were survivors of the ferocious fighting in Okinawa. 'They arrived in Yokohama peacefully, but with their combat habits intact. Every man was heavily armed, grenades hanging in clusters like grapes'. An anxious population witnessed their arrival. Another senior civilian advisor with the Occupation, Theodore Cohen, has observed that the Japanese were terrified of the victors' vengeance. Why would the American soldiers be any gentler than their own? In the two weeks before their entry, local radio warned women to take to the countryside. Conversely, on 29 August men with megaphones had passed through the streets of Yokohama to urge females to stay indoors. Cohen maintains that their fears were groundless: the Americans behaved with courtesy toward the suitably impressed Japanese, other than 'occasional rapes and drunken brawls'.[6]

The Japanese historians Eiji Takemae and Yuki Tanaka tell a very different tale, which they support with some horrifying statistics. The Americans 'comported themselves like conquerors,' Takemae insists, and indulged in a welter of violence, from vandalism and looting to drunken fighting, gang rapes, and other atrocities. In *Japan's Comfort Women* (2002), Tanaka contends that rapes were rampant from the first day of the Occupation in Kanagawa Prefecture, the location of Yokohama, and the large base at Yokosuka. Sick and retarded women were violated; teenage girls were raped in front of their parents and siblings.

According to Tanaka, the first reported rape occurred at 11.00 a.m. on 30 August, when two US marines on an 'inspection tour' entered a Yokosuka house and raped a mother and teenage daughter at gunpoint. The rapists had landed in Japan only hours earlier. Thereafter, the incidence of violent crime increased exponentially in the first few weeks of the Occupation, though it declined sharply thereafter. Statistics presumably sourced from the Central Police Office of Kanagawa Prefecture specify 1900 reported criminal cases by the end of January 1946, among which there were 58 rapes, though the data collection was probably faulty. Other figures obtained by the Japanese government's Central Liaison Office, whose function it was to confer with Allied GHQ, show Yokohama City police figures as specifying 957 crimes committed by GIs in Yokohama alone, in just one month from the beginning of September. Among them were 119 rape cases.

Many crimes went unreported, and few of the perpetrators were prosecuted. The picture of the American serviceman as the epitome of soldierly restraint is an idealised one, heavily tailored by censorship. After 19 September, the Press Code suppressed Japanese reportage of GI crime, deeming it contrary to the benevolent image of the Occupation.[7]

The Americans were not the only ones to take advantage of the chaos during those first weeks of 'peace'. Yuki Tanaka cites a public order report compiled by the Japanese military police, which states that on the evening of 4 September, three Australian POWs who had been released from their camps in Japan and were staying in transit in a hotel in Kyoto while waiting to be repatriated, visited a brothel in the eastern part of the city. Having enjoyed the establishment's services, the group forcibly took three of the prostitutes back to their own hotel, telling the protesting manager that 'Japan lost the war and your police have no power at all!' At the hotel, the women were gang raped by a group of drunken Australians whose number had swollen to seven. The women were returned to the brothel the next morning, minus their underwear, which the men kept as souvenirs.[8] The sudden freedom of men long under the thumb of the Japanese led to alcohol-fuelled violence that was not only perpetrated on the hated guards. In an unsubstantiated claim made in *The Sword and the Blossom* (1968), the POW Ray Parkin describes a local civilian being randomly bashed to death by some drunken Australians. It was his good Japanese friend Koko, a gentle timberman with whom he had worked in a labour camp.

Such events were more the exception than the rule. Fantasies of retributive justice had sustained many prisoners during their ordeal, but when the great moment of release came, they were surprised at how little they felt the desire to get even. POWs like Parkin just wanted to go home and get on with the rest of their lives. When the war ended, Parkin was working in a camp at Ohama, in far-western Honshu, about halfway between Hiroshima and Nagasaki. The amazing fact of their freedom filled the men with a disturbing exaltation, he remembers. Some 'revelled foolishly in the new feeling', entered the village, and 'marched possessively into houses'. Ohama's population was frightened, expecting the men to assert their 'right of rape and pillage due to the conqueror'. But Parkin asserts that, overall, the Australians exercised a self-control that surprised the locals. Destitute themselves, they gratefully received the newly acquired food and clothes offered to them by the liberated prisoners.[9]

Sex had been immediately established as the dominant form of human currency between Occupier and Occupied when the incoming Americans availed themselves of a short-lived system of 'Recreation and Amusement Stations', or 'RAAs'. These were little more than a domestic version of Japan's infamous provision of so-called 'comfort women' to service its forces in ruthlessly annexed parts of Asia. Two weeks before MacArthur's arrival, and with the tacit go-ahead of the Allies, the Security Section of the Ministry of Home Affairs secretly instructed governors and senior police officials of all prefectures to set up what were essentially state-sponsored brothels, to satisfy the appetites of the incoming foreign troops, many of whom were fresh from the privations of the battlefield. The idea was that a body of women, largely garnered from the urban working classes and the impoverished provinces, or those already working in the bar and brothel industries and recruited or coerced by businessmen and entrepreneurs, would be used to protect the honour of middle-class Japanese womanhood. It was to be a noble exercise in patriotism, in other words. In the blunt rationalisation of one police official, 'the American Army is coming to Japan. We fear that the Americans will molest our women – our wives and daughters and sisters. We need a shock absorber'. 'Female floodwall' was another metaphor used to describe officially endorsed prostitution, applied to the governmental goal of channelling a foreign torrent of sexual desire into a lumpen mass of female bodies 'to preserve the pure blood of one-hundred million'.[10]

The Americans took to the sexual hospitality with enthusiasm. A woman was to be had for the cost of a packet of cigarettes. The first RAA brothel, conveniently located not far from the Atsugi airbase, south of the capital, opened its doors the very day the Americans touched down in Japan. Business at the RAAs was hectic, with a staff of sex workers servicing from 15 to a scarcely conceivable 60 clients a day. One brothel, the 'Oasis', was located in the very centre of Tokyo, in Ginza. It catered to enlisted men only; others were set aside for officers. There were RAAs for black soldiers and RAAs for white, for the army that was to impress 'democracy' upon the Japanese was highly segregated.[11]

Yuki Tanaka's research indicates that perhaps 10,000 comfort women and prostitutes within and outside the RAA system were serving the Occupation troops in the Tokyo area alone, by the end of 1945. The prostitution rackets were by no means confined to the capital. Even in gutted Hiroshima, police sought out compliant local businessmen as early as September, encouraging them to recruit women then working in both licensed and unlicensed prostitution and, sometimes, directly hustling the women themselves. Following the arrival of an advance party on 26 September, American troop transports had entered Hiro Bay, near Kure, on 6 October. The following morning the troops disembarked and, by nightfall, several thousand soldiers were stationed in the area. The timing of the local procurers was spot on. Comfort stations were opened in Hiroshima that very day, with some 500 women on the job. An official report quoted by Tanaka says that, 'as expected, as soon as they were opened, all comfort stations were crowded with clients'. The local historian Takeshi Chida has remarked that elements of the female population of Kure-Hiroshima were so taken by the generosity and good cheer of the visitors that 'small gangs of Japanese girls quickly threw themselves at the Americans, and some became notorious in the eyes of the general citizenry'.[12]

WHILE THE AMERICANS were being warmly accommodated in Kure, the Australians who had volunteered for the Occupation were cooling their heels in military encampments in the South-

West Pacific. After the Australian government's announcement on 18 August that it was willing to contribute to an occupation force, it took the best part of six months for the first deployment in Japan. Prime minister Chifley did not announce the broad outline of the Commonwealth involvement until the last day of January 1946 and, even then, some of the detail had yet to be worked out. Disorganisation at GHQ in Tokyo as well as intra-Commonwealth jousting over the administrative core of BCOF itself, plus the priority placed on the repatriation of POWs dispersed throughout Asia, including Japan, led to a series of delays. Both the mounting and movement of BCOF, as Northcott himself lamented, had been adversely affected. In the meantime, a report in the Australian press that January suggested that a group of 40 Japanese newspaper correspondents were politely inquiring of the visiting American secretary of war Robert Patterson why it was even necessary to send British and Australian troops to Japan when 'the Japanese were getting on so well with General MacArthur and the American occupation forces'.[13]

The Commonwealth had actually begun planning for Japan's occupation while the war was still going. Robertson's biographer Jeffrey Grey has noted that a preliminary call for volunteers for an Australian brigade had gone out while the future BCOF leader was commanding the 6th Division in New Guinea.[14] The Australian army component of BCOF, the 34th Australian Infantry Brigade, under Brigadier R.H. Nimmo's command, had started concentrating in Morotai, the most northern island of the Dutch East Indies' island chain, in October 1945. The Brigade was composed of the 65th, 66th, and 67th Infantry battalions, made up from volunteers drawn from the remnants of various Australian divisions located in Borneo, Bougainville, New Britain, and Wewack. These were supported by an armoured car squadron; a field battery of artillery; a field squadron of engineers, signals, supply, transport, workshop, and salvage units; and medical, nursing, dental, and other administrative units. The Australian government had opted to provide the bulk of its contribution to the Occupation forces from volunteers within the Australian forces already serving abroad in the South-West Pacific. Enlistment was voluntary, and recruitment was strong, with 5800 servicemen volunteering to fill a quota of 3300, signing up for a tour of 12 months' duration (with the option of another six) as members of the AIF initial recruitment.[15]

The volunteers, many of them battle-hardened antagonists of Japan, had put up their hands for a variety of reasons. Some simply wanted to savour the fruits of victory. Tom Hungerford was still in Bougainville after an exhausting campaign of jungle warfare when a 'soft talking' recruiter lured him into joining BCOF: 'A year or so with a foot on the neck of prostrate Japan seemed like a pleasing proposition,' he recalls. Bruce Ruxton, in later life to become the belligerent president of the Victorian branch of the RSL (the Returned and Services League), cites an utterly prosaic reason for deciding to volunteer for Japan. In Balikpapan, after having been in the army for two years but with relatively little overseas service, Ruxton thought, 'I didn't want to go home yet.'[16]

Others saw the tour as the logical extension of their war service. Defeating Japan on the battlefield was one thing; bringing it to heel was to be the fitting sequel. The infantryman Terry Briscoe was in Tarakan, Borneo at the cessation of armed hostilities and volunteered for Japan because he wanted to participate in 'the final chapter of the complete surrender of this fanatical enemy'. A few Australians, according to one veteran, Les Semken, went there 'hoping to kill more Japs'. Some of their comrades took a more constructive line. Bill Towers wanted to encounter an alien people beyond the battlefield and outside the context of wartime hatred and propaganda. As he wrote to his mother, 'I wanted to find out why I was taught at school that the Japanese was the world's little gentleman, and ten years later … that he is a treacherous and uncivilized barbarian'.[17]

Volunteering was not a decision to be taken lightly. Steve

Macaulay had been in Bougainville for a year, after serving in New Guinea, when the ceasefire came. The abrupt end to the war had taken the troops by surprise; the men did not know what they were getting themselves into. They had no sure way of predicting Japanese resentment or resistance. The cynics among Macaulay's cohort said, 'You'll be sorry,' warning him in semi-jocular fashion that he would be found in bed with his throat cut. In the end, Macaulay's decision to go had a pragmatic basis. As he was low on priority points for discharge, he had resigned himself to more months in Bougainville; Japan provided an alternative to the drudgery of garrison duties somewhere in the South-West Pacific.[18]

In *The Phoenix Cup* (1947), British journalist John Morris' personal account of a tour of Occupied Japan, he comments caustically on glowing publicity given to the volunteer nature of the Australian contingent. Of the men with whom he had talked, Morris says, 'none had come to Japan for any other reason than that he could find no work at home'. He misses the point. As Les Murray observes in his verse novel *The Boys Who Stole the Funeral* (1980), military service was for many of the veterans 'their only proud employment ever'.[19] Soldiering in Japan seemed a good alternative to the humdrum struggles of post-war Australia. The comradeship and various excitements of active military service were so intense that the return to civilian life seemed like too much of an anticlimax.

Volunteers from outside the ranks of active servicemen were similarly motivated. During the long delay on Morotai, inactivity, uncertainty, and press criticism sapped morale, and a spate of resignations from the force left the 34th Brigade undermanned. Many men, about 2000 of them, simply changed their minds, and the force was opened up to the general population. Recruiting advertisements in the Australian daily newspapers preyed on youthful wanderlust. In one, headed 'Serve Overseas', a fresh-faced, slouch-hatted Digger is superimposed over a map of the

Eastern hemisphere, with lines spreading longitudinally from Australia to the Japanese archipelago. 'Recruits are urgently wanted' for Japan, says the advertisement, to become members of a 'world famous fighting force'. It was 'a splendid opportunity for keen young men to secure overseas experience whilst enjoying the benefits available to members of the wartime A.I.F' – a promise that proved to be hollow. Young men like Bob Christison who had just missed out on the war welcomed BCOF as an opportunity to put on the slouch hat and participate in the great tradition. The medico Murray Elliott, for one, 'felt guilty' about not fighting: 'anxious' to get overseas, he 'leapt' at the chance to go to Japan.[20]

The men lingering on Morotai spent their time as best they could. An island surrounded by a coral reef, with beaches of blindingly white, coarse coral sand, Morotai had its compensations. Steve Macaulay recalls the period nostalgically: 'There was plenty to do, nightly films, a "duck" [an amphibious jeep] to visit surrounding islands and plenty of fresh tropical fruit'. Then a young Intelligence officer with the 67th Battalion, T.B. Millar recalls lazy days spent plucking papayas from the tree. Murray Elliot lectured the troops on the horrors of contracting sexually transmitted diseases, tried to learn a bit of Japanese, and supplemented his small beer ration by concocting a dangerously potent liqueur, a sort of crème de menthe made by mixing absolute alcohol and peppermint oil, both extracted from the unit pharmacist.[21]

The irregular appearance of dated newspapers from home helped alleviate the boredom; in early December 1945, Headquarters Company produced its own newspaper, *Geisha News*, later renamed and revamped as *Be in It*. The war-crimes trials that were conducted on the island from November reminded the soldiers of the recent behaviour of some of the race whose homeland they were about to enter. A number of Japan-bound Australians attended the proceedings which, to their satisfaction, handed out several death penalties. On Morotai, Allan Clifton remembers, the men were constantly reminded of the wartime villainies of the Japanese, in addition to being told that they were 'unhygienic and disease-ridden and unfit to associate with'.[22]

Coming face to face with the enemy for the first time also brought with it the disconcerting knowledge that the Japanese were not the monsters of propagandistic lore. Supervising the Japanese medical staff who were tending their sick and wounded at a camp hospital in an isolated part of the island, the medical officer Dan Hart had the 'popular misconception' that they all look and act the same shattered: 'They are as variable as we are,' he tells his family in a letter home, dated 26 September 1945. As a doctor, he was impressed by their 'amazing' hygiene ('contrary to ideas held'). And, as he was the one 'European' doctor within several miles with responsibility of supervising the treatment of some 4000 prisoners, he was grateful for their willingness to co-operate. Hart has confided that the troops had to watch what they said about the Japanese in their letters, for to veer from the agreed 'truth' about them was to indicate that one had gone 'soft in the head'. Thus, in a letter from the same time, Hart reassures his family: 'It is undoubtedly true that this is the most barbaric race on earth.' This was the standard line. But direct contact with the Japanese had triggered the beginning of a *volte face* in response to them, which was to become manifest during the Occupation itself. Clearly, these eager-to-please men, at the very least, were not all 'maniacs and fiends'.[23]

There are only so many papayas to eat and lectures to attend. As the designated period of service did not begin until arriving in Japan, the men wanted to get moving. According to Tom Hungerford's account, the frustration of the men, in the great tradition of military scapegoating, focused largely on the Americans. MacArthur's vacillation on allowing Australians to participate in the Occupation was an acute source of annoyance. 'Japforce', as it was unofficially called, was becoming angry. "*What?*" roared indignant groups at the boozer, night after night. "*That Yank poofter?* Tell the *Aussies* whether or not they can go to Japan?

Bloody *hell*."[24] The men wanted ships to sail to Japan, and they wanted nominated sailing dates; they wanted a decision on the official date for commencement of service; and they demanded an unequivocal rebuttal of negative press reports. To make matters worse, Japanese POWs were using their latrines (though not, of course, those of the officers), and the men were tormented by fears that they would contract syphilis from the lavatory seats.

A strike, or 'jack-up', was planned by a small group of junior NCOs, who enlisted Hungerford's help. He had previously led something similar in a Darwin camp, and was considered an imperturbably effective troublemaker. On the appointed early January day, an orderly demonstration parade of around 1300 men was held outside brigade HQ. Tom Hungerford addressed the men over a PA, and was handed a list of requests written on a piece of Salvation Army Red Shield notepaper. He presented this to the colonel in charge, who pleasantly informed him he could be shot for leading what was tantamount to a mutiny. In fact, the brigade HQ defused the issue intelligently, and when Hungerford was summoned to appear before Brigadier Nimmo, he was praised for his sensible handling of the episode and invited to come to him directly, should he have any further complaints. Though suppressed by army censorship, the Morotai 'mutiny' provoked a visit by the minister for the army, Frank Forde. He arrived on the tropical island sweating in a suit and sporting a pork-pie hat perched on his head. Not for the last time did BCOF think that politicians were out of touch.

Gathered in various far-flung locations, the Australian components of BCOF were finally coming together. An ATIS advance party arrived in Tokyo as early as October 1945; the same month, members of the 88 Australian High Speed Wireless Troop departed Morotai for Japan to set up communication links to Australia and assist in the location and repatriation of Australian POWs in camps in Japan – a bittersweet process that included the identification and collection of the ashes of their comrades who didn't make it. Reconnaissance parties from the army and air force visited the BCOF areas early in the new year. RAAF personnel who enlisted in the British Commonwealth Air Group (BCAIR) had been assembling at Labuan Island in North Borneo, and experiencing similar frustrations to their brothers in the army. The men and equipment of 81 Fighter Wing, RAAF, eventually arrived in Kure by the end of March, before entraining for Bofu and Iwakuni, the RAAF bases in neighbouring Yamaguchi Prefecture. In September 1945, Australian ships had taken part in the recovery and repatriation of Allied POWs in Japanese camps. One of these, the HMAS *Warramunga*, entered the port of Kure on 1 February 1946; the local authorities were informed that the Commonwealth forces were about to take over from the Americans, and the city was ordered to make preparations to receive them.[25]

Truly, it had been a long and circuitous road to Japan. The Australian Occupation of Japan can essentially be dated from 13 February when, after a ten-day voyage from Morotai, the old Liberty ship *Stamford Victory*, carrying the first convoy of Australian Occupationnaires (some 1122 of them) entered the waterway of the Inland Sea, where it was joined by the destroyer HMAS *Arunta*, for passage to Kure Harbour. The Inland Sea has long been celebrated for its unsurpassed beauty. In the late 1870s, the Australian traveller James Hingston had written with exasperation: 'Nothing in the way of sea-coast scenery that I ever expatiated upon but was wet-blanketed by "Oh! You should see the Inland Sea of Japan"'. It was still beautiful in 1946, though the aspect changed dramatically as the ancient vessel arrived at Kure. From the deck, the war diarist of the 66th Battalion observed that the devastation was 'beyond description'. But so too was the 'satisfaction and happiness' with which the men contemplated finally setting foot on the soil of defeated Japan. On the wharf, a naval band struck up a selection of parochial favourites, including 'Waltzing Matilda' and 'The Road to Gundagai', as well as (prophetically) 'You'd Be Far Better off in a Home'. 'The long journey is over,' wrote the war diarist. 'Objective Nippon – reached.'[26]

A week later, the *Taos Victory* made the same journey, taking a second contingent of Australian troops into Japan. Word must have already got out about what lay at the end of the voyage. The final issue of the troopship newspaper, the single-sheet *Taos Digger*, published a short supplement titled, 'Your Japan'. Along with an ill-drawn map of the local region, it contained the following discouraging news, capitalised for emphasis:

> TOMORROW YOU ARRIVE AT KURE – what is left of JAPAN's greatest naval base. YOU are going into a DEVASTATED AREA and a climate more severe than any normal AUSTRALIAN winter. Do not expect bands, flag-waving or throngs of cheering people.

The supplement went on to remark that large numbers of Kure's pre-war population of 270,000 were drifting back to the ravaged city to make their homes in 'humpies'. These 'essentially native' people live at 'the lowest subsistence level'. It ended with:

> THIS is a poor country.
> THESE are a poor people.
> DON'T expect too much.[27]

CHAPTER THREE

In the City of the Dead

The Inland Sea is often likened to the Aegean because of its rich repository of maritime myth; however, Kure and its environs have never excited the traveller's imagination. Donald Richie didn't take to its chimney-belching coastline when he journeyed west along the waterway nearly 40 years ago, finding it emblematic of Japan's slow asphyxiation by aggressive industrialisation. As he writes in *The Inland Sea* (1971), his evocation of the passing beauty of the sea country that the Japanese call the 'Seto Naikai', even the ancient deities despised Kure and gave it a wide berth. Legend has it that the township was the lair of monstrous hairy spiders, 'big as automobiles', which would seize upon unwary travellers and carry them off into the hills behind, to suck them dry. 'With famous people going out of their way to avoid the place, with all sorts of horrid and pitiful tales surrounding it, one comes prepared for Kure,' Richie advises.[1]

But the Australians were hardly 'prepared' for Kure. They arrived to find a dump, in every sense. After BCOF's allocation of

Hiroshima Prefecture in December 1945, Northcott had recon-
noitred the area. He reported back favourably to all elements of
the force – Australian, British, Indian, and New Zealander –
stressing the importance of the naval base and the commodious-
ness of the barracks to be inherited from the Americans.[2] No
doubt Northcott wanted to boost the morale for the task ahead, at
a time when many volunteers were having second thoughts about
the enterprise.

But the rosy picture of the life and facilities that awaited the
men was something akin to a travel brochure that extols the virtues of an exotic resort which turns out to be a hovel. The majority
of the troops arrived from the sultry South-West Pacific Islands
into an icy, sleety shambles. Murray Elliott was a member of the
first consignment of troops on the *Stamford Victory*, on a voyage
that seemed a 'pleasant Pacific cruise'. Flying fish sped above the
low bow waves; days were spent in bathing trunks, playing cards
and chess. But the shipboard joie de vivre dissipated as Japan
approached, and the weather grew cold and overcast. As the
Stamford Victory entered Kure, Elliott gazed at a harbour ringed by
treeless hills that 'had been so altered by the intensity of the
bombing by the American Air Force that they appeared to have
been recently bulldozed into position'. At the wharves, a column
of black smoke rose into the sunless midday sky. Arising from a
huge stockpile of coal set aflame by American incendiary bombs,
it seemed to symbolise a cremation – a smouldering fire that
burned during the two years of Elliott's tour in Japan, defying all
attempts to extinguish it.[3]

Struck by its desolation, British Occupationnaires disembarking
at Kure on 1 April had nicknamed it 'The City of the Dead'. The
city's depressing impact on the spirits of the foreign visitors was to
become a persistent motif in BCOF testimony. Despite frenetic
rebuilding, Kure was still a mess several years into the Occupation.
Even the well disposed reacted against its dismal chaos, the oily
water, and the rusting debris. As late as 1950, the missionary's wife

Maida Coaldrake found herself in 'instant recoil' upon entering the harbour, when she travelled to Japan to join her husband Frank.[4]

Beginning his year teaching the progeny of BCOF in October 1949, Hal Porter found a frontier town pockmarked by war:

> splintery, treeless, stopgap, with side-streets of bare earth, weedy vacant allotments, out-of-plumb telegraph poles, and the wind-scoured look of a place run by the poverty-stricken from shards salvaged out of the rubble of holocaust.

Bomb craters could still be seen on the higher slopes of the steep hills behind the port, along with houses 'minced to rubbish', while down by the water's edge, an entanglement of rusted metal – girders, derricks, sheds, boilers, turbines – still awaited removal. The damage was spiritual as well as physical. The very streetscape was permeated with despair and trauma. As he makes his way down one of Kure's precipitous paths to the fleshpots of Hondori, the hub of the town, Porter invokes a local urban legend, that of the ghostly cries and imprecations of the tormented spirits of juveniles killed in the wartime bombing of the children's hospital.[5]

In February 1946, BCOF HQ having been established in Kure (they were soon to be moved offshore to Etajima), the bulk of the 34th Brigade headed about 20 kilometres west down the coast to Kaitaichi. These days, Kaitaichi is a suburb of Hiroshima, colonised by the gigantic Mazda motor plant; but, back then, it was a small, grubby, windswept seaside town. The troops were initially quartered in dilapidated wooden sheds that had been used for storage. Some were without floors, let alone luxuries like hot water. Snow lay on the ground, and the winter wind blew fiercely in from the sea. In August 1946, an officer newly returned from Japan, H.K. Wood, wrote for the popular press a bitter account of the spartan conditions he encountered in the 'peasant country' of Kaitaichi: 'In the unit with which I stayed,' he wrote, '20-odd men showered from two one-gallon canvas buckets, with water dipped from a 44-gallon drum under which a fire burned.'[6]

The appalling accommodation of those early Occupation days still gets the veterans' blood boiling. Brian Rose, a member of the Corps of Signallers, who arrived in Japan on 9 April 1946 aboard the *Duntroon*, ruefully recalls billets in a bombed-out brick building in Kure – 'no doors, no windows, and no top floor, just the walls'. Aircraftman Earle Morgan, a member of 77 Squadron RAAF who had been one of the first enlistments on Labuan Island, arrived at Bofu that March to quarters which should have been condemned. (In fact, they had been.) Gales howled through glassless windows, there was no drinking water, the showers and mess were located 200 metres away, and there were no internal toilets. The men were hopelessly ill-fitted for winter operations and dependent upon Comforts Fund parcels and handouts, as well as their families, for essentials such as gloves and scarves. Clifton Pugh's first letter home to his mother after arriving in Kaitaichi in February 1946 sees him making an '*urgent* appeal' (his emphasis) for a scarf – 'a good warm one' to ward off the 'devilish cold'. At Morotai, the volunteers had been outraged to be handed winter uniforms that included second-hand overcoats still showing signs of the stripes and the colour patches of their former owners. The Occupationnaires felt like tramps and imposters – not even proper soldiers, let alone conquering heroes. Dressed in cast-offs, scrounging for basic comforts, they were hardly better off than the derelict people of derelict Japan.[7]

VISITING OCCUPIED JAPAN in early 1947 with his friend, the painter Albert Tucker, the American-born writer Harry Roskolenko observed a quasi-feudal hierarchy of power and privilege. 'If General MacArthur is the unconscious Emperor-Elect,' he wrote, in an essay published in *Meanjin* that year, 'then every GI over the rank of 2nd lieutenant is a prince,' and the soldiers 'mere barons and dukes'.[8] Significantly, the Australians are not ranked at all. They were not 'serfs', for those were the common Japanese; but they were hardly noblemen, either.

The place of Australians in the pecking order was problematic. The American command was as impatient with opposition from bumptious Australians as it was with the Japanese. US president of the Allied Council George Atcheson habitually sought to put Australia in its place, railing – in the case of its vociferous opposition to SCAP giving the go-ahead to a Japanese whaling expedition in the Antarctic – against the 'venal' interests of a 'small nation'. The council met fortnightly in the Meiji Insurance building in central Tokyo, but it was viewed as a rubber stamp by MacArthur, as was the other body associated with the Occupation, the 11-nation Far Eastern Commission, based in Washington DC. With little on the agenda, the business of some of the council meetings was over in a few minutes, though sometimes proceedings could become quarrelsome. Disagreements between the ebullient Soviet representative General Kuzma Dervyanko and the Americans, on everything from labour and social policy to censorship, produced some volcanic arguments. As the Commonwealth representative, Macmahon Ball's preparedness to side with the Russians nettled SCAP. It also perturbed Ball's political boss, Dr Evatt. Tired of his minister and fed up with American derision, Ball left Japan in acrimonious circumstances in August 1947, to be replaced on the council, and as head of the Australian Mission in Tokyo, by the career diplomat Patrick Shaw, who was no mere cipher himself.[9]

In the field, SCAP was grateful for the Australian contribution but indifferent to its day-to-day operation. In February 1948, MacArthur told an Australian visitor, the soldier and academic T. Inglis Moore, that his countrymen in BCOF were 'putting on a very good show'. If that was the case, it was a performance the great man elected not to see, as he never flattered the provincial BCOF theatre with his presence. Then again, the Supreme

Commander never went anywhere much in Tokyo, let alone Japan, other than commuting between his residence in the American embassy and his headquarters in the Dai-Ichi building. The general saw Japan through the windows of the big, black 1941 Cadillac, acquired from a Manila sugar baron, now proudly displayed in his museum in Norfolk Virginia. Perhaps MacArthur could be forgiven for not even knowing where BCOF was stationed, as the map of occupied Japan used by General Charles Willoughby, his powerful Intelligence chief, revealed no divisional or brigade signs in the area allocated to BCOF.[10]

Upon assuming BCOF command from the more modest Northcott in mid-1946, Robertson sought to raise his men's status, largely by doggedly asserting his own. His self-importance verged on the absurd. The head of the British Mission, Sir Alvary Gascoigne, ridiculed him as a 'fantastic Australian' suffering from 'la folie de grandeur'. This was a view shared by many of Robertson's compatriots, including Macmahon Ball. 'His preoccupation with his status is nearly pathological,' Ball wrote in his dairy in November 1946. He simply had to keep up with the Joneses, especially if they came from Britain. Commonwealth House, the residence allocated to the Australian Mission in Japan, had been the Australian legation before the war. But it did not compare with the UK legation, according to Robertson. Australia required 'a first class embassy'. More than anything Robertson coveted a substantial residence in Tokyo. He stayed with Ball in Commonwealth House when visiting the capital, and also with Gascoigne in the compound at the British embassy. This would not do. 'I must have some place of my own,' Robertson insisted.[11] And not just any place – an 'A class house' befitting his rank and status. After some haggling, he was allotted the Siamese legation, taking possession in October 1946. Forced out of the residence when the Siamese demanded it back nearly three years later, Robertson refused MacArthur's offer of a suite at the Imperial Hotel. Eventually, another large home was found and suitably modernised for him, and he moved into it in April 1950.

Meanwhile, back in Kure, Robertson occupied the former official residence of the commander-in-chief of the naval base, a handsome Western-styled house with elegantly furnished rooms in the front, including an enormous dining room – in which Robertson could entertain his important guests and indulge his fondness for Scotch whisky – and simple Japanese rooms in the rear, where the servants lived and laboured. Robertson had an acute appreciation of the rituals and appearance of rank. They required, among other things, putting on a good show. In 1947, he lobbied the Defence Committee in Australia for a boost in his personal and entertainment allowance: he had three establishments to maintain, not only the Kure mansion and his official residence in Tokyo but also the General Officers Mess at his HQ on Etajima, in addition to providing hospitality to a train of distinguished visitors. In short, he had 'to maintain and enhance British prestige'. His habits soon became a cause for comment at home and abroad. In a wide-ranging attack, a November 1946 edition of the *Chicago Tribune* berated a 'self-indulgent general' crassly luxuriating in the comforts of power in a country still crippled by the ravages of war. Criticism came later in Australia, but was equally trenchant. When internecine squabbling about BCOF's behaviour broke out in the home press in 1948, the returned officer E.J. Thwaites described Robertson as living 'like a feudal baron'.[12]

Robertson's leadership of BCOF tells a tale in microcosm about Australian–British relationships. Nicknamed 'Red Robbie', for his flaming red hair and not his politics, Robertson had been an undeniably brave soldier. In 1915, he had spent his 21st birthday on Gallipoli and, the following year, he led the 10th Light Horse on a cavalry charge that ripped through the Turkish defences at Sinai. In World War II, he had commanded a brigade that chased the Italians across the Libyan Desert, and he was commander of the 6th Division in New Guinea when Japan surrendered. In a sense, he was the swaggering embodiment of the Anzac legend that seemed to express a new kind of independent and distinctive national character.

Yet, in some respects, Robertson was a picture-book parody of the colonial officer. He spoke with a plummy English accent and, on occasion, reportedly sported a monocle in Japan – an act which, according to a hero-worshipping profile published in the Melbourne *Sun* in 1954, improbably started a craze among senior American officers. He was a great Empire man, praising its 'valour, endurance and thrift' in a 1934 treatise aimed at shoring up vulnerable Australian defences in the context of a weakened British navy. Nonetheless, he also evinced a very modern Australian contempt for British assumptions. In Japan, Major General D.T. ('Punch') Cowan, the commander of the British–Indian Division (BRINDIV), was a particular source of irritation. Cowan had fancied that he, not Robertson, would succeed Northcott, and he resented Australian leadership of the force. He had commanded the 17th Gurkha Division in Burma for some years, fighting the Japanese; to now be led by an Australian was galling. In his unpublished reminiscences, Robertson rails against Cowan's superior attitude and his 'tendency to group all so-called Colonials and Indians as inferior races, to be kept in subjection by the English, who would never be commanded by such people'.[13]

In the early months of Robertson's rule, British sniffiness confronted Australian pushiness, and vice versa. 'Prestige' is a consistent motif of the Commonwealth contribution to the Occupation. The governments of the UK, Australia, India, and New Zealand had set down that it was the force's role not merely to 'represent worthily' the British Commonwealth and to 'illustrate' and 'impress on' the Japanese people 'the democratic way and purpose in life', but also 'to maintain and enhance British Commonwealth prestige and influence in the eyes of the Japanese and of our Allies'. Sometimes it seemed that self-image and self-importance were the only reasons the Commonwealth was in Japan. 'I have always maintained that the main purpose of the occupation forces is one of prestige', wrote Patrick Shaw in his report describing his visit the BCOF areas in May 1948.[14]

But prestige for whom? Robertson's anxiety to assert himself as the senior British Commonwealth person in Japan led to acute tensions not only with senior British military men but with officials as well – not least with the personal representative of the British prime minister at MacArthur's GHQ, Lieutenant General Sir Charles Gairdner. The pair fought a long duel of one-upmanship. When Robertson was promoted to lieutenant general in March 1947, Gairdner attempted to have himself promoted to full general. Robertson correctly discerned that the Englishman saw him as having 'no position or status in Tokyo at all'. This was a matter of cultural principle as well as administrative nicety – Robertson was a mere colonial. In the meantime, Gairdner apparently demanded a plane provided by BCAIR, the airforce wing of BCOF, and ordered the Union Jack painted on it, along with the name 'Eastern Monarch'. It seems Gairdner commandeered aircraft at will, using them to fly to Korea, China, Okinawa, and to Hokkaido to fish for salmon and hunt for bears. Reports back from the Ainu, the native people of Hokkaido, suggested that Gairdner's erratic marksmanship left numerous wounded and maimed bears wandering around the island. 'The Society for the Prevention of Wounded or Dumb Animals might find a greater scope among the UK personnel than among the Japanese', Robertson sneers in his reminiscences – a barb aimed at his other British bête noir, the de facto ambassador Sir Avery Gascoigne, whose wife had set up such a society in outraged response to perceptions of Japanese cruelty.[15]

The dissension stemmed not merely from a clash of Commonwealth cultures and individual egos. Britain prioritised confidential exchanges with the US over the wishes of what a Foreign Office official called Britain's 'obstreperous children' (Australia and New Zealand). Robertson's not unreasonable impression was that both Gairdner and Gascoigne were duplicitously working for the individual interests of the UK, counter to Commonwealth solidarity. The decision in late 1946 by the British government to withdraw its troops the following year, without any prior consultation, supports his view. The British had never relished the humiliatingly subsidiary role played by BCOF in the military governance of its areas of operation, which was essentially limited to regional surveillance to ensure that US directives were being faithfully enacted. The inheritors of a great heroic tradition had been reduced to the role of puffed-up policemen doing a local beat.

At the Foreign Office, Esler Dening (the first post-war British ambassador to Japan) thought that it had 'become increasingly clear for some time past that our occupation forces in Japan are serving no useful purpose', and that Australian 'vanity' was all that impeded the entire Commonwealth force from packing up and going home. British interest in the Far East had shifted to a focus on Europe, and the anticipated economic foothold in post-war Japan that would stem from participation in the Occupation turned out to be shakier than hoped. Britain opted out. Robertson heard the news second-hand from MacArthur, a blow that not only struck at his personal authority but that undermined BCOF as a whole. He would tell Macmahon Ball that both Gascoigne and Gairdner had 'double crossed him and generally treated him in a deceitful and contemptuous way'.[16]

Robertson got on rather better with the Americans than the British, though he refused to kowtow to them and objected to real or imagined signs of dismissive treatment. The Americans 'browbeat anyone they think is weaker than themselves', he remarks in his reminiscences. Overbearing and intolerant of dissent, they hold to 'the Christian doctrine of "he who is not with me is against me"'. Robertson made it clear he was going to stand up to the Americans shortly after his arrival in Tokyo in June 1946 to take over BCOF command from Northcott. Accompanying the latter on the laborious train journey down to Kure, he took exception to

Northcott's special coach, which had been drawn from a pool, being daubed with the legend 'US Army'. Robertson asked him why he had not replaced it with the BCOF badge. 'You will offend the Americans', was Northcott's reply. Upon assuming command, Robertson had the offending denomination erased. Pursuing the matter with the Eighth Army, Robertson succeeded in having a change made to all coaches and rolling stock, which were henceforth labelled 'Allied Forces'.[17]

To his credit, Robertson was also an indefatigable advocate for the status and conditions of his men. The main game in Japan (other than golf) was securing a better deal for his troops. Robertson tirelessly lobbied American GHQ to put his men on an equal standing with their fellow Occupationnaires. That meant standing up to the formidable MacArthur. Preparing for his first daunting audience alone with the famously magisterial Supreme Commander, Robertson says he was determined, having heard of MacArthur's garrulity, that for every minute the American talked during the interview, he would talk for a minute, too. He exceeded his own estimation, remarking that of the 75 minutes of the interview, it was his voice that prevailed for 'about forty'.[18]

This boast testifies to Robertson's relentlessly competitive ego, but also to his determination to have BCOF's voice heard where it really mattered. During his tenure in Japan, Robertson saw MacArthur officially no less than 67 times; 'Punch' Cowan, the one British general commanding Occupation troops, never enjoyed the privilege. Robertson also met with the Eighth Army chief, Eichelberger, on equally numerous occasions, doing BCOF's bidding over lunch or on the golf course, leading the American to describe him as 'both a scrounger and a moocher'. Even Gascoigne, mindful that the British troops were dependent on him for their rations and general amenities, was impressed by the way he successfully dealt with GHQ. Despite their disagreements, he wrote to Robertson in August 1952, 'I always recognised the magnificent show that you were putting up for the Commonwealth'. Gascoigne particularly complimented the manner in which the Australian 'managed to get everything [he] wanted from the Americans, and yet keep on good terms with them'.[19]

Well, not quite everything. At his first audience with MacArthur in Tokyo, Robertson took up the vexed issue of the geographical location of BCOF. According to his account of the meeting, the Supreme Commander assured him that the BCOF constellation of locations in western and southern Japan – Hiroshima and Yamaguchi Prefectures, plus Shimane, Okayama, Tottori, and the four prefectures comprising Shikoku Island – was not permanent, and that Robertson was 'quite at liberty to go about Japan and see if there was an area which I would prefer'. Robertson's use of the first person singular is indicative. The principle of divide and rule was at work, and he relished the thought. 'He thought perhaps I might like Nagoya, or even Kyushu,' the Australian wrote. 'He did not think I would be interested in Hokkaido'.[20] In fact, it was Kobe that Robertson coveted. It was a prestigious area of old British commercial interests, and it was adjacent to the cultural marvels of Kyoto, which had been spared the wartime bombing. But BCOF remained substantially in its nether region to the bitter end. Robertson had to make do with SCAP agreeing to the stationing of a detachment for guard duty in Tokyo and a small British Commonwealth 'Sub-Area' established in Kobe in October 1946.

DESPITE ROBERTSON'S EFFORTS on their behalf, his men always felt like second-class citizens. Compared with their American counterparts, who were living it up in the capital, they were hayseeds from the sticks. Earle Morgan remembers travelling to Tokyo with a squad of RAAF to take part in an Empire Day march, going from Bofu all the way to Tokyo on a train usually reserved for American personnel. The trip still rankles: 'They were served their meals in a dining car, but we were not allowed in until they had all finished, and then we got what was left over.' Like most Australian Occupationnaires in Tokyo, Morgan noticed 'how well the Americans were looked after', and marvelled at the lavish amenities at their disposal, including nightclubs, cinemas, ballrooms, lounges, roof gardens, and dining and grill rooms. To Cyril Stringer, a petty officer aboard the *Warramunga*, the little America of downtown Tokyo was 'a revelation', after Kure and Hiroshima, 'like walking out of a primitive village into the heart of New York'.[21]

The wealth and power of the conqueror contrasted with the plight of the conquered; while oxen-drawn carts were still to be seen plodding down the main streets, the emporia of Ginza stocked imported goods at fabulous prices. Like most of his comrades, Ian Wood, of the 65th Battalion, had such a good time doing guard duty during his Tokyo stint that he was sorry to leave, making the parting observation that 'the Yanks ... appeared to own' the city. This was not just a case of an envious Australian soldier griping: civilian visitors to Japan were also struck by the contrast in conditions. 'To come to Tokio [sic] from Kure is like paying a visit to one's rich relations,' wrote Dorothy Drain of the *Australian Women's Weekly*, who covered the Occupation in a series of articles in mid-1946, travelling to Japan with the first shipment of Australian female nurses and AAWMS, the Australian Army Women's Medical Service.[22]

Even bombed-out Osaka had superior amenities, according to an Australian soldier, H.K. Wood, who visited there after six weeks in the Kaitaichi–Kure area. The city had been gutted by B-29s, but any substantial buildings left standing the Americans simply made their own: 'Building after building, six, eight stories high, flew the Stars and Stripes. Each building was steam-heated, a cosy refuge from the biting winds. Each had its army of Jap cleaners, girls in national dress waiting on the US soldiers.' The latest Hollywood movies were on continual show, with occasional 'date nights', when a soldier could take along a girlfriend – 'European or Japanese'.

There were no furtive meetings in back lanes, no brawls with 'back-alley Japs'. Wherever one went, Wood wrote, lighted arrows directed one's path to the nearest US-army coffee shop.[23]

Back in bleak, miserable Kure, where amenities were few and unappealing, the troops were forced to spend their free time 'wandering the streets like lost souls', in the words of the 66th Battalion official war diarist. Such comforts and diversions as might be had (other than those laid on in the brothels) were off limits. The men couldn't even have a haircut in a Japanese barbershop, let alone a meal or even a cup of tea, without breaking the rules. Wood paints a depressing picture of demoralised troops hanging around the 'dingy town' and scoffing beer bought on the black market. By May 1946, the men were moaning that they had been falsely promised that 'every facility' would be provided for 'seeing Japan', but the organised 'sight-seeing tours' had never eventuated.[24] Escape from the 'City of the Dead' and its wretched suburban limbo seemed impossible.

Touring the BCOF area that July and August soon after assuming command, Robertson was appalled by what he saw and reported to JCOSA on the urgent need for better amenities, facilities, and quarters. The situation improved after the move of Brigade HQ from Kaitaichi to Hiro in July, following the departure of BRINDIV to Okayama. (HQ took the 66th Battalion with it; the 67th remained in Kaitaichi, while the 65th moved east of Kure to Fukuyama.) But the Hiro barracks, once inhabited by Japanese soldiery, had been built for 'a smaller race of men', Robertson observed. The general particularly shuddered at the squat toilets: 'The ordinary sanitary pedestals usual to European people,' he wrote with disgust, 'were not even in production in the country'. Conditions in Kure itself made Hiro look like the Hilton. As the stifling, acrid summer of western Honshu settled over the men, some Kure-based elements of the force lived in crude corrugated-iron sheds. 'Had I been a private soldier in one of those units at this time,' Robertson reflected, 'I should have felt rebellious against the whole thing'.[25] Nature, for once, did the men a favour. When some of the barracks were severely damaged by a typhoon that blew through the area, new ones were constructed.

Things could only get better. As 1946 wore on, the Australian Canteens Service was improved; a local broadcasting station was set up in Kure; the service postal units got their act together; and the sporting energies and abilities of the young men of the force were directed into organised meetings and competitions. Movies also provided a diversion. The Australian Cinema Unit established a series of mobile or fixed cinemas, with American films greatly in favour. Visiting performers, including some big names, entertained the troops. Towards the end of the Occupation, the American harmonica virtuoso Larry Adler, witch-hunted out of his home country, performed a recital broadcast on the BCOF shortwave station WLKS – even Occupied Japan was more accommodating than McCarthyist America. BCOF itself spawned several theatre ensembles, such as the Brindiv Players, the Hiro Players, the Etajima Repertory Society, and the Iwakuni Dramatic Society. The BCOF Repertory Society staged Noel Coward's *This Happy Breed,* one of several productions reviewed by Hal Porter for *The Gen,* the monthly journal of the Army Education Service. Porter says he went to the theatre expecting 'to stumble once more upon amateurs plunging to dramatic suicide', but emerged pleasantly, if patronisingly, surprised.[26]

The birth of the newspaper *British Commonwealth Occupation News,* or *BCON,* gave the force a voice. Published from the Mainichi offices in central Osaka, the first edition appeared on 9 April 1946, and it ran for the next four years. When the writer Miles Franklin received a copy of the first edition in the mail, sent by her friend Frank Ryland, a BCOF journalist, she thought it a 'funny little paper' that might 'grow into a powerful journal'. Grow it did – in circulation, at least. By mid-1948, more than 50 BCOF personnel were employed in producing the broadsheet newspaper six days a week. *BCON* drew on international news organisations such as the Reuters World Service, the monitoring organisation Radio Press (operated in Osaka by second-generation Japanese Americans, the 'Nisei'), along with special correspondents in Japan and Australia. Its circulation of 12,000 was small by comparison with the *Pacific Stars and Stripes* (over 80,000 copies), but enough to enable a wide BCOF readership. 'In view of its prestige value', Robertson desired it be read outside the force, recommending it be sent to Japanese schools where English was taught.[27]

Determined that Commonwealth personnel, languishing in what some of them unkindly called the 'arse end' of Japan, should partake of some of the privileges of the American conqueror, BCOF developed a network of leave hostels for service people and their families, subsidised by the Amenities Fund. These were strategically situated in places of cultural and recreational interest, usually as far as possible from the Commonwealth zones – establishments such as Gloucester House and the Sumitomo Villa at Kobe; a resort hotel on Lake Biwa, near Kyoto; hotels in the *onsen* (spas) at Beppu, on the island of Kyushu; the Lakeside Hotel by Lake Chuzenji, above Nikko; and the Marunouchi Hotel in central Tokyo. But the jewel in BCOF's crown was the vast Kawana Hotel, located two hours south of Tokyo on the typhoon-prone Izu Peninsula – not far from Shimoda, where the momentous arrival of the American 'Black Ships' in 1853 signalled the end of Japan's long seclusion. It was Robertson himself who had petitioned the US military leadership for the Kawana as a suitably prestigious leave hotel. Macmahon Ball drily observed that the BCOF commander jubilantly communicated the news of its requisitioning 'like a small boy who has achieved a great triumph'.[28]

No doubt Robertson coveted the Kawana's two golf courses, with their grand vistas of Mt Fuji one way and the ocean the other, as an opportunity to engage his grand recreational passion. It was common to come across a pack of brigadiers, as well as Robertson himself, out on the links. There they hacked and sliced away, assisted in their endeavours by the hotel pro, Chick Chin. Yet the hotel was run on democratic lines: every member of BCOF was entitled to at least a week's holiday each year at one of the leave centres, and many lucky young private soldiers made it there.

The first BCOF guests started arriving in June 1947. To Jim Grover, a country boy from the West Australian wheat belt, the hotel was 'a palace', especially after the dreariness of barrack-room life in Kure. Golf in the morning was followed by a few beers before lunch, then swimming or horse-riding, tennis or billiards, with a sauna and a massage thrown in. New arrivals were warned not to be obnoxious not only to fellow guests but to the staff drawn from the 'indigenous population', especially the waitresses and caddies. This was a stipulation that proved beyond some Australians. The Army Education Service's Major Arthur John recalls the unedifying spectacle of a medical officer who, after depositing three balls into Sagami Bay, flung his club after them. When his partner remonstrated, he threatened to throw his caddy, a young Japanese woman, into the sea, too. The young waitresses were part of the appeal of the place. One Occupationnaire recounts a party of male guests taking a couple with them on a picnic to a lake nearby, 'to help us arrange the tables'. It was a most enjoyable day, apparently: 'contrary to what you may think, we behaved ourselves like the gentlemen we were brought up to be. Ahem!'[29]

But for all these ostensible improvements to their tours of duty, the sense of inferiority remained with the force, and frustration was never far away. The showing of the British film *Great Expectations* was a mocking selection in the circumstances, as was Coward's *This Happy Breed* for that matter. The army tried to engage the troops with activities and programmes offered by the Army Education Service, based in Kure. Its director, Arthur John, organised visiting lecturers, such as T. Inglis Moore and the well-known naturalist Crosbie Morrison, editor of *Wild Life*. But that was not really the kind of 'wild life' the men wanted.

On 14 April 1947, the HMAS *Manoora* neared Sydney Harbour, carrying home 1018 officers and troops from Kure for discharge in Australia. Among them was a young private, Clifton Pugh, the illustrator for the troopship newspaper *The Manoora Times*. Along with some of Pugh's sketches imagining the delights awaiting the men in Sydney, the last edition of the paper included a list of ten 'BCOF Commandments'. Home was in sight; they had left Japan behind. By 1947, 'year two of the Atomic Age', the troops felt free to express, albeit comically, their sense of grievance and their envy, along with a little residual guilt:

BCOF Commandments

AND it was in the year two of the Atomic Age when there appeared in Japan a mighty vision, and all who awaited knew and understood; who came after shall know and understand.

Thou shalt not blackmarket.
Thou shalt not use stamped hundreds.
Thou shalt not love thy housegirl better than thy wife.
Thou shalt not steal the sergeants' beer.
Thou shalt have no leave.
Thou shalt have no amenities.
Thou shalt not rely on the Australian Amenities Service.
Thou shalt not trespass into the American zone.
Thou shalt not envy thy American brother.
Thou shalt not have fresh vegetables for weeks and weeks.

AND when these things came to pass, there was great wailing in the land of Nippon and they took up their pens from their desks and wrote to the newspapers; and there was great consternation, and gloom was upon us, but the position changeth not.

THEN it came to pass that a great empire heard of these tribulations and sent the amenities mission from Australia; and the Mission fathers made a long report and nothing happened.

AND it was at that time that the great prophet said: 'I've had it,' and packing up his goods, he went forth from the land of Nippon into the clear, blue sunlight.

The Australians also could not resist a parting shot across the bows at their Supreme Commander Douglas MacArthur, smug in his Tokyo court, who hadn't bothered to pay them a single visit as they laboured in the atomic wastelands of western Japan.

The General's Prayer

Our general
Which art in Tokyo,
MacArthur be thy name,
Thy kingdom is off limits.
Thy will be done in BCOF as it is in Tokyo,
Give us this day our daily directive,
And forgive us trespassing into the American zone
As we forgive postal for jettisoning our mail,
And lead us into insanity,
But deliver us from Eta Jima,

For thine is the kingdom,
The power and the glory,
For the period of the occupation.
Salaam![30]

CHAPTER FOUR

Bile, Spit, and Polish

T ravel, as the American writer and critic Paul Fussell reminds us, is work. Deriving from the Latin *tripalium*, a tri-staked rack or instrument of torture, a traveller is one who endures *travail*: painful, laborious effort.[1] 'Real' travel is still usually associated with danger and difficulty, risk-taking, and individual resourcefulness; by contrast 'tourism' is deemed passive, recreational, hedonistic. This is one reason why soldiers on their foreign tours of duty can be seen as the ultimate travellers. What, then, do we call the Occupationnaires of post-war Japan? Certainly not travellers, in the word's original meaning. They weren't quite putting their bodies on the line – their duties were more mundane than that. They are more akin to what the French call 'travailleurs' – workers or labourers involved in doing a job that many found dreary and even demeaning.

BCOF performed many useful tasks during that first year of the Occupation. After completing its initial deployment, the force settled down to begin its essential operations of sea, ground, and air patrols – a variety of related Intelligence tasks, including (in the early, uncertain days) road reconnaissance, to seek out resistance elements and potential guerrilla activities; checks on illegal immigration; the control of black marketeering and smuggling activities; the confiscation of narcotics and other contraband; port and dock control; the demilitarisation and dispersal of repatriated Japanese servicemen; the collection of weapons; and the disarmament and disposal of hidden enemy ammunition and equipment.

Both skilled and hack work had to be done to get the region back into some kind of working order. Soldiers were engaged in various clearing, building, and maintenance tasks, in concert with a force of Japanese workers that totalled more than 40,000 at its peak, in October 1946.[2] The signalman Jim Grover expresses pride in helping rebuild Japan's shattered communications system; a modern telephone exchange as well as the Force Radio Station was built in Kure. Other tasks were more basic, but just as essential. The hammering Japan had taken by B-29s had left the place a mess. As Brian Rose recalls, 'Hygiene was practically nil and the place was on the nose. If anyone wished to relieve themselves, in whatever capacity, man, woman or child, then they did so in the gutter at the side of the road. One of the first jobs of the occupation force was to erect public toilets.'[3]

It is not only good killers that make good soldiers; though desperate courage may be one of the military virtues, soldiering also entails more humdrum abilities and duties. Nevertheless, erecting lavatories is not quite in the same league as scaling the rocky slopes of Gallipoli under raking Turkish fire. This is the kind of comparison, sometimes sarcastically uttered back in Australia, which undermined BCOF. As commander-in-chief, Robertson did his best to provide the force with some panache. Disdainful of the BRINDIV Commander 'Punch' Cowan's routine of being escorted 'by four Gurkhas loaded with Tommy-guns as a personal bodyguard such as he had in the jungles of Burma', Robertson boasted that he walked unarmed through the streets of Kure, and right through Japan, often alone and always unafraid.[4] Given his own fleet of cars, squadron of Mustangs, and penchant for making bombastic speeches, Robertson's criticisms are a touch hypocritical. In any case, his best efforts made little difference. The harder he tried, the more fatuous both he and the force looked. BCOF's reputation for mediocrity settled irresistibly in the minds of outsiders and came to dominate its self-image as well.

Even the few major events that occurred during the Occupation were not, in themselves, fashioned by human agency. One of the biggest stories covered by *BCON* was the huge earthquake, one of Japan's most powerful ever, that rocked the country at around 4.00 a.m. one freezing morning, just before Christmas in 1946. Swamped by the ensuing tsunami, parts of Wakayama and Shikoku were particularly badly affected; 1000 people perished. The quake also caused considerable damage to BCOF facilities in Kure and the area around the BCAIR base at Iwakuni. The guidebooks had warned them that they were venturing into an earthquake zone, but it scared the living daylights out of Australians who had been sleeping contentedly in their beds. The most memorable image in *BCON*'s extensive coverage of the catastrophe is a story describing 'soldiers in pyjamas' dashing out of their barracks into the cold – not the stuff of derring-do.[5]

Yet some BCOF endeavours were of historic, if not quite heroic, significance, and others were dramatic and even tragic. Rescuing Japan from its pit of feudalism and bringing it into the light of democracy was the lynchpin of SCAP policy. When Japan went to the polls to elect members of the Diet's House of Representatives on 10 April 1946, the American military government recruited patrols of Australian observers and interpreters on polling day and during the week preceding, ensuring that the vote was free of intimidation. There was a certain idealism motivating the BCOF engagement in this enterprise, especially as Japan's women were voting for the first time. Pitied as downtrodden, as well as being idealised as decorous, the women of Japan were regarded somewhat paternalistically (the Occupationnaires were not feminists) as deserving of 'a fair go'. A constant refrain in Australian responses to Japan was that the country consisted almost of two distinct tribes. 'It seems strange that this race of Nippon, producing shy, demure, very feminine little women', wrote Alan Queale in the Australian War Memorial's *As You Were* series in 1947, 'has bred so many vicious, violent, ugly little men'.[6]

The extreme distrust of Japanese men was the main reason why such a high priority was placed on the wholesale repatriation and demobilisation of the nation's servicemen, as they filtered back into Japan from the various battlefields in the Pacific and mainland Asia. Approximately eight million Japanese military personnel were either repatriated from foreign theatres or demobilised from the Japanese home forces. Not unreasonably, it was feared that any armed local resistance such as might arise during the Occupation would come from this quarter. The returned servicemen were trained in the arts of combat. Shamed by their surrender, some may not have accepted the absolute fact of their country's defeat. Some 620,000 Japanese repatriates, about half of them civilian personnel, were processed within the nine BCOF prefectural areas of responsibility by mid-May 1946 – 100,000 of them in Hiroshima Prefecture alone.

One of the major centres for the reception, customs search, medical examination, and demobilisation of returning Japanese was located at Hiroshima's port, Ujina, for which the Australian 67th Battalion, based in Kaitaichi, had responsibility. It was an affecting if ironic sight. From at least 1894, when Japan's Supreme Imperial Headquarters moved to the Hiroshima Castle compound (the emperor Meiji moved, too, for a time), Hiroshima functioned as a vital staging base, sending soldiers and supplies off to the various military ventures that expansionary Japan embarked on over the ensuing decades. When the Japanese returnees arrived at the Ujina wharves, they first had to pass though two tall wooden columns at the head of the pier – Ujina's pillared gates. On the left pillar, bold Japanese characters read: 'Let's do things cordially; don't lose heart; keep up your spirits.' The right said, 'Repatriates, thank you for suffering such hardship [for us] you have all suffered such hardship.' They then entered the splendid *Gaisenkan*, 'The Hall of Victorious Return', built to welcome home the nation's all-conquering armies, outside which stood two ancient stone lions pilfered from China.[7]

Actually, the ex-servicemen caused few problems. Most slipped back into mainstream Japanese life, though not to the adulation of the civilians. They had lost the war, and were at least partly to blame for the nation's current misery, and their return in such vast numbers added to the burden of a population already suffering severe hardship. From Singapore and the South-West Pacific, from Burma and Thailand, from China and Manchuria, these defeated and dejected men had returned to a country quietly resolving to rebuild anew. Collecting their meagre bundles, writes Allan Clifton, who observed the demobbing ritual, the returnees went to the railway station to board trains to take them to their homes, which were all over Japan. Many did so with reluctance, worrying how family and friends would receive them. The Japanese government had routinely sent the next-of-kin of soldiers or sailors believed to be missing in action notifications of their 'glorious death' in battle. The living POW – but departed 'hero' – might already have been enshrined at Yasukuni, and his family might already have received a bereavement payment from the government. They may have received a box containing hair, or a fingernail, or even bones; a gravestone may have already been erected; his name would have been marked 'deceased' in the family register. He was, in effect, dead. No wonder many POWs undertook the final journey home with trepidation. Some of the Ujina returnees lingered in central Hiroshima, just a kilometre or two away. 'Their uniforms did not distinguish them from the crowd,' Clifton writes, 'for many denizens of the "atomic desert" wore similar clothing'.[8] There was simply nothing else to wear.

While the returnees were re-entering Japan, the Koreans, along with ethnic minorities such as mainland Chinese and Formosans (or Taiwanese, as they would now be known), were being shipped out. The Koreans had long been entrenched in the Japanese community. In the hard years after Korea's annexation by Japan in 1910, many thousands had gone to the imperial centre to escape famine, oppression, and unemployment. By 1938, some 800,000 Koreans were resident in Japan, and nearly 20,000 ethnic Koreans were residents of Hiroshima. Many of them, forcibly brought from their homeland to labour for the Japanese war effort, had been among those wiped out by 'Little Boy'. They were given no funerals or memorial services, and it was not until 1999, after years of agitation, that the monument to their loss was accepted into the hallowed grounds of the city's Peace Park.

Like the Japanese, BCOF tended to regard the Koreans as a race of irrepressible hotheads. Accordingly, they were blamed for many of the problems and disturbances of Occupied Japan, from political agitation (including riots and communist-inspired strikes), to the black market, smuggling, and other crimes. In 1946, the 65th Battalion, based in Fukuyama, was responsible for escorting tens of thousands of Koreans by rail to ports in western Japan, such as Hakata and Moji, for return to Korea. Finding life even harder in their homeland, many deportees tried to return to Japan almost immediately, and several thousand succeeded. Shipping and shore patrols thus became an important operational task. In fact, packing off the Koreans was to BCOF's detriment, for they proved a fertile source of information. If the Japanese knew where all the sequestered weaponry was, they were not letting on. Spurred, at least in part, by a desire for vengeance on their colonial masters, the Koreans made voluble and valuable Fifth Columnists.[9]

Western Honshu and the islands of the Inland Sea were littered with dangerous war junk – shells and bombs; depth charges and torpedo warheads; land and marine mines and, also, many tonnes of cordite and other high explosives; small arms; cases and boxes of ammunition and dynamite; plus fuses, shell casings, and so on. Japanese confidantes told Allan Clifton that immediately before the Occupation, large caches of weapons and ammunition had been 'secreted away in remote, inaccessible places, against the day when the Japanese nation would rise in righteous anger and throw out the "hairy foreigners"'. This was idle talk, but BCOF set foot on its area of operations quite literally worried about the ground beneath its feet. Parts of the countryside were eaten up with caves and catacombs storing explosives and ammunition; the actual landscape was rather more volatile than the populace. One huge magazine on Etajima – the home of BCOF headquarters, no less, – contained some 70,000 tonnes of highly dangerous material. The Etajima tunnels, according to Les Semken of the 10th Australian Bomb Disposal Platoon, which performed much of this potentially lethal work, were 'huge things, like huge warehouses dug into the sides of the granite mountains'.[10]

The picturesque little islands of the Inland Sea were deadly. The reason Okunoshima, up the sea lane towards Fukuyama, did not appear on maps from the late 1930s had nothing to do with its tiny dimensions. It was the secret location of a factory dedicated to the execution of chemical warfare. During the Occupation, it became known as the 'Burning Island': many thousand tonnes of poison gases and ordnance, including mustard-gas bombs, were destroyed by burial, burning, or sinking offshore, in a BCOF operation codenamed 'Operation Lewisite'.

On the island of Onasamishima on 22 October 1946, Corporal J.R. Sewell and sapper F.J. Smith were present when a boat loaded to the hilt with high explosives and pyrotechnics, and manned by Japanese labourers, caught fire. Many were killed when the explosives detonated, including Smith. Murray Elliott says he had heard and felt the tremendous explosion as far as ten kilometres away, on Miyajima. Elliott set out in his unit launch to investigate, aiming for a column of smoke rising high over Onasamishima. He arrived at a beach to find an Australian NCO, who turned out to be Sewell, holding a human head under his right arm. 'This is my mate, this is my mate', he cried. Elliott remembers how the eyes looked more alive in the decapitated head, and more startled, than those of its bearer.[11] Though badly concussed, Sewell had rescued several survivors from the water, an act for which he eventually earned the George Medal.

The medal was awarded posthumously. Almost exactly one year later, on 15 October 1947, Sewell and two comrades, sappers Bramley and White, travelled to Muroto on the Pacific coast of Shikoku to defuse a marine mine loaded with high explosives that had been discovered washed up on a local beach. At Kochi Station, they were met by local field security sergeant, Derek Hopper of BRINDIV's Dorsetshire Regiment, who sent them on to the mine location, in company with a Japanese interpreter and a local policeman. Later, the news came through that the mine had exploded, killing Sewell, Bramley, and a large number of Japanese. These included more than 20 children and the recently married interpreter, who had edged close to the scene to have a look. In company with a Sergeant Spalding, Hopper rushed to the site, where he witnessed a scene from hell:

> Sergeant Spalding and I went down to the beach. There was a large bonfire to light up the area. Remains were being collected and taken to a nearby fish shed. I sent Sergeant Spalding off to find a Roman Catholic Priest and a Clergyman. I went to the shed to see if I could locate any identifiable remains ... A local doctor, Lt Smith and myself went though the remains. No rubber gloves were available, I would hate to do it again. There was nothing large enough to identify. A few children's hands and feet were found and put into shoe boxes for identification.
>
> The remains were put into three coffins. There were about thirty bodies involved, twenty-three being children.[12]

The third member of the Australian party, sapper White, had been knocked unconscious by the blast. When he came to, part of a human head lay beside him, though he could remember little else. In the confusion and shock of the immediate aftermath of this terrible tragedy, he could not be located. Apparently, no one present among those uninjured was willing to take care of him. Finally, he was found in the house of three women, who had cleaned him up as best they could and lain him down on a futon. The three good Samaritans turned out to be local prostitutes.[13]

The good works and occasional dramas of the first year did little to strengthen BCOF's fragile self-worth and general sense of bilious irritation. BCOF had 'military control' over its area, but military government remained the sole province of the Americans. Real power was centralised in SCAP. While BCOF exercised immediate authority over the local civil population, its role was that of the monitor and the enforcer, in making sure that the SCAP reform program was enacted. The Commonwealth men initiated nothing; they enforced laws and directives formulated elsewhere. The strict ban on fraternisation did not help.

To many Japanese, the men of the Commonwealth force assumed the look of oppressors, while the Americans were hailed as saviours. A critical article published in the London *Times* by the newspaper's Tokyo correspondent in February 1947 highlighted the cancerous sense of self-doubt running through the force. With the activities of commanders limited to 'petty details of procurement', the troops felt they had no proper soldiering task to perform. According to the *Times* report, one of the 'most popular subjects of debate throughout the B.C.O.F. area was: "Why are we in Japan?"' It was a question that gnawed away at the soldiers. Sifting through the pages of *BCON*, one is struck by the note of desperation in much of the reportage of BCOF endeavours. In the lead story of the 30 November 1946 edition, a report of the opening of radio WLKS by the commander-in-chief Robertson, it is his praise of the 'efficiency' of the troops that is headlined.[14]

'Efficient' is not an adjective one would primarily associate with the Anzacs. 'Devil-may-care', yes, or even 'effective', but never merely 'efficient'.

'Operation Foxum', conducted in September 1946, illustrates the ignoble nature of some BCOF activities. The American Military Government of the Chugoku Region requested Australians of the 34th Brigade enforce two SCAP directives related to the enforced democratisation of Japan, with which the Americans suspected the local prefectural governments were not complying. Phase 1 of the operation, Directive 519, related to education; Phase 2, Directive 642, related to prostitution. This conjoining of imperatives was made even more bizarre by the wording of the secret brigade orders. These orders directed BCOF personnel, including interpreters from CSDIC, the Combined Services Detailed Interrogation Centre, to 'visit simultaneously as many schools and houses of prostitution as possible'.

For Phase 1 of 'D Day' (for that is what the orders call it), teams of soldiers from the battalions at Fukuyama, Hiro, and Kaitaichi were to raid schools, paying close attention to the libraries and text books to determine if any of the texts housed therein contained 'militaristic and ultra-nationalist propaganda', Shinto doctrine, or 'pictures derogatory to an Allied Power'. In fact, the raids unearthed little direct evidence of violation of the SCAP edict, though the official post-mortem on the operation noted that of 26 schools (both primary and secondary) that were inspected, 'only two were actually working', many of the libraries having been damaged or destroyed by fire. However, the raiders did not come away totally empty-handed, managing to identify a few texts deemed suspect, including one obviously explosive tome entitled *British Misdeeds in India*.[15]

Phase 2 of 'Foxum' was trickier. Having disbanded the RAAs by the end of 1945, SCAP outlawed all forms of public prostitution in March 1946. SCAP Directive 642 (it issued plenty) asserted that licensed prostitution was 'in contravention of the ideals of democracy and inconsistent with the development of individual freedom', and also ordered the Japanese government to nullify all contracts and agreements binding women to prostitution. This did little to stamp out the business, which continued to flourish unofficially and unregulated. Sex workers and desperate women were driven into street solicitation; in Tokyo, the *panpan*, the tarted-up, Western-styled woman-of-the-night catering to the prowling Allied soldier, became a symbolic figure of the Occupation, and a humiliating reminder to returned Japanese soldiers of the totality of their defeat. Nonetheless, it was a laudable policy that BCOF pursued with alacrity, albeit somewhat hypocritically, given the number of its men who were prostitution's avid clients. But the force was faced with an uphill task, for the industry was deeply embedded in the official landscape of Occupied Japan. Allan Clifton, who took part in the operation in Hiroshima city, inspected a brothel, where he recognised three of the young women as the serving girls at a party given in honour of several officers of his acquaintance by a high police official.[16]

While the soldiers of BCOF were slightly sceptical of the American faith in 'democratisation', it did take operations such as 'Foxum' seriously when Japanese non-compliance affected the way they were seen and treated. An intelligence report dated October 1946 notes 'a large number of old type text books' in the staff room of a primary school in a town in Shimane Prefecture known for the boldness of its students. The report cites the incident of a 12-year-old schoolchild following a BCOF officer along the road, behaving 'in a very insolent manner'. The officer hauled the boy in before the school's senior master, who was warned that he would be removed if no improvement was shown in his pupils' behaviour. A few days previously, a pupil from the same school had thrown a stone at the same officer, for which a written apology was demanded from the miscreant's parents. The 'obvious lack of respect' toward Commonwealth personnel, the report states, is especially manifested in 'giggling and whispering' among younger Japanese and the 'insolent behaviour' of young primary school children. The grandsons of the Anzacs, the 'terrible, laughing men in the slouch hats' who inspired the men of the Second AIF in the recent war, had been reduced to chastising primary school children and bringing teachers to heel.[17]

AS IF TO COMPENSATE for the lack of an outlet for more impressive soldiering, BCOF strove to keep up appearances. Among the force's most significant activities were ceremonial parades and guard duties. A major parade and fly-past took place in Kure on Anzac Day 1946, and the first momentous Australian guard mounted in Tokyo a couple of weeks later. Putting on a show of force became progressively prioritised as the Occupation wore on. The Australian Defence Committee had reaffirmed the prestige value and the demilitarising duties of the force when it reviewed its future in April 1947. Numerically, however, BCOF was in terminal decline. At the end of 1946, BCOF had numbered 37,021 personnel, of whom 11,918 were Australians. By the middle of 1948, after the completion of the staged British, Indian, and New Zealand withdrawals, that number was estimated to shrink to well under 7000 – almost all Australian, but with substantial reductions to the Australian component to come by the end of the year. The 65th and 66th battalions had sailed home to Australia by that Christmas, leaving just the under-strength 67th. Yet Australia persisted with the force, despite its shrunken size and duties that were becoming mainly formal. The symbolism of putting on a good performance was imperative, especially given the Australian government's determination to influence the drawn-out process of the peace settlement with Japan.[18]

The massed marches and the fly-pasts gave an illusion of strength, and the increasing emphasis on in-barracks drill – or 'square bashing', to use the derogatory British military slang –

instilled a sense of purpose, especially among the young reinforcements who replaced the mostly experienced soldiers of the original Commonwealth force. As Bob Christison, who arrived in the country in January 1947, remembers: 'Our initial training in Japan comprised six weeks of parade ground drill – all day, every day whatever the weather.' A newcomer to the 65th Battalion, Ian Wood took to the regimen with relish. 'Now life is all spit-and-polish. Polished bayonets, hat badges, buckles and white webbing are compulsory ... ' Outside observers considered the emphasis on military punctilio unnecessary and anachronistic. On his visit to the Australian area in Kure, John Morris notices 'an air of useless efficiency', noticeable because it is so 'peculiarly British'. 'I felt that I had been transported backwards in time,' Morris observes, 'into that closed and narrow military world which I had imagined had disappeared'.[19]

BCOF thus confounds one of the sustaining legends of Australian martial discourse – the idea that the Australian military manner is modern and democratic compared with that of the hidebound English. In the Changi POW Museum in Singapore, one of the wall panels illustrates, and comments on, the diverse theatrical productions of the famous Changi Concert Party. 'Each camp produced their own shows – the British tended to put up conventional plays, while Australians concentrated on vaudeville.' The observation has a neat, if oblique, military application. The Anzacs (so the legend says) more than made up for their lack of textbook discipline with individual rough-and-tumble resourcefulness and confident self-reliance. Indeed, they *celebrated* their lack of spit-and-polish, performing best when it counted most: in the deadly vaudeville of battle. Naming their main parade ground in Kure (formerly the Japanese Naval Parade Ground) 'Anzac Park' signified BCOF's sense of its lineage. But it also referred to a benchmark against which the Occupationnaires were inevitably bound to fall short. There is a faint note of contempt in Frank Clune's description of the Australian role in the Changing of the Guard in front of the Imperial Palace in Tokyo in September 1948. In demilitarised Japan, 'the only display of militaristic huff-huff' is provided by 'representatives of an Army renowned for dash in battle, and never till now renowned for parade-ground precision'.[20]

Never mind – the Australians were as skilled on the parade ground as they were on the battlefield. They caused 'a sensation' in Tokyo, Clune remarks, and their Changing of the Guard became 'one of the mustn't be missed impressive spectacles of Tokyo under the Occupation'. As the palpable contempt for the British army in the Great War reveals, it is a trait of popular Australian military historiography to assert superior virtue over ally as well as enemy. The tendency to big-note emerges in BCOF testimony in the insistent, and rather sad, claim that the Australians paraded better than the Americans. 'Even the Yanks themselves admit they can't reach our marching standard,' writes Ian Wood of his rostered tour in Tokyo on guard duties. As the men in their spotless khaki drill and white webbing swing down Marunouchi to the tune of 'Waltzing Matilda', on the way to the vast public plaza outside the gates of the Imperial Palace, 'Each man felt a surge of pride for his Australian nationality.' The men revelled in the spectacle and the performance. 'Every morning we faced a barrage of cameras. We didn't mind – in fact, we were proud of it.' The whole scene, he writes, gave an impression of 'vitality, youth and strength which absolutely captivated the Americans'.[21]

Whether the Japanese were as captivated is another matter. By early 1947, according to the *Times*, the Japanese had taken to viewing these Commonwealth parades with 'mild contempt'.[22] Perhaps the novelty had worn off; or perhaps they didn't know who they were actually looking at. In a complimentary article written for *BCON*'s 1948 Christmas issue, the Australian Japan specialist and sympathiser Peter Russo cannot resist a sarcastic shot at BCOF's pretensions:

You are enormously proud of the snappy guard change the Australians carry out in Tokyo. If so, prepare for a nasty shock. The believe-it-or-not feature is the number of Japanese who positively did not know the guard was Australian. They thought it came from a crack American regiment, especially trained and equipped for precision work of this kind.[23]

In fact, the men of the British Commonwealth had always been a mystery to the Japanese. In December 1946, BCOF intelligence noted that only a small fraction of Japan's best and brightest, the students of Tokyo Imperial University, knew that the Dominions were in fact independent. For their part, many of the folk in the villages and towns of Hiroshima Prefecture did not even know the nationalities of the men making up the force.[24]

If the Australians made an impression on the Japanese at all, it was a negative one by comparison with the resplendent Americans. The Australians were hyenas feasting on the American kill, undeserving pretenders who made a lot of noise but were irrelevant to the future of the country. The Americans may have destroyed Japan, but now they were in the process of making it anew, into something better than before. The Kure resident Noboru Ota remembers the awe with which the population witnessed their arrival into the area, months before BCOF, in October 1945. 'When I saw a convoy of Americans jeeps and heavy vehicles, stretching endlessly into the distance,' he remembers, 'I thought, now I understand the reason why we lost the war.'[25]

The Americans were charming and generous, as well as powerful, and they quickly won over the locals. They were a hard act to follow. The Australians seemed uncouth by comparison, ill-educated and ill-disciplined, dressed in shabby uniforms, and sporting 'large hats like cowboys'. BCOF censorship of Japanese mail late in 1946 revealed some writers harking back nostalgically to the Americans, whom they considered 'more kind and attractive' than the Australians, who were looked down on as 'grandsons of uncivilised convicts'.[26] Dreadful stories of Australian barbarism had circulated among a population that had had little contact with the rest of Japan, let alone exotic creatures like Australians. They were prepared to believe the worst. In *Goshu* (1965), written by the Occupationnaire Stephen Kelen, an elderly female Japanese imagines 'redheaded, bearded, hairy barbarians of gigantic proportions, who killed men without reason, raped women regardless of their age and social position, and ate children for their tender meat'. This nightmarish scenario may be disregarded as a novelist's fancy, but it was based on rumours overheard by the servicemen themselves, and it is supported by the recollections of POWs like Ray Parkin, who was labouring in a coal mine beneath the Inland Sea when the war ended. According to Parkin, the sudden release of hundreds of Allied prisoners after the Japanese capitulation scared the hell out of the provincial population of western Honshu. Local women were warned that if they consorted with the Australians, they would give birth to kangaroos.[27]

The note of desperation in the expression of pride in their formal appearance outside Hirohito's palace reveals the extent to which the Australians were susceptible to believing the negative publicity that accompanied them in Japan and followed them home. They knew they couldn't cut the mustard, either with regard to their fellow American Occupationnaires, or by comparison with their feted national forerunners of battles past. Their poor morale is unusual in Australian military history, though it has a significant contemporary correlation in the American occupation of Iraq, where a similar sense of feeling both sidelined and second rate, along with the derision of their Allies, reportedly undermined the self-confidence normally associated with the Australian soldier.[28]

The Anzac Day controversy of 1947, when BCOF was denied the opportunity to parade in front of the Imperial Palace and ceremonially reveal its links to the most hallowed Australian military tradition of all, illustrates its predicament. Here was a potential good news story for the Australians in Japan that turned into a PR debacle. The main character in the fiasco was the journalist Richard Hughes, later to become the legendary Hong Kong-based China-watcher. Finding himself out of a job during 1947 and 1948, Hughes accepted the unlikely role as the manager of the Tokyo Foreign Correspondents' Club, a post that brought with it the not-to-be-sneezed-at inducement of free board and half-price drinks. The Tokyo Press Club was a slightly disreputable place, a hangout for all the journalistic detritus that washed ashore on Japan during the Occupation. Billeted in the club during Hughes' tenure, John Morris thought he had landed in 'a cross between a waterfront sailor's bar and a brothel', and he caustically observed a group of newsmen who had been 'knocking about the Pacific for years and had lost what civilised standards they ever had'. In *Foreign Devils* (1972), Hughes is more indulgent of the crowd of war-weary correspondents, commentators, and 'implausible rogues and magisterial scoundrels' who congregated in what he ironically calls 'an outpost of the free world'.[29]

But at the time of Anzac Day 1947, Hughes was still in employment, a relatively inexperienced journalist ('young and headstrong and stupid') covering the Occupation for Australian newspapers. When in early April he got wind of a BCOF order stemming directly from Robertson himself, which drastically curtailed the Anzac Commemoration Services that were to be conducted in the Imperial Plaza, he knew he was on to something. The reason for confining Anzac Day services to within rigid unit boundaries, according to a leaked Defence Department document, was 'in deference to Japanese sensitivity'. This naturally made the story all the more irresistible to a newsman with Hughes's instincts. It was bound to arouse outrage. Apparently BCOF's leadership considered that the still touchy Japanese would be offended by such a show of force, especially as Anzac Day fell on the day elections were being conducted for the Diet.

Robertson was also unconvinced that he could provide proper security to guarantee the due solemnity and dignity of the occasion, especially as BCOF personnel were required to help supervise the election. The plaza was a popular spot for the kind of demonstrations and noisy electioneering that the Japanese are still fond of, but which was especially vehement in the febrile days of the newly democratic Japan. The issue became even more delicate with the suggestion that it was the Americans who were behind the restrictions – an incorrect insinuation that prompted an unseemly denial from the head of SCAP's Government Section, General Whitney. The headline of one of Hughes's pieces on the issue is telling: 'BCOF "Muffs" Opportunity'.[30] Here was an opportunity to fly the flag and impress the Japanese that had been wasted by a pusillanimous deference to logistics.

Under popular pressure – and a stern intervention from the army minister, Cyril Chambers – the 67th Battalion, then garrisoned in Tokyo, was finally given the go-ahead to conduct a full-dress march-past on Anzac Day, after a dawn service at its quarters in the Ebisu Barracks. But the issue didn't end there: a couple of days after the event, Hughes told the Australian public that the march-past had not in fact been held in the usual public ceremonial space, as promised, 'but in a secluded avenue leading from the plaza', which fronted the palace walls but was 'shielded by trees from public notice'. The plaza was deserted on the big day, and surprised official guests were diverted to this 'hidden rendezvous'. The Australian public had been misled, and BCOF had been relegated to a side street. 'It was as though', Hughes remarks, 'the Anzac Day ceremonial in Melbourne had been switched from the Shrine to the Albert Park lagoon'.[31] Once again, BCOF had been cast into the shadows and excluded from the greatest national narrative of all.

'WHY ARE WE in Japan?' The question became more insistent the longer the Occupation went on, and the character of the force changed, becoming younger and less motivated. As Macmahon

Ball had loosely told George Atcheson as early as May 1947, the Australian troops in Japan 'did not know really what they were here for and consequently were not serving a useful purpose'. The mien of the Japanese was itself a source of confusion. The first Australian troops who went to Japan were shocked by what Stephen Kelen called the 'honeyed friendliness' of the people. Japanese behaviour at home just didn't tally with that of the war zone. Some senior soldiers, like the English officer F.J.C. Piggott, wondered if their 'apparent docility' was 'another example of Oriental cunning', a tactic to make the homesick visitors demand their early withdrawal 'on the grounds that there is no work to do.'[32]

Like the British of the Raj, BCOF was acutely aware of its vulnerability. The force was grossly outnumbered. Carolyne Carter's research reveals that the ratio was something like 500 to 1 at the beginning of the Occupation. After the numerical swelling of the force throughout 1946, the figure was still in the order of 250–270 to 1 by the year's end.[33] In British India, the Mutiny of 1857 had deeply entrenched the line between coloniser and colonised, and hardened dislike and distrust of 'the natives', leading to a withdrawal of all but the most official and superficial contact with them. There was no such massive disturbance in Japan, but Australian suspicions about the Japanese population lasted well after the demilitarisation process was achieved.

At senior military levels, the Australians never stopped distrusting the Japanese or viewing the Occupation as the final operation of a long military campaign. As late as December 1946, after six months in the BCOF commander's job, Robertson was unwilling to be put into social, or even diplomatic, situations where he would have to shake hands with a Japanese – he even refused to attend a Tokyo welcome for the visiting eminent Roman Catholic Cardinal Gilroy because one of the hosts was the Japanese Archbishop of Tokyo.[34] For all its desire to rebuild Japan, the Chifley government was unbending in its commitment to non-fraternisation. In late July 1949, MacArthur's 'Occupation

Instruction No. 5' stated inter alia that, as the Occupation had 'gradually changed from the stern rigidity of a military occupation to the friendly guidance of a protective force', Occupation personnel needed to be 'indoctrinated in an attitude of friendly interest' towards the 'indigenous peoples'.

Even Robertson wondered how this directive could be met without a considerable degree of fraternisation. Yet despite a recommendation to the contrary by its Cabinet Defence Committee, the government decided not to alter the existing policy. The general public seemed to concur. The SCAP directive relaxing all restrictions on existing fraternisation and permitting free intermingling with the Japanese was interpreted by the popular Australian press to pose an unwelcome problem for BCOF that threatened Allied unity itself. The Melbourne *Herald* headlined its report 'MacArthur's "Kind To Japs" Order Poses Dilemma'.[35]

Like timid travellers, the Australians in Japan often suspected they were at the locals' mercy. Was the hand offered in friendship an overture of entrapment? Peter Russo warned that the seeming passivity of the vanquished Japanese was in fact a highly effective means to a selfish end. Russo saw it as a strategy of self-defence not unrelated to the native sport of *ju-jitsu*, 'a cult which pervades the mental, as well as physical, reactions of the Japanese', and which the foreigners needed to come quickly to grips with – 'the knack of knowing how to utilise someone else's superior strength or knowledge to help himself'. He continues: 'You overcome the opposition of a Japanese and push him along triumphantly. When you're well down the course, you discover that somehow you've been pushing him precisely in the direction he wants to go.'[36] Gullivers in the land of Lilliput, the Australians learned the lesson that physical presence and ostensible power were no guarantee of mastery, and that the dextrous, determined Japanese still pulled the strings on their own turf.

An anecdote told by T.A.G. Hungerford suggests the depths of Australian suspicion of the Japanese, the extent of their cultural misunderstanding and, quite literally, their inability to read the signs. As that first bitter winter of 1946 turned to spring, Hungerford and two or three of his comrades would borrow a jeep on Sunday afternoons and explore the green farmlands behind Kure. One afternoon, driving through a picture-book landscape of long rising valleys and terraced fields, they chanced upon a solitary pedestrian, about 60 years of age. He turned out to be the genial schoolteacher from Kure whose acquaintance would alter Hungerford's attitude to Japan. The man's spoken English was exemplary; the Australians had hardly a word of Japanese between them. Ignoring the prohibition on mixing with the local people, they accepted his offer to visit his house, which was 'tourist-pretty' in a traditional way: white plaster and dark wood, with a straw charm on the front door, upon which paper strips of crimson Japanese characters were pasted. Hungerford remarked admiringly on the characters to one of his mates, who replied: 'How'd you know it doesn't mean, "Fuck the Aussies"?'[37]

PART TWO

Occupation Blues: disturbing the peace

CHAPTER FIVE

Tabi No Haji Wa Kakisute

It is a truism of travel that people do things in foreign
countries that they would never contemplate doing at home.
The Japanese have a saying for it – *Tabi no haji wa kakisute*.
This translates roughly as: 'The shame incurred while travelling
can easily be discarded and forgotten.' Travellers, in other words,
are shameless. Abroad, they enjoy the *frisson* of the illicit, the
feeling of liberation that comes with breaking the constraints and
taboos of home. This manifests most odiously in predatory male
sexual behaviour, committed either singly or in groups. Think of
the calculating paedophile on the prowl, or the bacchanalia of the
sporting team cutting loose on an end-of-season trip. And think of
the rampant lawlessness of soldiers on tour.

The provenance of the saying may have something to do with
the sense of release felt by the Japanese people in foreign parts,
freed of the shackles of their overpopulated islands and rigid
behavioural codes.[1] This is a view to which the Chinese might
incline. When the news broke in September 2003 that a group of

400 Japanese men had flown to the southern Chinese city of Zhuhai, checked into a luxury hotel, and brought in 500 local prostitutes for a three-day orgy, the Chinese press erupted. The tawdry episode was magnified into an international incident at a time of heightened tensions between China and Japan, occurring at around the time of the anniversary of the 'Manchurian Incident' of 18 September 1931, which marked the beginning of China's 14-year-long struggle against Japanese military occupation. Humiliation was heaped upon humiliation. The Zhuhai orgy invoked a primary source of dissension between the two countries, the Nanking massacre – the six-week slaughter of up to 300,000 citizens, after the city fell to the Imperial Japanese Army on 13 December 1937. One of the features of the 'Rape of Nanking' was the extent of sexual atrocity that accompanied the killing. Individually or in gangs, tens of thousands of rapes were perpetrated on young girls, pregnant women, and the elderly. Rape was often followed by mutilation and murder; some surviving women were spared to serve as prostitutes for the Imperial Army. There are stories of Chinese men being forced to commit incest, of sons forced to rape mothers, and fathers their daughters; some were made to have sex with corpses.

The Japanese rapist-murderers in Nanking were enacting a transhistorical, transnational pattern of the sexual humiliation attendant on military domination, ranging from the routine ravishing of the women of conquered tribes, described in the Old Testament; to Roman rape and robbery as an instrument of imperial policy; to the diabolical vengeance of the Red Army, as it swept towards Berlin in early 1945; to random episodes of American sexual terror in Vietnam; to the pack rapes committed by Serbian paratroopers on Bosnian Muslim women fleeing their land in the 1990s.

The BCOF element of the *Shinchugun* – or 'advancing stationed army', as the Japanese euphemistically called the Occupation forces – cannot be charged with anything remotely resembling the

Nanking atrocities. Occupation veterans would rightly be appalled at such a comparison even being contemplated. Most of them behaved considerately toward the local population and chivalrously towards the women. When informed they were coming, the local population moved to keep their girls locked up inside their homes, according to Shizuo Inoue. But they needn't have worried, because the visitors behaved 'like gentlemen'. From the historical vantage point of 2004, one Australian veteran, George Martin, says that the force instilled into the Japanese 'that the victors of war can behave with discipline, compassion and in a humane and civilised manner, toward a defeated enemy'.[2] This assessment is hardly disinterested, of course; old soldiers have a tendency to gild the lily. Clearly, however, many Occupationnaires went about their work in a manner that was beyond reproach.

The veterans with whom I have talked or corresponded wonder how – based on the hard evidence of the behaviour of the Japanese Imperial Army throughout Asia – things may have been different if Japan had triumphed and the roles had been reversed. I asked Allan Wells, a member of the 66th Battalion who went to Japan as a 19-year-old, what he thought the Occupation achieved for Japan. His only reply was: 'I believe we did not treat them as they would have treated us.'[3] A visit to the museum in Seoul's Seodaemun Prison, where the Japanese Imperial Army dished out a hideous menu of punishments to Korean independence fighters over decades of brutal occupation, attests to the validity of this point of view.

By what measure, then, do we judge the BCOF years in Japan, so punctuated by spasms of racial and sexual fury? As bacchanalia or bastardry? By any reasonable assessment, Robertson's stated desire to have the force set 'a first-class example to the Japanese people' was unevenly met. To expect this body of mostly young men, few of them well educated, and many of them unworldly, to perform as unofficial ambassadors, or in today's jargon 'role models', was always a false expectation. An Australian makes a telling comment in Stephen Kelen's novel *Goshu*. 'I didn't come here to save the Nips from themselves,' he remarks, 'I just came here to see how they live, have a bit of fun, adventure'. The contingent was young and inexperienced. At the time of its initial recruitment, the average age of officers of the 67th Battalion, for instance, was just 26 years, and of the other ranks, 23; only 3 per cent of the soldiers were married.[4] As BCOF evolved, it got younger and younger. Some of the reinforcements were 18- and 19-year-olds who were champing at the bit, having missed out on the 'test' of the battlefield. Added to this mixture were ne'er-do-wells able to infiltrate the force due to inadequate screening at home, and the potential for trouble was acute.

The Occupation disrupted the natural circumstances of human intercourse. Japan became topsy-turvy land; usual standards of behaviour didn't apply. Inhibitions were shed and scruples discarded. 'The ruins were one huge playground,' Donald Richie says in his Occupation novel *Where are the Victors?* (1956), 'where everything forbidden was now allowed and clandestine meetings were held under the noonday sun.'[5] Richie was writing about American behaviour in Tokyo, where a semblance of civilised life was in place and conventional diversions were to be enjoyed.

Post-war Kure was an altogether rougher frontier. The city exhibited the moral squalor of small-town garrison life, as memorably captured by Albert Tucker in his depiction of wartime Melbourne in *Victory Girls* (1943), with its sordid imagery of painted women in the clutches of grotesquely grinning American soldiers. Bede Wall, who had sailed for Japan in May 1946 as a virginal 19-year-old, a shy Catholic boy from Sydney's northern suburbs who 'had never been outside the Heads', recalls one comrade who indulged his ravenous appetite for 'sailor girls', Japanese schoolgirls so called because of their sailor-like uniforms. On one occasion, he was discovered in the barracks with a young schoolgirl and her mother. The men were not fussy about where they had sexual relations, or with whom. Kure may have been 'Sin

City', in the words of one BCOF veteran, the cartoonist Les Tanner, but it was not exactly some sumptuous seraglio of the *Arabian Nights*. One of Bede Wall's favourite Kure brothels was a dingy dive located by a local graveyard near Point Camp, with the unlovely nickname 'The Cemetery'. Down by the docks at Ujina, according to Allan Clifton, Australians and their partners repaired to disused refrigerating chambers which, 'like army latrines', were occupied by numerous rutting couples at the same time.[6]

Some Occupationnaires behaved with the single-minded intent of sex tourists. An admittedly overworked lot with an impossible job to perform, the military police of the Provost Corps often turned a blind eye to their trysts. Sometimes they themselves were involved. Murray Elliott and his staff were first staged at Point Camp, a dismal collection of draughty, bomb-damaged buildings located by the sea, just down the coast from Kure towards Hiroshima. Strolling idly through an abandoned chemical laboratory within the camp one morning, Elliott came across a mounded roll of army blankets and gave it a nudge with his foot. An aggrieved male voice told him to 'bugger off', after which the naked figure of a young Japanese girl sprang up. 'She was probably about fourteen years of age,' Elliott remarks. While the girl hid her face with her partner's slouch hat, he emerged to admit to Elliott that he had smuggled her though the entry gate, and that, yes, the sentry on duty was his mate, and both were in fact provosts themselves.[7]

Australian mateyness sometimes extended to men sexually swapping their girlfriends – and on the same *tatami*. Bede Wall remembers he and a friend picking up two girls at Tokyo Station and spending the night with them in a single room somewhere in the suburbs, along with an American and his companion, all 'sleeping' on the same floor together. Occasionally, the girls were a cause of dissension between the men, who fought over their prey. Steve Macaulay, who was also based at Point Camp, recalls a violent argument over one teenage girl, also aged about 14, who had been secreted into the barracks via a tunnel, thus avoiding the guards on the gate. Shots were fired and a serviceman was wounded in the leg.[8]

The hedonism of Occupation life seems slightly shocking even today. The new-fangled cameras that were the playthings of these military tourists were put to some interesting uses. One of the BCOF wives remembers a colleague of her husband's proudly revealing his homemade collection of pornography in the mess one evening. Included among the usual snaps of festivals and snow scenes were nude photographs of his wife, his 18-year-old daughter, and his house girl.[9] The gendered paradigm of the Australian Occupation is that of the aggressively heterosexual male Occupier imposing himself on the female Occupied. But the licentiousness extended to other forms of sexual expression frowned on, or out-lawed, at home. Like other Occupation taboos, Australian female promiscuity in Japan is only frankly broached in fictional narra-tive. A notable example is Hal Porter's novel *A Handful of Pennies* (1958). In an episode based on the case of a Nijimura female teacher cashiered for contracting gonorrhoea from her Japanese black-market contact, Paula Groot, a Tasmanian woman teaching the BCOF dependants, seduces her housegirl's brother, simply because she can. Her logic is impeccable: 'since thousands of men played the double-backed game with Oriental women, she was justified in exchanging flesh with an Oriental man'.[10] Unfortunately, her young lover had contracted syphilis from a local brothel worker who had in turn caught the disease from a South Australian Occupationnaire who had picked it up in Manila.

The complex web of sexual promiscuity created by the interna-tional disorder of war claimed many victims. In the novel, Paula, in her turn, catches the disease and is sent home, along with an army padre discovered engaging in sexual relations with a Japanese bar boy, a fictionalisation of another actual BCOF scandal involving a scoutmaster. The padre, Hamilton, who taught reli-gious instruction at the dependants' school, had also acquired a boy lover in the form of the school captain, a strapping youth named Maxie Glenn. Padre Hamilton's sexual difficulties are related in Porter's characteristically sniggering manner, but with some sympathy, for 'the complicity had been dual' in the relationship with Maxie.[11] The subterranean homosexual cultures of the Australian Occupation of Japan, including relations within BCOF itself and between the Occupationnaires and the Japanese, have yet to be thoroughly excavated and examined. No veterans I spoke to disclosed any such activity. If homosexual relations did occur, they insist they took place outside the Australian cohort. Bede Wall remembers the 'every night occurrence' of young Japanese boys waiting outside Point Camp to be entertained by the Sikh soldiers of the Indian contingent who shared the encampment. But he claims the Australians stuck to the straight and narrow. In Hungerford's novel *Sowers of the Wind,* the young soldier Andy Waller, fresh from the slums of Redfern, frankly sets out an agenda of sexual conquest that many men tried to meet. On the voyage from Australia, Waller had bragged to a group of appreciative listeners 'just what he was going to do to the Japanese when he got to Japan – particularly to the women ... When he had arrived he had been at pains to consolidate this opinion.'[12]

Andy Waller is articulating an attitude that historical and personal accounts of the Occupation tend to shy away from. Liberated by the medium of fiction, the Occupation novelists relentlessly exploit the theme of conquest. Hungerford's Bosch-like portrait of BCOF folly and immorality in *Sowers of the Wind* caused its nervous publisher, Angus & Robertson, to withhold its publication until the Occupation was well over. In *Pattern of Conquest* (1954), L.H. Evers likens the Australian rule of Kure to classical stories of ruthless rape and pillage. A conquered city 'is always burned, looted, and its women ravished,' an Occupationnaire of scholarly disposition tells his doubting comrades. The 'pattern of conquest' is unvarying: Kure now is 'suffering its martyrdom, and you and I ... are the instruments of its agony'. The city had been destroyed, and its population reduced to serving the conqueror: 'There's a good imitation of slavery for you.' Destitute women had to sell their bodies. And 'as for the looting – tell me one soldier who doesn't get his roll off the black market'.[13]

Fiction, of course, has a tendency to play up the louche and lurid aspects of military life. But it also tackles touchy subjects head-on. What Hal Porter privately called the 'hushed-up scandals' and 'moral defoliation' of the Australian Occupation provided the BCOF novelists with ample raw material. 'You can get away with murder here quite easily,' Clifton Pugh wrote to his mother ('Mumsie') in August 1946, in feigned astonishment at the antics of the wild element in the Australian contingent. 'All one has to do is bring the Nip inside camp limits, put a couple of packets of cigarettes and a chocolate in his pocket then shoot him – no effort.' Pugh hastens to add that he wasn't talking from experience.[14] One would hope not. It may be that the young Pugh was trying to impress 'Mumsie'; maybe he wanted to give her a shock from a safe distance. No doubt he is exaggerating. But people did get away with murder in Occupied Japan, both figuratively and literally. *Tabi no haji wa kakisute.*

CHAPTER SIX

Crimes and Misdemeanours

Official military unit diaries make for mind-bendingly dull reading. Logged tersely and impersonally, the record of the diurnal doings of the men tests the patience of even the most engaged reader. The BCOF diarists were obsessed with the weather. As the saying goes, there is a lot of weather in Japan. Routinely making my way through the war diary of the 123 Transport Platoon for the June–September quarter, 1947, I back-pedalled from the entry for 15 June, 'Weather Report – Dull, Tendency to Rain'. My racing eyes had skated across this entry for 10 June: a medical inspection conducted on a Japanese girl aged eight, who had been 'criminally assaulted', on the evening of 9 June, by an Australian soldier. 'Condition of child serious.' I also almost overlooked the finding of a court martial held in Hiro for Private Mervyn William Allen in the 65th Battalion's Routine Orders for 15 October 1947, wedged as it was between an item on how much the regimental dinner cost and the notice of a sale of a stock of tennis equipment. Allen was found guilty of murdering a Japanese civilian, one Kawabe Rihei, at Onomichi the previous November. 'Sentence: To suffer penal servitude for the term of ten years.'[1]

Shocking details like these whet the appetite: one starts hunting these documents with grim voyeuristic intent, ignoring the individual tragedies behind the outrageous facts. The 123 Transport Platoon war diary's report for the quarter previous had noted a letter of gratitude from a certain Mr Goichi Nishio, thanking BCOF for the timely and effective assistance rendered his daughter after a motor accident. His daughter Momoko had been run over by a car, escaping death due to the 'kind and heroic conducts' [sic] of three BCOF soldiers. Nishio-san's letter, translated into English by a Japanese, describes the Australians' conduct as 'a good example for us from the viewpoint of social justice'.[2] This is a touching story, but cynicism intrudes: were the chivalrous Australians criminally responsible for the accident in the first place? Judging from the documentation, the careless motorists of BCOF seemed to bowl over unsuspecting Japanese like nine-pins. The road carnage on Etajima is the subject of facetious concern in one of the BCOF publications, *Gloom*, in a letter addressed to 'Dear Sir, or Gook':

> Why the temporary War Cemetery at Kure isn't packed with the bodies of Eta Jima drivers and their victims is a mystery to me. These gentlemen drive their jeeps and trucks down the Koyo road in a manner reminiscent of the peace-time "Wall of Death" at the local fairground. Fast driving is wizard on proper roads but the Koyo Road was only built for aged Japanese and their children to walk along.[3]

An official BCOF HQ list of 'Major Accidents' for the period October–November 1948 cites numerous examples of horrific 'accidents', some resulting in charges of manslaughter. On 25 October, a Japanese cyclist in Yoshiura, on the coast between Kure and Hiroshima, was killed in a hit-and-run by a staff car driven by a sergeant from BCOF Workshops. In the same little town two weeks later, seven Japanese were struck by a 'recklessly driven' BCOF vehicle, which took off from the scene before the culprit was apprehended. Two of the victims died in hospital. One was a pregnant woman, the other a young girl.[4]

The reports of the BCOF Provost Services, especially those detailing the work of the Special Intelligence Bureau, which worked in close liaison with the Japanese civil police, tell a similarly sobering story of BCOF crime. An official 'History of the BCOF Provost Services', dated 2 April 1948, details a catalogue of serious offences committed on or by members of the force, including homicide, rape, armed robbery, breaking and entering, larceny, and other crimes, including black marketeering. Several of the major investigations resulting in arrest involved major crime by Australians – the rape of a Japanese woman in Kure; the aforementioned murder in Onomichi; the wounding of a Japanese female, committed by a member of the 65th Battalion; the body of a Japanese woman found in a staff car down by the Kure docks, with the consequent charging of a driver from the Base Transport Pool; the fatal beating of a Korean national in Okayama by a member of the 67th Battalion; a hit-and-run near Kure, in which a four-year-old girl was killed.[5]

Things did not improve after that report was written. A résumé of BCOF provost activities for the month ending 31 May 1948 cites an incident involving three Australian soldiers visiting a Japanese dwelling in search of prostitutes. Disappointed, they trashed the place before finding their quarry. Two young women were raped. The résumé for the period ending 28 January 1949 records that two Australian soldiers travelling in a jeep in company with an interpreter held up some locals at bayonet-point and demanded sums of money; one of the Japanese was struck several times by the weapon. A later résumé, from early 1951, cites an act of sodomy committed by an Australian serviceman on a Japanese boy, who also suffered a fractured skull in the assault.[6] Some of the most repellent crimes, and the most worrying to authorities, were committed during the first months of the Occupation. In July 1946, two Japanese schoolgirls were attacked in Kure by three Australian soldiers, 'recognised by their hats'. Predictably, the men were 'very much under the influence of alcohol'. They emerged from the dark and set upon the girls, striking them with blows to the face and body. One of the girls was pushed into a deep gutter, snapping her left leg, which had to be amputated. The official report of this abhorrent incident called it a 'dastardly' and 'cowardly' crime that brought the entire force into disrepute, and observed that the base commander had asked for an appeal for cooperation to apprehend the offenders. They were never identified.[7]

The Japanese also committed crimes, both against the Occupation and against one another. Some stole; assaults were committed on BCOF servicemen, sometimes provoked and sometimes not; and the women who slept with the Occupationnaires (along with the men who worked and consorted with them) were often treated abominably. The 'History of BCOF Provost Services' notes the arrest of 2537 Japanese and 563 BCOF personnel, up to April 1948. Despite these figures, there is substantial evidence to suggest that the Japanese may have been more sinned against than sinning. Carolyne Carter's excellent research into crimes and misdemeanours in the BCOF areas indicates that, as she puts it, 'the general pattern of violence under the occupation was dominated by acts committed by occupation force personnel on the Japanese'. The commander-in-chief's official report to JCOSA on 'incidence of serious crimes' committed by BCOF personnel against Japanese civilians for the period May 1946–December 1947 lists 289 assaults, 57 rapes, four cases of manslaughter, and three of murder. The report for the period January 1948– September 1951 specifies 233 assaults, 23 rapes, four cases of manslaughter, and a single murder.[8] No reliable statistics are available for the initial settling-in months of February, March, and

April, but the anecdotal evidence suggests that more than a few Occupationnaires released the pent-up pressures of war and ennui when they set foot in Japan.

We will never know the extent of Occupation crime accurately. The strict Press Code ensured that the press would not circulate bad news stories of the BCOF, in Japan at least. With the relaxation of censorship after the Occupation wound down and officially ended in 1952, local regional newspapers, such as the Hiroshima-based *Chugoku Shimbun*, suddenly started publishing reports of BCOF iniquity, especially to do with road accidents. The trial and eventual suspension of the prosecution of an Australian serviceman who had run over and killed a toddler was a big story in August 1952. The following year, a Hiroshima newspaper reported the shocking news that that no fewer than 90 people in Kure alone had been killed in Occupation-related accidents, and stories about bereaved families seeking compensation for the untimely death of loved ones at BCOF hands became commonplace. The latter would have been lucky to receive a single yen as, according to an *Asahi Shimbun* report in June 1953, the Kure Municipal Council was complaining that BCOF owed it ten million yen in local electricity and gas taxes. The BCOF, it seems, had shot through without paying its bills.[9]

THERE WERE PLENTY of bad eggs among the Australian component of BCOF, but was the contingent as a whole *that* bad? Certainly the conspicuous misbehavior of the Australians provided the Allies with a convenient scapegoat on which to pin the more general ills of the Occupation. Both the Americans and the British had their reasons for disapproving of the colonials from Down Under. The broader cultural reputation of Australians as a bunch of rowdies from a country rooted in its convict past seemed to precede the Occupation and to colour responses to them during it, and during the historical reckoning that has appeared since.

The November 1946 article in the *Chicago Tribune* condemning Robertson's self-indulgence claimed that the Australian troops were the 'worst' disciplined in Japan, at least partly because its leader's excesses encouraged an 'anything goes' attitude that approached anarchy. 'The Australians are out of control and should be sent home', the article asserted.[10] This not-uncommon American view was apparently shared by the Japanese, and it still prevails.

An almost automatic association of the Australians with criminality has led to lapses in accurate Japanese historical accounting of the Occupation. In *Rape and War* (1995) and *Hidden Horrors* (1996), English-language versions of a work first published in Japan in 1993, Yuki Tanaka, an excellent scholar, retails a ghastly story told by a Hiroshima prostitute about the Australian soldiers 'who landed at Kure … in November 1945'. Claiming that the Australians were 'the worst' in Occupied Japan, she alleges that young women were dragged into jeeps, taken to the mountains and raped: 'I heard them screaming for help nearly every night'. But the Australians had not even arrived in Japan in November 1945. The rapes must have been perpetrated by the Americans who were ensconced in the prefecture at the time. A fairly obvious chronological discrepancy went undetected – the Australian reputation as 'the worst' of all the Occupation troops gave the story a kind of mythic credibility.[11]

Yet indisputable documented facts do tell a dismal story of casual episodic Australian violence. Allan Clifton was also of the view that his countrymen were 'the worst-behaved' of all the troops in Japan. Clifton's Intelligence role within CSDIC, a specially raised unit composed of translators and interpreters to assist BCOF with general field security, brought him into close daily contact with Japanese, including many who shared his leftist political leanings. As he remarks in his story of his year (1946) in Occupied Japan, *Time of Fallen Blossoms*, it also brought him into 'monotonously regular' contact with female victims of Australian rape, and to young men beaten to a pulp simply because they were 'Japs'.

Evidence of the bashing of men and women 'for the sheer joy of it', the 'setting fire to brothels from pique at being refused entrance', the robberies 'with and without violence', and the high incidence of random vandalism of property lead the Japanese to start calling the Australians *Yabanjin* – barbarians.[12]

It is in a chapter entitled 'Yabanjin' that Clifton makes his allegations of pack rape. The chapter begins with Clifton standing beside a girl lying unconscious on a hospital bed. She had just been violated by 'twenty soldiers' and left abandoned 'on a piece of waste land'. Clifton's prose is precise but theatrically dramatic: 'The hospital was in Hiroshima. The girl was Japanese. The soldiers were Australians.' Episodes such as this undermine the central constructive and punitive aspects of the entire Occupation project – the enlightened West 'civilising' the backward Japanese, and the relentless commitment to punishing the wartime iniquities of the Imperial Army through a series of war-crimes tribunals. Clifton makes it plain that the perpetrators were not aberrant 'apish creatures', but unexceptional Australian men drawn by their position of immense localised power into performing despicable acts. Assisting the police with their investigation of the rape of a woman in her own home by an Australian soldier, Clifton is 'amazed and shocked' to be confronted by a tall, handsome 'lad' aged 21 or 22, such as one might see at home 'in flannels on a cricket field, or at tennis in any middle-class suburb; the pride of doting parents and the quarry of pretty women'.[13]

Its startling content attracting the interest of the press, *Time of Fallen Blossoms* infuriated the authorities. His fellow interpreter Les Oates, who was working for the BCOF's legal section at the Kure HQ at the time of the book's publication in 1950, recalls that the Australian government considered suing Clifton for defaming the Australian troops, and made discreet enquiries about the alleged incidence of rape. Significantly, it did not pursue the matter. At the time of the controversy, Clifton's commanding officer during the time he was attached to the 67th Battalion, none other than Captain T.B. Millar, was approached by the press for comment. He refused to oblige, instead making a detailed statement designed to rebut the allegations and discredit the man who made them, which he passed on to the military authorities. In the statement, dated 13 March 1951, Millar thinks 'attacks on women' could not have occurred, because, as he says:

> There was no need for them, as there was a vast army of professional and amateur whores only too willing to oblige the occupation forces in return for a cake of chocolate, a packet of cigarettes, or less.

This is a funny way to suggest that all was well. Rape was apparently unnecessary because there were ample women who were desperate enough to sell themselves for a packet of smokes.

The attempt to defame Clifton himself is a measure of the military's concern. Clifton's duties were confined to interpreting, Millar remarks, because as an investigator, he 'could not be relied upon to keep to the subject under inquiry'. More damningly, he was a communist sympathiser who had 'a liking for the Japanese ladies'. Apparently, he used to boast about his conquests, several of which took place on a houseboat borrowed for the purpose. Clifton's own attitude to Japanese women, Millar pointedly contends, 'was not that of the devout well-trained occupation soldier, but *more aggressively sexual than most Australian soldiers in my unit* [my emphasis]'.[14] The wording is calculatedly ambiguous, in describing the predilections of a whistler-blower on Australian rape, but the reputation of the Digger was more important than Clifton's own good name – or, for that matter, than the suffering wrought on Japanese women.

Many BCOF men remain dismissive of claims of sexual criminality in Occupied Japan. When Yuki Tanaka alleged Australian rape at a conference in Canberra in 1993 (citing the flawed testimony of the Hiroshima prostitute as partial evidence), veterans were incensed. Speaking on behalf of the Victorian RSL, Bruce Ruxton decried Tanaka's 'outrageous lies', and said that 'there was no such thing as rape in Japan'. A letter-writer to *The Australian* concurred, stating, 'No rape, Tanaka San, only the natural thing since Adam and Eve'. At the time, the elderly Clifton sprang to Tanaka's defence, while recalling that the threats he received at the time of the publication of *Time of Fallen Blossoms* forced him to flee Melbourne for Tasmania. So did a disinterested party, a former Army Reserve sergeant, M. Bernard Carroll, who provided the telling testimony that he had been able to access the BCOF court-martial files in the late 1950s, which revealed nothing less than 'a tale of "raping, looting and pillaging"'.[15]

Is Clifton a reliable witness, or is he an emotive writer with an axe to grind about the Australian inability to forge a rapprochement with Japan? Les Oates, a fellow BCOF interpreter who knew Clifton well, recalls that his nickname was 'Padre' because of his dogmatism and tendency to preach at people. Having his own account of Australian pack rape in Hiroshima coupled (in Tanaka's account of war crimes *Hidden Horrors*) with the erroneous testimony of the Hiroshima prostitute encourages scepticism. Nevertheless, Clifton's job did bring him into direct exposure to what he says were 'countless' incidents of serious crime, and he also had indirect knowledge of them from the provosts, from intelligence reports, and from the stories of fellow interpreters from other units. Equally knowledgeable and not one to sensationalise, Oates, for one, believes Clifton's claims to be valid.[16]

There can be little doubt that the official statistics severely underestimate the actual amount of serious crime. Typically, as Clifton confirms, many sexual assaults went unreported. The victims were wary of reporting such incidents and of pressing charges. Fear, a sense of personal shame, and the potential for unwelcome publicity and family disgrace were strong disincentives. Moreover, there was a feeling abroad that the perpetrators would not be brought to account. It was an Occupation after all; this kind of thing occurred as a matter of course. The *Shinchugan* was beyond criticism and beyond justice. The Japanese woman raped by the handsome young Australian in *Time of Fallen Blossoms* is reluctant to have the culprit punished: ironically, the ten years' penal servitude the Australian receives at a court martial is later quashed, back in Australia, 'because of insufficient evidence'.[17] Carolyne Carter's investigations tend to support Clifton's account. A BCOF intelligence report for the month of December 1946 criticises the Japanese police for not doing their duty in handing on to the Military Police reports of crime committed by the Occupation troops, which 'led the Japanese thinking that Military authorities are not concerned with troops' crimes against them'. On the contrary, the provosts were more than willing to pursue and charge serious offenders. However, the sentences duly imposed by courts martial were not severe. Carter provides the examples of rapists receiving ten years' prison then reduced to five, and of a convicted murderer given ten. Long-term prisoners were discharged from the military, and sent home to a civil prison to serve their term. Yet, as even the military admitted, 'sentences imposed by Court Martial in Japan were often mitigated or quashed in Australia'.[18]

What price did BCOF put on a Japanese life? Working with the provosts in and around Iwakuni as an Intelligence officer, Hugh Cortazzi (later a British ambassador to Japan) recalls a bad traffic accident involving a BCOF truck with an unauthorised driver behind the wheel, speeding criminally, running down and killing two children on a narrow street. The driver was eventually convicted of manslaughter, for which the sentence was a risible three months' imprisonment.[19]

IT WAS NOT ONLY the Japanese who were victims of Australian crime. There was some low-level friction with the GIs – a dance-hall donnybrook or two, usually incited by simmering envy of American power and popularity, and fuelled by alcohol.

Sometimes, it took a more serious turn than the throwing of a few ill-directed haymakers. In May 1948, a group of six inebriated Australians, including five airmen and one soldier, were heard 'loudly disparaging America' on Yarakucho station in central Tokyo before they 'very brutally assaulted' a senior American officer as he attempted to board his train.

Australian relations with the British and the New Zealanders during their tenure in Japan appear to have been relatively good. Attitudes toward the Indians were more complicated. Robertson's irritation at BRINDIV commander 'Punch' Cowan's arrogance turned a crusty conservative into a temporary republican sympathetic to the newly independent India. Knowing Cowan, he understands 'why the Indians were so anxious to get rid of the Englishmen from their country'.[20]

Resentment at British assumptions of superiority also led an Australian airman, Flight Lieutenant James Hawes, into an ambiguous solidarity with the Indians. In a letter home from Iwakuni in early May 1946, he informs his family that he has been given a billet in British quarters already accommodated by an Indian squadron leader, then in hospital. 'I don't think he will be coming here to stay as the RAF do not billet Indians with their own men. Whether they consider an Australian and an Indian are on a par, is something I have to learn.' Hawes tells his family that he is 'not too snobbish to share a room with an Indian', though he admits he would be 'a bit embarrassed if he was a turban man … and had the big top-knot of hair'; he is relieved when the 'Indian wallah' goes in with a fellow Indian upon his return, and an Australian ends up sharing his room.[21]

The exoticism of the Indians could lead to nastier responses than mere embarrassment. On the night of 30 August 1947, antagonism erupted into a fatal firefight between two units of Australians and Indians housed in neighbouring camps in Hiro, in which one Indian was killed and three wounded. What took place between the Australians of the 14 Works and Park Squadron,

Royal Australian Engineers, and the Indians of the 653 Indian
Plant Company, Royal Indian Engineers is unclear. Nor is the
event especially elucidated by the circumspect report handed down
by the official Court of Inquiry. The court found that animosity
had existed between the two units for a 'considerable period', and
that the firefight was its 'culmination'; 'several cases of ill-treatment
of Indians by Australians had been already reported, but the
officers responsible had taken no action'. The climactic 'disturbance'
was commenced through 'the action of unknown members' of the
Indian unit 'in molesting an Australian soldier and Japanese
female'. Just exactly what they did is unspecified. (Other
documentation suggests this initial incident took place 'on a hill
behind the two camps'.) Whatever it was, it brought a violent
response from the Australians. The armoury was forcibly opened,
and the Australians started shooting. The Indians returned fire.
The Indian sapper Mani Ram, who took no active part in the
fight, was killed – whether deliberately and by whom, the court
could not determine.

Members of the Special Investigation Branch who ventured
into the Indian camp to conduct enquiries found themselves encir-
cled by angry Indian soldiers chanting in their own language
something like, 'Death to all Australians'. It was not a shining
moment of Commonwealth amity. Six Australians and three
Indians (one of the latter under orders) were found to have fired
live ammunition; all but one of the Indians were charged with
'misconduct'. The court criticised negligent and ineffective
Australian leadership and the damning detail that both the
Australian guard commander and his second-in-command were
absent from duty. It also noted the 'excessive drinking' by the other
ranks which led to 'the excitement of the moment' being 'enhanced
through lack of self control'.[22]

Race was clearly a factor in the internecine BCOF violence at
Hiro, and in other, less dramatic, flare-ups with their
Commonwealth counterparts. The 'notorious' bigotry identified

by Eiji Takemae as characteristic of the Australian contingent extended, he says, from the Japanese to the Indians, whom they 'tended to regard as just another "aboriginal underclass"'.[23] Takemae is extrapolating here; he is rather more assiduous in pointing the bone at Western racism than in identifying it among his countrymen and women. Nonetheless, the 'Battle of Hiro' illustrates the unedifying tendency of Australian malfeasance in the Occupation to be expressed in racial ways. A report of the episode published in the Sydney *Daily Telegraph* several weeks after the event quotes an Australian soldier blaming the trouble on the 'cheeky and arrogant' attitude of the Indians after their Independence that August. Who did they think they were? In a military expedition devoid of battles, that the one Australian firefight in Japan led to the death of an innocent ally is nothing to boast about. Not surprisingly, BCOF secretly sought to suppress any further publicity of the unsavoury incident.[24]

CHAPTER SEVEN

Anything Goes

Behind the lines, Australian conduct in foreign military theatres has not always been edifying. The unruliness of the Diggers of the Great War has become part of the Anzac mythology, tolerated as the untamed national character expressing itself on the international stage. The men of the new world were refusing to bow before the old. If their memoirs are to be believed, the Australians ran amok among the hapless 'Gyppos' en route to Europe, and terrorised the 'niggers' of Colombo on the way home. (They seemed to behave rather better when on leave in Britain; possibly the forbidding presence of Mother England kept them in check.) Touring the pyramids near Cairo before embarking for Gallipoli, A.B. Facey witnessed a drunken Australian military tourist being told by a guide that the candle flame by the entrance to one tomb had never been allowed to go out, and had been burning for over 1000 years. With that, the Australian gave a puff, and out went the candle. '"There, it is out now," he said.'[1] In Vietnam in the 1960s, the gauche larrikin of the First AIF became somebody more disagreeable altogether – a serial hater who relaxed by sculling cans of Foster's Lager, engaging in some 'horizontal refreshment', picking fights with the Americans, and generally giving the locals a hard time.

In Occupied Japan, Australian military exuberance degenerated into displays of contempt for a recently defeated Asian people. Quite apart from the assaults and rapes was the ruinous cultural violence of men misbehaving simply because they could. Allan Clifton writes:

> It is an ugly sight to see a truckload of twenty or thirty of one's fellow soldiers descend like ravening wolves on a row of market stalls, grabbing fistfuls of tawdry trifles, overturning counters, and punching anyone who looked as though he (or she) might resent it.[2]

Alcohol was almost always involved. The Australians 'carried a heavy animus against the Japanese', according to the American observer Hebert Passin, 'and had fewer inhibitions than American combat veterans about displaying it'. On assignment in Fukuoka, Passin was appalled by the spectacle of a group of four capering, red-faced Australian soldiers drunkenly amusing themselves at a train station by forcing the crowds on the platform to line up and bow to them as they walked back and forth. Along with Japanese repatriates from mainland Asia, bone-weary old men and women were 'obliged to remain standing up and bow every time an Australian soldier passed in front of them'. An Intelligence Report for February 1947 cites constant Australian mockery of the cultural practice of bowing as a reason for its decreasing use by the Japanese as the Occupation progressed. That the Japanese had stopped bowing before BCOF was then taken as a sign of their calculated insolence. They couldn't win.[3]

The Occupationnaires had had no expert training about Japan, or detailed advice about their role there. T.B. Millar remembers giving lectures about Japan to the assembled force waiting on Morotai, even though it was a subject of which he was 'only marginally less ignorant than the troops'. 'We were almost totally unprepared to be an army of occupation,' Millar recalls, 'and were given almost no instruction in what was expected of us.' *Know Japan*, the guidebook specially produced for the force under Northcott's direction, could not have been much help. Northcott's foreword, dated February 1946, told the men that, 'although we may not like the Japanese people, we must learn something of their life and customs' in order to help them civilise themselves. With this altruistic ambition specifically in mind, *Know Japan* was designed to provide 'essential background to an understanding of Japan and its people'.[4]

So what did the ignorant Occupationnaire get to know about Japan? Enough to make Northcott's non-fraternisation edict, printed in full before his foreword, unnecessary. Like most travel guidebooks, from the Baedekers of the 19th century to the Lonely Planets of today, the book contains just enough empirical detail to give the suggestion of factuality and objectivity. There are substantial sections on geography and topography, on climate, and on flora and fauna, as well as on industry and commerce, agriculture, fishing, and transport, along with some data about the Hiroshima region specifically. (Giving the population of Hiroshima as the pre-Bomb figure of 340,000 seems fatuous.) There is a list of national holidays and festivals, and some rudimentary commentary on Japanese aesthetics. In the two central chapters on political organisation and social life, the trenchant critiques of emperor-worship, State Shinto, the warrior creed *Bushido*, and the practice of *seppuku* seem fair enough and probably even necessary given the military and historical context.

But where *Know Japan* really reveals its ideological colours is in its analysis of the Japanese national character. In a masterpiece of crude Orientalist ethnography, this is reductively stereotyped as a 'mass-produced product' labelled 'Suzuki-San', the Japanese version of John Citizen. Self-disciplined and obedient, but with a 'taste for power', Suzuki-San never loses his inherited and socially conditioned ideas of 'masculine and racial superiority', ideas that are imbibed, like mother's milk, from an early age. 'And so' – the leap is made as blithely as this – 'in later days he may have become one of the braves who took part in the rape of Nanking', or one of the 'slave-drivers' on the Burma–Thailand Railway. Recent tragic history lives on, personified by the Japanese man-in-the-street.

The subtext is clear, and a warning to the soldiers of BCOF not to drop their guard. Living in such a conformist and repressive social system, Suzuki's self-abnegation occasionally breaks down, and pent-up personal frustrations boil over into incoherent rage. En masse, the Suzuki-Sans of Japan express themselves in wars and revolutions, 'or in a fanatic attempt at world domination'. The woman's position in this volcanic human landscape is necessarily marginal, confined to staying at home uncomplainingly while her husband 'varies his pleasures with a visit to the geisha-house'. But the Occupationnaire should beware. The final item in the last chapter of the book, an apocalyptic survey of serious diseases prevalent in Japan, from dysentery, to typhoid, to malaria, to scrub typhus, and even the Plague, is a brief reference to venereal disease and the 'great risk ... in associating with Japanese women'.[5] Evidently, many of the men did not make it to the end of the book; reading about Suzuki-San must have killed them off.

As a BCOF intelligence report from early 1947 suggests, many troops were 'just not interested in the Japanese in any deep sense of the word'. The tendency was to view them as 'a semi-native people' whose formal manners and customs made them appear 'stupid or rather laughable'. Only two categories of Japanese were recognised, according to the report: pretty girls and 'bastards'. More damningly, the report goes on to assert the callous indifference to the contemporary daily life of the Japanese, quoting the 'cynical' but 'not entirely' false view that 'the only interest of troops in the economic chaos is the exploiting of it'. That urge to exploit found two principal outlets. One was in the rampant recourse to official or unofficial prostitution, as desperate women fed the sexual appetites of the Occupationnaires to provide for themselves and their families in a society bereft of breadwinners; the other was in the *Yami'ichi*, the black market. These twin compulsions meet together in the figure of Andy Waller in *Sowers of the Wind*, who 'knew all the best places to black-market, and was on speaking terms with the girls in half a dozen brothels', who 'rarely had less than fifty pounds' in yen on him, who had 'never earned more than fifteen shillings a week', and for whom 'the Occupation might go on for ever'.[6]

Few of the now elderly veterans like to reflect openly on the VD issue; it was always somebody else that copped it. The president of the NSW BCOF Veterans Association, Air Commodore Ken Skillicorn, was so incensed by the focus on sexual diseases in the documentary *The Forgotten Force*, when it was released in 1994, that he wrote an aggrieved letter to the makers, Film Australia.[7] However, the veterans become loquacious when it comes to discussing the illicit black market. Almost all Occupationnaires were into 'wogging' in some form. 'They had their girl friends and "wogged" their canteen goods, I suppose – we all did', Allan Clifton admits. Gordon Leed, who did three tours of duty in Japan as a stoker aboard the destroyer the HMAS *Quiberon*, policing the smuggling rackets on the waters of the Inland Sea and out in the Sea of Japan as far as the coast of Korea, remarks that sailors became so proficient at 'the game' that they were able to save most of their navy pay and live off the market. 'The soldiery stationed in bases ashore were into the business before us,' he writes, 'but it did not take us long to catch up'.[8]

Storehouses and service installations in the BCOF areas were widely dispersed and stretched the manpower available to guard them. Often made of ageing wood or rusted iron, they were also hard to secure. Abject poverty among the local population made Occupation largesse all the more desirable. On the night of 22

July 1946, a group of youngsters attempted to raid a BCOF store. The piquet opened fire, wounding two of them. They turned out to be just 11 years of age, mere children.[9] Petty pilfering of stores, (mainly essential items such as food and blankets) by Japanese workers attached to BCOF was not uncommon, and large-scale theft by organised gangs of goods sold for profit on the *Yami'ichi* took place. Many of the gangs were identified, but others soon took their place. Much of the merchandise that found its way onto the black market, often in clandestine transactions 'down a dark alley', originated from within BCOF.

Members of the force were prohibited from selling, bartering, exchanging, or disposing to the Japanese any goods emanating from any of the services or amenities of any arm of the force. But the soldiers treated the instruction with the same contempt as that of the rule forbidding fraternisation, of which, of course, black marketeering was a form. Before May 1947, when a special Occupation currency, British Armed Forces Vouchers, was introduced (thereby deterring the accumulation of excessive amounts of yen), the local currency in which the troops were paid had much less purchasing power outside the canteens and amenities of the force, which encouraged the selling of Occupation rations and goods 'on the black'. Australian troops made a killing selling cigarettes, chocolate, condensed milk, and the like to the Japanese at an enormous profit.

Becoming enmeshed in the 'marketo', as the Occupationnaires called it (mimicking the English usage of the Japanese), presented soldiers with a moral conundrum. 'The spectacle of soldiers trying to drag the last possible yen' from struggling local people, many of them mothers with sickly children, outside Hiroshima railway station repelled Allan Clifton.[10] But to some, it was a business opportunity that was not to be missed – like playing the stock market. When to sell and when not to sell? One contributor to *Gloom* dramatises the quandary in mock-Shakespearean soliloquy:

To sell, or not to sell: that is the question;
Whether it is better to eat your canteen ration
Or sell it on the Black Market,
To take the meagre prices offering at present,
Or wait until there is a boom? To sell: to keep:
That's all; and by decision to say we end
The torment of our frail and human mind
That now besets us, 'tis a benediction
To the troubled soul.[11]

Clifton Pugh was no procrastinating Hamlet. He was into the black market from the word go. In the first paragraph of his first letter home to his mother from Japan, he is quoting rates of currency exchange and how much a blanket is worth on the black market – 300 yen, at 48 yen to the Australian pound. Playing the market becomes a kind of addiction. Rejecting his mother's offer of money to make him stop, he remarks about the 'strong effect' it has on him, as a stimulating antidote to the boredom of garrison life. His only concerns are about getting caught, and about how to spend the small fortune he is rapidly acquiring. 'I have been working on a large scale in the "Black",' he tells his mother, in a letter dated 17 April 1946, 'making over a thousand yen a night, maybe I am taking risks but the risk is worth taking. The only blue is to realise on the money …' One could not buy all that much with the Japanese yen, as the Japanese knew only too well. Pugh is hard pressed to find ways to convert his pile of cash, but that does not stop him wanting more. 'Tell me is sugar still rationed?' he asks in that same April letter, letting his mother know it is worth more than gold in Japan. 'If you could just post cake tins full up as much as possible it will mean big money.'[12]

Pugh was a young private soldier from a modest background trying to set himself up for life after the army, so perhaps we can excuse him exploiting Japanese desperation. One is less forgiving of the three senior RAAF officers who were part of an Australian gang smuggling precious sugar into Japan. Hugh Cortazzi, who gave evidence at their court martial while working from the BCAIR base at Iwakuni, has described their 'ingenious scheme', eventually exposed by a Japanese informant. It involved arranging for Australian ships on their way to Kure to rendezvous off Iwakuni with a fishing boat: 'The sugar was unloaded into the boat and smuggled ashore for sale. The Australian gang then bought cultured pearls to smuggle back into Australia for sale at huge profit.' At the court martial, the RAAF officers were treated leniently by their fellow officers, receiving the puny penalties of loss of seniority and promotion. They 'did not give a damn', Cortazzi remembers: most of them were awaiting demobilisation anyway. Unsurprisingly, the Japanese involved in the scam received prison terms.[13] The Occupier displayed its commitment to democracy by having one law for itself and another for the Occupied.

One especially wicked exploitation of supplies was passing off weak tea as penicillin to local people anxious to deal with the many outbreaks of various viral infections, including venereal diseases, that swept the Occupied areas. Murray Elliott, who at just 24 years of age served for a time as the commanding officer of the Australian Convalescent Depot on Miyajima, heard rumour of this disgraceful activity sometime in 1946. Sixty years later, he cannot conceal his contempt at the memory. Making money at the expense of the Japanese was an irresistible temptation. In *Sowers of the Wind*, T.A.G. Hungerford personifies this nexus of greed and hate in the form of the Australian serviceman Ron Prothero, whose loathing for the Japanese (he had two brothers perish in Changi) translates into trafficking in drugs and medicines, as well as supplying weapons to rebellious Korean labourers, hoping for a vicarious Japanese kill. Dan Hart, the medical officer with the 65th Battalion – and Murray Elliott's friend for 60 years, stretching back to the Occupation (he had done a three-week locum for him on Miyajima in 1947) – tells the story of a major who established for himself a 'palatial set-up', complete with a Japanese mistress and a cache of black-market material, including penicillin, plundered from BCOF stores. When this grasping individual's nest was discovered, he was summarily cashiered – or 'bowler-hatted', in Hart's delightfully archaic term.[14]

Some of the black-market activity was connected with the need to facilitate illicit domestic arrangements with local women. Again, illustrations are best sourced from fiction. In *Sowers of the Wind*, Andy Waller has a wife of sorts who puts up with him 'for the food he brought her'. In the same novel, the central character, McNaughton, has to 'wog like hell' to set up his girlfriend Fumie in a rough cottage in bucolic mountain country above Kure, having bought her out of contracted slavery as a 'hostess' in a sleazy downtown dance hall. This was a situation possibly based on one of Hungerford's BCOF pals, who 'had to wog like the hammers to hell to foot the bill' to get his girl out of a cabaret and into a couple of rooms in the town.[15]

The picture of what L.H. Evers in *Pattern of Conquest* calls the 'rape of Kure', based on his personal observations as signalman and invigorated by a lively imagination, centres on the tragic consequences of naïve young Australian men getting in over their heads in black-market crime in order to secure the continued affections of Japanese femmes fatales. After the introduction of the currency vouchers meant that he couldn't use his stash of yen to buy up big on canteen rations to sell on the street at inflated prices, Mark Foster (a parson's son) finds himself financially unable to maintain his liaison with the manipulative Canadian-educated Tohana. Desperate, he combines with a vicious comrade in a line-construction unit, nicknamed 'Honest John', in a plan to sell bags of sugar to Japanese hoodlums. The scam goes horribly wrong, and Honest John bashes a black marketeer to death. Mark's falling out with Honest John becomes complete when the latter insinuates himself into Tohana's affections. Enraged, Mark sexually assaults Tohana and, later, back at the camp, shoots Honest John dead as he returns from one of his nightly assignations. Lurid and overdrawn, alternately moralistic and salacious, and full of incredible coincidences, *Pattern of Conquest* succumbs to the sensationalist tendencies of the popular war novel. But its essential theme, that Occupied Japan was a place 'where civilised society has gone off the rails', is supported by both the documentary and anecdotal record.[16]

BCOF men would sell anything for cash. Brian Rose relates one rich symbolic method of fleecing the local population. The shuddering response to the local use of human excrement as field fertiliser is the most insistently registered form of Australian negativity toward Japan during the Occupation. No BCOF narrative fails to mention the 'honey carts' drawn by bullocks, which carried nightsoil collected and emptied into large wooden barrels for use in home gardens and on the paddies. They made most Australians hesitant to touch the local food, which they were forbidden to do, in any case. The country stank, literally. That is the main thing many Occupationnaires remember, when they think back on Japan: they automatically associate it with shit. But this malodorous local farming practice was seen by one of Rose's commercially adventurous comrades as a golden business opportunity. Having participated in the building of new latrines for the men soon after his unit's arrival in Japan, he starts selling 'the contents of the toilets' to the honey-cart man.[17] The Australians were recoiling from a stench created, at least partly, by themselves.

CHAPTER EIGHT

Home Affront

Like all armies, the Australian military has always been protective of its reputation, and has resented criticism. The outrage at a fleeting reference to Australian boasts about atrocities in Robert Graves's Great War memoir *Goodbye to All That* (1929) is a case in point. Furious, the federal executive of the Returned and Services League advocated censoring authors 'who defame Australian soldiers'.[1] Only the good stuff was permissible. This is an expectation still reliably met by popular Australian writers on war, for whom the mythology of Anzac and its associated legends remain irresistibly seductive. Australians are proud of their armies.

Anxious about the impact of his disclosures and his pro-Japanese sentiments, Allan Clifton had held back writing *Time of Fallen Blossoms* upon his return to Australia at the end of 1946, waiting to let what he calls the 'private prejudices born of lost sons, husbands and close friends' run their course. Angus & Robertson delayed publishing Hungerford's *Sowers of the Wind* because of fears of the censor, but the company was also concerned about the prospect of negative public reaction to such an unpleasant presentation of the national character revealed in Japan. Hungerford had completed the novel by 1949; it won a fiction competition awarded by the *Sydney Morning Herald* that year, earning its author the handsome sum of 1000 pounds. But the novel did not appear until 1954, well after the Occupation was over. The same year, the other major novel by an Occupationnaire, Evers's *Pattern of Conquest*, appeared. The reasons for the hiatus are unclear, but may be found in a remark near the end of the novel, made by the astute old soldier 'Pop' Manning. 'The folks back home will be shocked and hurt if they ever find out about their Army in Japan,' he remarks.[2]

Yet controversy and allegations of impropriety had dogged BCOF from 1946, at least. On Morotai in January 1946, the war correspondent Stewart Legge had sympathetically reported that members of the 34th Brigade awaiting transport to Japan were irritated by 'discouraging comments on their role coming from the mainland' and indignant at suggestions that it was 'on its way to a sightseeing tour'. Rumours of venereal disease among the troops were already circulating and they hadn't even made Japan yet. T.A.G. Hungerford remembers that men had started receiving 'anxious letters from mothers and wives and girlfriends – sometimes with clippings from the papers', asking if 'Japforce' had been put together from troops 'the army just didn't want back in Australia, and was sending them off somewhere to cool down, or recover from whatever they'd caught – VD being the inference – or change their politics.'[3]

Criticism of the force, in particular the charges of immorality, continued throughout the Occupation, giving way to the legend of press negativity towards BCOF. In fact, the newspapers were reporting criticism that came within the ranks of the force itself, and was significantly fuelled by attacks from veterans' organisations. To the latter, BCOF was always a gimcrack outfit that simply didn't command the same respect as that of the fighting forces.

In the first months of the Occupation itself, Australian press coverage of BCOF was strongly supportive of the men, if not the overall enterprise, as soldiers started filtering back home with horror stories of conditions in Japan. Headlines like, 'A Soldier from Japan Says it's Hell at Kure', and, 'How Long Must This Be Endured?' made it seem as if the Australians were garrisoned in the Warsaw Ghetto. One returned officer, H.K. Wood, wrote in August 1946 in the *Sunday Sun & Guardian* that a 'no hoper from the worst Australian slum would hesitate before living in the normal Kure home'.[4] As usual, the comparison was with the Americans, living the life of Riley in civilised places like Osaka, Kobe, and Tokyo. Much of the press criticism had a political motivation; the conservative daily press, notably Frank Packer's *Daily Telegraph*, was antagonistic to the socialist inclinations of Ben Chifley's federal Labor government.

The government was returned in the September 1946 federal election; but the negative impact of the press reportage can be measured by the fact that the army minister (and briefly prime minister, after Curtin's death), Frank Forde, lost his seat. The BCOF controversies continued unabated after the ballot. *Smith's Weekly*, the sporty, Digger-worshipping, pro-White Australia tabloid with a largely male readership, blamed the debacle on the Labor government. In October 1946, it ran a sensational cover story on the national 'scandal' of broken promises and broken men, of tragic shipments of 'physical and mental wrecks' arriving back in Australia from Japan. Troops who had gone to Japan 'believing they would be a swagger outfit, dressed, paid and quartered in a style designed to impress the Japanese' found themselves living like the natives. They were 'conquerors on coolies' pay', with a daily allowance about one-third of that of the American GI, living in derelict conditions, neglected by the government, drinking themselves stupid and, quite literally, bored out of their brains.[5]

Even immorality could partially be excused by the lack of planning given to the provision of basic amenities, especially in the early winter weeks of the Occupation. The *Sunday Telegraph*, in an August 1946 article headlined 'Australian Sufferings in Kure', cited the lack of amenities and amusements as the reason why the soldiers turned to Japanese girls met 'on the streets'. Girls who, it must be added, were 'of a very low type, diseased'. (It was the Japanese women, of course, who were commonly blamed for the prevalence of sexual disease.)[6] This was a mealy-mouthed argument. Yes, the amenities were poor, and the troops were not exactly bombarded by an array of entertainments. But they were a group of inexperienced young men living in a strange country, made all the more enticing by the fact that the Commonwealth authorities, in their wisdom, had forbidden all but official contact with the local people. The women were cheap, accommodating, and available. No up-to-date Hollywood film or night of popular song would ever compete with the tender flesh-and-blood attractions lying outside the rough masculine squalor of the barracks. An editorial in the Melbourne *Age* put its finger on the issue in April 1948: an army of occupation anywhere, it states, 'is exposed to influences that only the faithful among Milton's arch-angels could resist'. No amount of education courses, hobbies, entertainments, discussion groups, and amusements could alter the fact that thousands of young men were stationed in a bleak area 'with the knowledge that little more than a routine of formal obligations is required of them'.[7]

These are remarkably considered observations for the time. The more popular view of the Occupationnaires was that they personified the evil of promiscuity that seemed be the curse of the feverish post-war world. Diseases such as syphilis and gonorrhea were regarded with the same sort of fear and alarm that led to the AIDS public-awareness campaigns of the 1980s. In January 1946, the New South Wales Ministry of Health placed a large advertisement in the press, headlined 'Face the Facts about Venereal

Disease', reminding people of the consequences of 'every promis-
cuous sexual act', which only something called 'clean living' could
prevent. The controversies swirling around the men of BCOF were
thus very much a symptom of the Zeitgeist, and account for their
reputation as a bunch of (in the bitter words of one veteran)
'whoremongers and syphilitics'.[8]

Unfortunately, statistics didn't help BCOF's cause. The com-
parative figures relating to the Australian contraction of venereal
diseases in the BCOF areas vary, but they are uniformly high. By
the end of December 1946, the British historian Peter Bates suggests the total number of VD cases in BCOF was 8090, of which
the Australian contingent were responsible for about 55 per cent
– well above the 32 per cent of the overall force it represented. Just
how many of these cases were *re*infections (which were common)
is unclear. It may also be true that the Australian process of identification, the reportage, and the treatment of venereal diseases was
superior to that of the British, Indians, and New Zealanders. But
according to Jeffrey Grey, the alarming statistical picture considered by JCOSA at the end of August 1946 told a similar story.
During the months of June and July that year, the Australian proportion of VD cases averaged over 64 per cent of the BCOF total,
or twice the Australian percentage of bodies on the ground.[9]

Some reasons for the high figures were submitted in mitiga-
tion, both at the time and since. The Australians occupied a
particularly devastated area; they don't come more devastated than
Hiroshima. The desperation that drove women into prostitution
was particularly acute there. More intent on highlighting Japanese
turpitude during the war than Australian misbehaviour after it,
the returned serviceman's advocate Bruce Ruxton has suggested
that Japan was already 'one big brothel' when the Australian forces
(of which he was a member) arrived. This is insulting hyperbole,
but certainly Kure, as a major naval base and port, had an
infrastructure of prostitution already in place, and alternative recreational outlets were meagre. And, as JCOSA itself somewhat

hopefully ventured, the Australian force was rather younger than its counterparts, and hence, 'more irresponsible'.[10] But the picture was far from pretty, and was made worse when the beleaguered force also came under fire from an unexpected quarter – a veterans' organisation. When the federal president of the Legion of Ex-Servicemen, Barry McDonald, used the phrase 'morally rotting' to describe the Australians in Japan, the major Sydney dailies sat up and took notice. Further published allegations about high rates of venereal diseases and the illegitimate children of Australian servicemen being cared for in a Hiroshima orphanage followed. Support for them came from an apparently impeccable source – the Melbourne barrister E.J. Thwaites, recently returned from Japan, where he had served as a captain in the Australian forces and on the prosecution team of the War Crimes Tribunal. Thwaites's criticisms of ill-disciplined, ill-trained troops with too much time on their hands indulging in a range of unhealthy activities were front-page news in papers such as the *Sydney Morning Herald*. The troops 'were not a good advertisement' for their country, an assessment that was pure poison in Australia.[11]

Resisting a public inquiry, Forde's successor as army minister, Cyril Chambers ('a dentist by profession', as Robertson noted with distaste), responded to the furore by announcing he would send three army chaplains-general to Japan to conduct an investigation. Cynics suggested that these worthy individuals might lack the knowledge to delve deeply into such unseemly matters as black marketeering and venereal disease. In response, Chambers added another two members to the party, Major-General C.E.M. Lloyd, a former businessman, and the journalist Massey Stanley. Presumably, these were people with the necessary expertise to probe economic exploitation and sexual dissolution.

The 'Sin Busters', as they were dubbed, arrived in southern Honshu in the Japanese spring of 1948 to a chilly reception, and worked independently over a few weeks to produce two separate reports. The chaplains remark in their report that the men of

BCOF did their best to help them produce an accurate account. Les Oates, who was there and knows what transpired, takes a different view, remarking that the delegation, like another all-party delegation of politicians that took place a couple of months later, was 'carefully shielded from reality'. That may explain the breathtakingly sanguine nature of the reports. The chaplains ambiguously found that 'the degree of promiscuity in Japan is no greater than would have been the case in Australia'. Black marketeering, for its part, was dismissed as 'occasional personal barter'. Speaking at a lunch upon his return, one of the chaplains says he 'never saw a drunken soldier', and that the 'magnificent' troops were 'the best behaved' he had ever seen; they had been 'grossly defamed'. For its part, Lloyd and Stanley's report was more comprehensive, but equally tepid. As an Occupation force, BCOF's record was assessed to be 'conspicuously clean', compared with others around the world.[12]

To capitalise on the clean slate obligingly provided by these reports, a delegation of politicians led by the Labor parliamentarian Leslie Haylen travelled to Japan in July, where they spent six weeks seeing things for themselves. Upon his return, Haylen unleashed an attack on negative newspaper coverage of BCOF. Speaking in the House of Representatives on 2 September, Haylen savaged 'vicious' and 'unsubstantiated' reports of the misbehaviour of 'lonely and homesick' men who are 'sweating it out in a climate which is intolerably hot and humid for three months of the year, and equally harsh in the winter'. It is time, Haylen thundered, that we 'cease libelling the fighting men of our country'.

That the Occupationnaires were not strictly 'fighting men' is a nicety overlooked by Haylen. Instead, he concluded his speech by implying that BCOF was a kind of distant front-line of national defence, invoking the terrifying arithmetic of an overpopulated Asia ready to pounce on vulnerable White Australia: 'We are only 7,000,000 compared with 1,000,000,000 people in countries to the north, and we must not make ourselves look ridiculous.'

Unsurprisingly, the men of BCOF were encouraged by this speech.[13] In the end, the parliamentary delegation to Japan attracted public attention for something other than its rebuttal of the improprieties of BCOF. It made the mistake of going to the palace to see the emperor. When the delegation met Hirohito and Haylen shook his hand, 'all hell broke loose', as he remembered later. What was a minor faux pas at worst, and no more than a gesture of courtesy, was turned into an act of dire treachery. To relatives of those thousands of POWs who had suffered in Japanese hands, observed the *Sunday Sun*, the action was akin to 'shaking hands with murder'.[14] Therein lies the real rub of home-front suspicions about BCOF. People in Australia did not like any interaction of *any* kind with the Japanese.

There seemed to be almost as many official investigative field trips to Japan to check up on BCOF's wellbeing as there were members of the force itself. The army minister Cyril Chambers went on his own 'tour of duty', as he called it in his report to the prime minister, at the end of 1946. The minister observed 'a notable absence of spiritual and moral outlook on the part of the troops' in the Australian areas. That September, the coordinating authority for the BCOF medical services, Major-General S.R. Burston, made a comprehensive tour to gain insight into 'the general health' of what had earned the reputation as a sick force. Struck by the men's poor morale, Burston thought the answer was to have good, clean, wholesome Australian women working in the canteens and clubs, to boost soldierly 'contentment', and stop them wandering the streets 'with the almost inevitable result of fraternisation with Japanese women'.[15] He was offering a 'female floodwall' of his own, an ironic reversal of the one put into effect by the Japanese authorities when the lusty GIs arrived in Japan. Contact with their own kind might prevent the men from consorting with the natives.

With supreme inelegance, commander-in-chief Robertson had said as much, a couple of months before Burston's visit, in a letter to prime minister Chifley. The force faced a 'feminine problem' that needed fixing. The three or four hundred women in the Australian formations were mainly the nurses and members of the AAMWS, the Australian Army Medical Women's Service, confined to the hospital, away from where most of the servicemen were located. The men lived 'a kind of monastic life except when they fall for a Jap girl in the street'. Things were different in the hospital environment, with the availability of 'normal feminine society'. There, the men and women engaged in healthy pursuits (though some of the men must have been ailing), such as talking and having picnics. An influx of more women drawn from the AWAS, the Australian Women's Army Service, Robertson implored the prime minister, would not only cover 'our essential typing, clerking, telephoning etc.', but would also end the 'monastic ritual' and its unhappy flipside of soldiers going with the local girls and contracting sexual diseases. The saving in medical and social costs alone would be great.[16]

His request was denied, as was a follow-up demand for civilian female workers, though in time, nearly 50 civilian women were granted permission to work with the Australian Army Canteens Service in Kure. Duties included working as stenographers and clerks in the Canteens Service offices; managing gift shops and dependants' stores; acting as receptionists in BCOF hotels and coffee shops; and working as 'hostesses' in officers' and other ranks' clubs. The Red Cross and the YMCA also supplied a small number of female representatives. The YMCA women supervised transit hotels and leave, ran coffee shops, and organised an exhausting array of wholesome pursuits like table tennis, darts, and other kinds of games, picnics, concerts, and dances. Much of their time, according to Roma Donnelly's original research, was 'spent talking to the troops about home and listening to their problems'. The contribution of the female members of BCOF was praised by Robertson (in an article in the *Women's Weekly*) as giving 'the only touch of home life' for the troops, in providing 'some relief from otherwise strange and bewildering surroundings'.[17]

BCOF never received the number of Australian women Robertson wanted. However, over time, the ratio of females to males did improve, especially after the arrival of the wives and their children, and the female teachers to educate them. But did the presence of more women provide the restraining and civilising effect on the moral and social life of the men that was officially envisaged? The numbers of women, such as they were, peaked well before the claims of turpitude made by Thwaites and others were publicised in 1948, which suggests not. The arrival of the BCOF wives and dependant children in 1947 had an impact, but mainly on the immediate lives of those concerned.

It probably saved a few marriages. One of the BCOF wives, Mary Bleechmore, who gave birth to two children in Japan, remarked in retrospect, in 1991, that the value of allowing soldiers to be reunited with their wives could not be overestimated. Many had barely seen their spouses during the upheaval of the war years. 'How the marriages would have survived without this coming together I do not know,' she observed. The coming of the wives may also have had an inhibiting effect on the husbands. Paddy Power, an English nursing sister who met and married an Australian lieutenant of the 66th Battalion in Kure, says, with a glint of amusement, that 'the behaviour of the men changed when their wives came'. (Though many continued to keep Japanese girlfriends 'on the side'.)[18] But the influence of the women on the force at large was negligible. The BCOF families tended to live in a self-contained bubble, removed from the force, and even from Japan itself. As for the unmarried women workers, their numbers were small compared with the superabundance of their Japanese sisters. Faced with the choice between a cup of tea at a Whist night run by the doughty ladies of the YWCA, or a few beers and a night on the *tatami* with one of their local girlfriends, many servicemen, unsurprisingly, elected the latter.

THE YOUNG, SINGLE MEN of BCOF were entitled to feel alone, let down and maligned by their homeland. Lacking the anchor of a settled family life in Japan, many of them were at sea. During the Occupation, some very large claims were made on their behalf, such as Leslie Haylen's ludicrous reference to the extremes of the Japanese climate, to milk them some sympathy. A *Smith's Weekly* article describing a shipload of 'physical and mental wrecks' returning from Japan on the *Taiping* quoted the ship's surgeon's comparison of garrison life with the battlefield and the prison camp. 'The ambition of men in action was to get out alive. In Kure their ambition is to get out sane,' he told *Smith's*. 'Ex-prisoners of war serving with the occupation forces declare prison life was easier to take than the nothingness of Kure.'[19]

It is doubtful if any survivors of the Burma Railway would have swapped Kure for slave labouring in the jungles of the Japanese prison camps. Yet the Occupationnaires may have felt as abandoned as the soldiers in Vietnam in the late 1960s, fighting not only the enemy but also their homeland and, ruinously, themselves. There is a famous photograph of an American GI in Vietnam, face contorted in anguish, hands clutching at his helmeted head – a helmet bearing the legend, 'I'm Not a Tourist, I Live Here'. Home front opposition to the war in Vietnam, and vicarious civilian pain at its manifest tragedy, left a legacy not only of deflation but of deep bitterness and abiding alienation. Something similar occurred in Occupied Japan, leading to antisocial attitudes towards the local people and self-destructive behaviour.

'Nowhere in the world have I seen a place more likely to breed neurosis than Kure,' observed the ship's surgeon in *Smith's Weekly*. Troopships returning to Sydney during 1946 contained numbers of what the newspapers called 'neurosis patients' and 'anxiety' cases, men who were subject to 'fits of depression'. Some were considered so dangerous that when the ships docked, police kept relatives, well-wishers, and other onlookers away. The psychiatric invaliding of BCOF was 'unusually high', Carolyne Carter contends, and the problem 'seems to have been greatest in the Australian contingent'.[20]

When Major-General S.R. Burston inspected the area in September 1946 on behalf of the military medical services, he made an unpleasant discovery. Visiting the psychiatric ward of one of the major service hospitals, he found that of the 18 patients with acute disorders, 17 were Australian. BCOF medicos recognised the link between criminal or aberrant actions and anxiety, depression, and other forms of mental illness, but took a cynical view of psychological disturbance. A BCOF psychiatric report for the quarter ending September 1947 diagnosed 'fairly simple behaviour problems in late adolescents'. 'Almost without exception', medico-legal problems were 'precipitated by excessive drinking in unstable individuals'. The patients usually pleaded idleness or lack of amenities. While there is 'some validity' to their claims, the professional opinion holds to the view that 'inadequate inner resourses [sic] and initiative are the real cause'. The problem, the report concludes, 'is more an educational and social one going back to pre-service days'. For his part, Major-General Burston argued that poor screening at the enlistment stage allowed too many undesirables into the force. (Possessing a criminal record seems not to have debarred some from being accepted.) None of the psychiatric patients he came across, he said, should have been enlisted.[21]

The suicides and attempted suicides of BCOF troops were a distressing manifestation of neurosis. The official statistics record 77 deaths in BCOF from the period of the contingent's arrival in February 1946 to the end of June 1951. Of these, 58 were classified as 'accidental', about half of which were motor vehicle accidents, and the rest, a range of other fatal mishaps. These included four persons 'struck by train', four 'accidentally drowned', four who fell to their deaths 'from building' [sic], one from a fall 'type unstated'(perhaps the senior officer who, one veteran has told me, fell down a flight of stairs 'dead drunk'), and one 'shot dead by fellow soldier'. Of those remaining 19, only four are defined explicitly as suicides.[22]

Dark rumours abound in BCOF veterans' circles of young servicemen from other ranks wanting to kill officers who were bastardising them, but ending up killing themselves instead; of 'accidents' being the result of murder (by both fellow Australians and by Japanese); and of shooting 'accidents' actually being suicides. It is difficult to determine the truth or otherwise of these allegations. Too much time has passed – memories have become clouded; pasts have become distorted, mystified, fictionalised. Official BCOF records on these matters are woefully inadequate.

Many BCOF suicides remain inexplicable. The CSDIC linguist Colin Funch is still perplexed by the suicide of an unnamed colleague in Kure that defied explanation: 'Those who had just had lunch with the man cannot recall that he was in any way agitated … it seems the incident was quite spontaneous.' Dan Hart, the medical officer of the 65th Battalion who went on to become a leading ophthalmologist after the war, and who is still as sharp as a tack in his mid 80s, has personal knowledge of two suicides that seem to sum up this fraught and upsetting aspect of the Occupation of Japan. One was a young private in Hart's battalion, Edward Nathan. Born in Alexandria, Egypt, Nathan had enlisted at Royal Park in Melbourne a few months before the war's end, in March 1945. At Fukuyama, as Dan Hart remembers him, he was a cheerful and smiling character, the star turn at the camp concert, crooning the popular 1940s ballad 'Gomen Nasai' ('Forgive Me'), with its lilting lament 'won't you forgive, won't you forget'. A few days later, on 4 July 1947, Eddie Nathan climbed up a hill near the camp, aimed a .303 at his brain, and pulled the trigger with his toe.[23]

Another suicide Hart recalls is equally distressing. It happened on 1 July 1946, an eventful day in Hart's working life. Having very recently dealt with the local threat of a cholera epidemic, he had just started inoculating the troops at the battalion base in

Fukuyama with a serum derived from rat's brains, hoping to guard against the deadly strain of encephalitis B that was endemic in areas of the Inland Sea. Word came to the camp of the death of an Australian soldier. He had been run over by a train at nearby Daimon, a little stop on the main national line of Honshu, which connected Tokyo to Kyushu 1000 kilometres to the west. Hart and a comrade drove hurriedly to the site, to find the Tokyo Express stopped at the tiny station. Agitated Japanese railway officials were anxious to get it going again; they like to run the trains on time in Japan. The Australian had apparently walked forward and placed his head across the line with shocking deliberation as the express train hurtled towards him. He made a terrible sight. Hart and a comrade had to delve under the train to collect the pieces of the dismembered corpse, including the head, which had somehow remained stuck to a front wheel of the train. 'A subsequent inquiry confirmed that the train death was a suicide,' Hart writes, 'but did not find why the poor chap had done it'.[24] The serviceman who died had been the batman of one of the lieutenants of the 65th, the Norwegian-born Fred Ness, who had once fought a fist-fight with the infamous Melbourne criminal Squizzy Taylor. The young man was Private Kenneth Ernest Becker. Like Eddie Nathan, he was just 20 years old.

PART THREE

Japanorama:
on tour

CHAPTER NINE
At the Kawana Hotel

I n an enterprise so fixated on 'prestige', it was imperative for the Australians to display concrete evidence of their power. They may have ruled BCOF, but they hadn't much to show for it. Kure and Hiroshima rate as booby prizes on the historical scale of plundered and sacked cities. Ultimately and fittingly, it was a hotel that proved that the Australians were really somebodies in Occupied Japan. In 1936, when Baron Kishichiro Okura completed the redevelopment of his Kawana Hotel as the Japanese equivalent of an elite European country retreat, it was probably not in his reckoning that, a decade later, his showpiece would be managed and occupied by Australians.

A pioneer of Japanese tourism and president of the Imperial Hotel in Tokyo, Okura liked to plan on a grand scale. The Kawana was originally modelled on an English country estate. But its palm trees, swimming pools, and two manicured golf courses reaching down to Sagami Bay and out to the blue Pacific suggest sunny California, rather than England. Maybe that is what drew Marilyn

Monroe there in 1954, with her new husband, Joe DiMaggio. Today, the Kawana proudly displays a photograph of the honeymooners posing for the camera on the hotel terrace. Alongside it is another beaming celebrity guest of the 1950s, John Wayne, who visited Japan to film *The Barbarian and the Geisha*, John Huston's version of the liaison between Townsend Harris, the first US consul general after the country's re-emergence, and his self-sacrificing Japanese consort, Okichi.

The Australians of BCOF cannot compete with Marilyn Monroe and Joe Dimaggio, let alone John Wayne. There is no photographic record of their presence in the Kawana's cabinet. Yet all the veterans and their dependants who stayed there remember the Kawana with awe. Mind-boggling amenities usually granted only to millionaires and movie stars could be enjoyed for a pittance. For Bruce Fisher, who enjoyed a holiday there in November 1948 as a teenage BCOF dependant, to be at the Kawana was to be a part of history. Now a retired policeman living in Melbourne, Bruce still has a photograph of his family with Lieutenant General Robertson, taken in the magnificent Kawana dining room, toasting Princess Elizabeth upon the birth of her first child, Prince Charles.

By the third anniversary of the hotel coming into BCOF hands, February 1950, it was the sole survivor of what had been a national network of 16 leave hostels. Guests celebrated the occasion by indulging in an exhausting 'gala weekend'. This included a reception and cocktails, a dinner offering oysters, entrecôte à la Béarnaise, and a 'glace Mt Fuji', followed by dancing and a variety show, then a buffet luncheon the next day, a concert by the Nippon Symphony Orchestra and, finally, a special showing of the popular British feature film *The Red Shoes*, based on a Hans Christian Andersen story about a woman who cannot stop dancing. Meanwhile, outside, in the wrecked cityscapes of Japan, barefoot and famished infants rummaged through the Occupier's garbage bins for scraps of food.

Also excluded from the Kawana's moveable feast were the Nisei, the second-generation Japanese-Americans, who comprised a large proportion of the interpreters, translators, and administrative personnel of the Army of Occupation. This was a public-relations disaster. In September 1949, damaging press reports in the US and Japan suggested that the Australians had erected a 'racial bar' to exclude American officers of Japanese descent, as well as black American servicemen, from its rest hostels. The *Nippon Times* quoted the American commander of Yokohama Special Services complaining that it was 'impossible' for a Nisei or a Negro to stay at the hotel. Given that General MacArthur's own HQ contained several officers of Japanese lineage, this was an embarrassing prohibition, to say the least.[1]

Apparently it was not only at the Kawana that the Australian colour bar applied. In November 1949, the Japanese American Citizens League Anti-Discrimination Committee wrote from Washington DC to prime minister Chifley, alleging an Australian 'whites only policy' which denied Nisei access to BCOF facilities in the Hiroshima area while welcoming 'Caucasian Americans', and threatened to take the matter before the United Nations Commission on Human Rights. The committee claimed that American scientists and technicians of Japanese ancestry stationed in Hiroshima were barred from Australian-operated clubs, canteens, and other recreational facilities. Many of these American Nisei 'now so curtly denied facilities by Australia' had served 'faithfully and loyally' alongside Australian troops during the war as interpreters attached to ATIS. That they had become 'the objects of her prejudice and discrimination' was a 'bitter commentary upon the Australian sense of justice'. Actually, the official Australian attitude to the Nisei during the Occupation was carried over from the war. Recalling his own stint working with ATIS, alongside the Second AIF in New Guinea in 1943, Faubion Bowers said that the 'color prejudiced' Australians 'wouldn't touch the Nisei', and wanted nothing to do with them 'in any form'.[2]

Naturally, both BCOF and the army minister Cyril Chambers vehemently denied any refusal of access to Australian-run facilities, either pertaining to the rest hostels, BCOF cinemas, schools, or housing. All exclusions were justified by the need to make the most of limited resources that were already overused and overcrowded and, in any case, 'full-blooded' Aborigines among the troops were allowed. (Given that the Australian government prohibited the enlistment of Aborigines in BCOF, this number must have been almost nonexistent.) With regard to the Kawana Hotel, some Americans were 'accepted', but only when accommodation was available and, even then, according to BCOF, only 'those who are specially close to us'. The official denials were half right. In a letter to the Department of External Affairs, the head of the Australian Mission, Patrick Shaw, clarified the issue: 'As I understand it, no person of Asiatic race other than nationals of British Commonwealth countries are allowed in any installations run by BCOF.' Under this ruling, Shaw went on, 'American nationals of Japanese racial descent are excluded from BCOF rest centres, which accept a number of Americans'.[3] The White Australia Policy had been shipped offshore, to post-war Japan.

THE GREAT EUROPEAN EMPIRES of the 19th century were built on travel. Conquest meant movement, then occupation, followed by colonisation. In our contemporary era, the colonial administrators and their military enforcers have virtually vanished, replaced by vast numbers of globe-trotting tourists, largely from affluent countries, who crave 'authentic' and 'unspoiled' native cultures, while demanding infrastructure to support their fleeting presence. Long before the advent of mass tourism as we know it today, E.M. Forster's *A Passage to India* linked the ostensibly innocent practice of 'sightseeing' with colonial domination. After a tedious performance of *Cousin Kate* at the British-only Chandrapore Club, followed by a rendition of the anthem of the

Army of Occupation, which reminded all present that they were 'British and in exile', the English visitor Adela Quested expresses her frustration. Adela is in India to meet her prospective husband, the magistrate Ronny Heaslop, but her impulses are those of the tourist. She doesn't want *Cousin Kate*; she wants to see the 'real India'. Anxious to accommodate her, the Indian Dr Aziz arranges the calamitous visit to the Marabar Caves, which ends with her falsely charging him with indecent assault, his incarceration and trial, and the entrenchment of divisions between Occupier and Occupied. Two years later, an embittered Aziz reviews Adela's desire to see the 'real' India as a 'pose'. 'No sympathy lay behind it'; she merely wanted to have the country laid on for her private benefit. 'Seeing India', Aziz thinks, 'was only a form of ruling India'.[4]

The Occupation of Japan was built on this kind of colonial appetite for foreign spectacle. From the desire of young servicemen to 'see the world', to a travelling press corps reporting the event for home consumption, to the wives and children who formed distinctive expatriate communities such as Nijimura, Australia's Chandrapore, the Australians evinced attitudes of possessiveness toward the country they were occupying and its seemingly servile people.

The most revealing individual example is the unlikely figure of W. Macmahon Ball. Unlikely, because Ball, politically and intellectually democratic, and cynical about SCAP's motives and methods in Japan, might have been considered capable of transcending an indulgence in newfound power and privilege. Ball went to Japan a well-educated and well-travelled man – a true internationalist. He had studied abroad for years, on Rockefeller and Carnegie Fellowships, and had established a distinguished academic career at home. His first book, *Possible Peace* (1936), pondered a new international order in Europe and the Pacific. As a well-regarded analyst of Nazi ambitions, he wrote reports for the ABC and the BBC following a tour of the Sudetenland, guided by members of the German army, at the time of the Munich crisis of 1938. (He visited the Sachsenhausen concentration camp, apparently the first foreigner to do so for years.) During the war, he was the Commonwealth Controller of Short Wave Broadcasts, the precursor of Radio Australia. In 1945, he went to San Francisco as an advisor to the Australian delegation at the United Nations Conference. Prior to going to Japan in April 1946 as the Commonwealth representative on the Allied Council, he served a stint in Jakarta, or Batavia, as it was known, as a political representative of the Australian government in the Netherlands East Indies, which was then enduring a tumultuous struggle for independence. Macmahon Ball was no mug. The American leadership in Japan regarded him as a troublemaker, but he impressed people such as the journalist Mark Gayn, who considered him 'one of the most brilliant original thinkers in official Tokyo'. Faubion Bowers was to describe him, rather ambiguously, as 'one of the intellectuals of Australia, a country of very few intellects'.[5]

However, the crass seduction of status, combined with lingering war-derived animosity, could narrow the broadest outlook and destroy the best intentions. After his tenure in Japan, Ball became an advocate of closer Australian relations with Asia, leading, in mid-1948, to yet another 'Goodwill Mission' to several Asian cities. But during his Tokyo posting, he never felt comfortable with the Japanese, and he had to be cajoled by MacArthur into having all but the most formal dealings with them. In his diaries, he describes telling the general that he felt 'rather shy' and 'squeamish' about making direct contact with them, 'because this almost inevitably involved the exchange of social civilities'.[6]

Like Robertson, Ball sought to have his status reflected in bricks and mortar. Soon after arriving in Tokyo, he complained about the house he had been allotted, on the basis that 'a Japanese family were overlooking us from one section and internal architecture and furnishings were jimcrack [sic]'. Accordingly, he demanded 'one of the best houses irrespective of who was now occupying it'. But it was out of Tokyo, enjoying a spot of R&R, that Ball revealed a domineering attitude toward the Japanese. A strong dose of power turned this Melbourne academic, the son of a country clergyman, into a martinet. Arriving at the mountain *onsen* at Yumoto for a weekend away, Ball was angered by the Japanese hotel owner's refusal to hand over rooms that his office had pre-booked for himself and his entourage. The hotel owner told the furious Ball that he had received the request too late. 'At this point I told him that there could be no further discussion, that he must show me immediately to our rooms,' Ball writes. 'He still tried to fob me off with inferior rooms.' Ball's order was met, but when the hotel owner complained, the Australian warned him 'that if he continued to behave in this way it would probably be necessary to take the hotel over from him altogether'.[7]

By his own admission, Macmahon Ball was a 'gauche' golfer, but he seems to have tolerated his free holiday at the Kawana Hotel, despite finding fault with the 'severe' architecture of the structure. He must have been comfortable enough, as he and his family were given Commander Robertson's private suite. While lodging at the Kawana, Ball travelled up the coast of the Izu to the nearby resort town Ito to inspect a 'huge rambling house' set in a big attractive garden that was to be made available to BCOF. But Ball declared it 'useless'.[8] Why? Because it was all of half a mile from the beach.

HAVING SURVIVED two common Japanese calamities – fire and bankruptcy – the Kawana Hotel has changed little since the Australians moved on. These days, its clientele consist solely of Japanese golfers, and its tariffs are way over par. On a personal visit to the hotel in 2006, the links seemed to be deserted, though the day was fine and sunny and, out on its vast, silent lawns, it was not hard to conjure the sight of Australian children cavorting in the pool or running off to the stables. I was taken around the establishment by the hotel's cheerful PR man, Kato-san, who has worked there for decades. He ushered me through the sumptuous lounges with their huge marble fireplaces, before taking me up into the tower, with its view of the island Oshima and its active volcano to the south, and of Mt Fuji, looming serenely to the west. Kato-san's knowledge of the hotel's history was encyclopedic: he knew all about its BCOF days, having escorted a nostalgic Australian return visitor or two, over the years. 'Now I have something special to show you,' he said confidentially, leading me down deep into the bowels of the hotel, into a cave-like storeroom housing boxes of the cigarettes that are as essential to a Japanese golfer as a set of clubs. He pointed at some barely legible scrawl chalked on the wall. Close inspection revealed some hieroglyphs of a bygone age, when the Kawana was in the hands of the interlopers from an outpost of the empire, the Australians of BCOF. Barely discernible was the legend, evidently an old shelving marker, 'PIMM'S'. It was like chancing upon a Rosetta stone of one of the more curious neocolonial enterprises of the postcolonial age. The Australian role in the Occupation of Japan is not identified by some memorable catchphrase or grand public statement. 'PIMM'S', with its anachronistic suggestion of ruling class affectation, is as definitive as any.

CHAPTER TEN

A Passage to Japan

Among the Americans, the Raj-like nature of the Occupation could hardly escape the notice of its more self-aware participants, though they tended to keep quiet about it at the time. Years later, Faubion Bowers claimed to have been 'ashamed and mortified' at his personal participation. 'I and nearly all the Occupation people I knew were extremely conceited and extremely arrogant', he remarked in 1984, 'and used our power every inch of the way'. Donald Richie, who worked as a typist and, later, feature writer for the *Pacific Stars and Stripes* (it was he who interviewed the BCOF Commander Horace Robertson about his Hiroshima performance), draws on a brace of highly significant historical parallels in identifying the hypocrisy of SCAP's democratic project. The Japanese, he writes in his private journal, 'are treated like blacks in the American south, or like the "natives" in Forster's *A Passage to India*'. In his novel *Where Are the Victors?*, Richie dwells on how the accessibility of power in Occupied Japan turned unassuming provincial Americans, men and women who were 'nobodies' at home, into overbearing brutes. 'It wasn't that the glorious Occupiers were cruel,' concluded one woman attached to SCAP, 'they were merely thoughtless.'[1]

Ruling Japan liberated people from the obligations of decent behaviour; they had a licence to please themselves. 'What happened to Americans abroad?' Richie asks. 'They changed somehow. The fellow in the fields of Arkansas or the hills of Tennessee would have been a nice guy. But here he became a monster.'[2] Richie might just as easily have been talking about the Australians of BCOF, men and women from a remote and isolated country thrust into positions of almost unimaginable influence. Travel doesn't always broaden the mind; often it has the opposite effect, narrowing the outlook and shrivelling sympaties. Of course, the Australian contingent had its share of 'nice guys'; the wonder is that there were so many. But there were 'monsters' as well. Roaming virtually at will in Allied-only train compartments, the extended BCOF family represented, at its worst, the prototype of the contemporary caricature, the 'Ugly Australian' tourist in Asia.

Some of the more 'ugly', unpleasant Australians in Japan were women. The figure of the racist colonial wife is one of the staples of imperial discourse. Fictions of the British Raj are populated by snobbish, churlish *memsahibs* who embody the evils of occupation and provide a convenient scapegoat for imperialism itself. In India just to be with their husbands, confined to the domestic space and stripped of a constructive role even in that limited sphere (given the preponderance of home help), the fictional *memsahib* is stereotypically driven to extremes of race hatred that outdo the worst of the men. The documentary record suggests that, by contrast, the most vicious female Australian interlopers in Occupied Japan were in fact working women, whose transient involvement with the country encouraged the casual exercise of influence.

As a reporter for the London *Daily Mirror*, Lorraine Stumm was Australia's first accredited female correspondent during World War II. In company with vast numbers of the world press, in

September 1945, Stumm flew into Tokyo still angry with the Japanese. As she explores the streets of Tokyo, she finds herself kicking people out of the way, 'pathetic creatures' and 'sly devils' who 'never stepped aside for us or showed any sign of humility in their defeat'. In the eyes of a woman who is obsessed with her own appearance, that these largely destitute people were so 'miserable, underfed and badly dressed' is presented almost as a racial failing. 'In Tokyo I never looked crisp and tailored,' Stumm, who later became the fashion editor of the Sydney *Sun*, complains. Having regarded the Japanese as 'a race of laundrymen', she is appalled by the poor quality of the laundry service at her luxury hotel, a foible she encourages an Australian soldier to remedy by having him threaten to shoot the hotel's staff. Her callousness towards the Japanese as 'beaten, wrecked [and] utterly dependent' extends to vagrant orphaned children wandering the city streets and 'living like rats' in bombed buildings. Stumm has no protective sympathy for these bereft and vulnerable children, some of them infants, just frustration that they had evaded the strong arm of the law.[3]

Of all BCOF texts, the victor's mentality is no more wretchedly illustrated than in the letters home (to her mother) of Annetta Chisholm, a young, middle-class woman from suburban Melbourne, who sailed to Japan in October 1947 to serve with the YWCA for almost two years. Life in Japan is a hectic round of social engagements, tireless touring, and relentless souvenir hunting. But Japanese culture is kept at arm's length. Expected to take a bath during a rare stay at a Japanese hotel, she makes sure to keep her 'scanties and brassieres' on, a bizarre concession to modesty. What she calls 'fratting' is reduced to a minimum. Japanese men give her 'the creeps', so her interaction is limited largely to her house girls, who are given short shrift if they do not conform to her standards of efficient slavishness. One, a 'lazy little beggar', is sent packing; the others she tolerates, despite their tediously tricky Japanese names, which she finds hard to learn. The 'best singer in BCOF', by her own estimation, Chisholm performs her favourites, 'My

Prayer' and 'Ave Maria', at concerts and church weddings. Occasionally, she condescends to teach Christian hymns and Christmas carols at the 'Jap YW', but her sense of Christian charity is not inexhaustible: at a Christmas party for 'Jap children', the 'little boys were just as repulsive as their old men'. After a year in the country, she cannot bear 'to touch a Jap, even a child'. Visiting the shrines on the island of Setoda, she recoils from the sight of ailing, poverty-stricken children 'so covered with sores they were positively revolting'.[4]

The BCOF wives were angels compared with the likes of Stumm and Chisholm, but their very presence invoked distasteful cultural memories of a hegemony that most had assumed had passed into history. While it was the practice of Imperial Britain for the wives and children of soldiers garrisoned in far-flung parts of the empire to be quartered in cantonments near the barracks, it was a new phenomenon in Australian military history.

Frank Clune, for one, had reservations about the anachronistic nature of the innovation. An otherwise tireless advocate of the Occupation's role in pulling the Japanese out of what he calls 'the primitive ooze', Clune suggests that the experiment 'was not 100 per cent satisfactory'. This is his polite way of saying it was a big mistake. On the one hand, the presence of the dependants 'added considerably to the practical problems of the Occupation'. Housing had to be constructed (nearly new dwellings were built, and more than 100 Japanese houses were renovated by Japanese contractors under the supervision of BCOF engineers), arrangements had to be made for the medical care and education of the dependent children, amenities had to be provided, and an adequate supply of household goods, including food, guaranteed. But it was the effect of the enclave experience on the women that really bothered Clune. The prolific home help drawn from the impoverished local population engendered unwelcome attitudes of slothful superiority among the wives. Instead of providing a working example of 'the Democratic way of life' to the Japanese, Australian women were themselves ruinously taught 'the feudalistic way'.[5]

Underlying Clune's misgivings is an ideology of occupation that sees it as 'man's work'. The women not only got in the way of the practices of rule, their presence was an unnecessary indulgence that only made relations with the Japanese all the more problematic. Other male visitors to Nijimura marvelled at the luxuries enjoyed by the women, and at the degree of snobbery in the settlement.[6] It was not only men who commented on this. The purported pampering of the BCOF wives became a matter of public interest, especially when Robertson's own wife lambasted them upon her arrival back in Australia, asserting that they were being 'spoiled' by having too much attention lavished on them.

Returning wives found themselves in the position of having to defend themselves from the impression that they had turned into some kind of collective Lady Muck. A *Woman's Day* feature quotes one woman's aggrieved belief that Australians had formed 'the wrong idea' about them and that they had not been 'spoilt'. Yet they cannot hide their wonderful suntans and their strings of Japanese pearls. 'Japan', a returned wife is quoted as saying, had been 'one long holiday'; another described their 'false life' there. Looking back, many BCOF people remember the wives with cynicism. According to the Englishwoman Paddy Power, the Australians 'were not used to having servants', and some abused the privilege. Jennie Woods, a BCOF wife who was employed while she was in Japan (first in the Pay Corps and later with the YWCA), writes that some of the housewives, albeit a minority, exploited their house girls 'woefully', working them to the brink of exhaustion. 'A number of the women would not permit their girls to have chairs to sit on in their kitchens,' Woods recalls, 'as they said, "Oh, they sit on the floors at home, why not here?"' A welfare worker with the YMCA/YWCA, Joan Haigh expresses her frustration with the Occupation wives' inability to deal appropriately with their domestic staff, and with their general assertion of their superior situation in Occupied Japan, which had made her and her fellow workers' lives in Japan 'a misery'. 'For some inexplicable reason they seem to think that we of the YM/YW are also here at their beck and call', she writes, adding that she and her colleagues didn't see themselves 'as domestics to be ordered about at the whim of any of the Dependants'.[7]

Yet it was not the women who originally insisted on having servants provided. It was BCOF itself that saw domestic staffing as a necessary reflection of the force's prestige within Japan. As with the Raj in India, it was considered undignified for the Occupation wives to perform menial domestic tasks, especially during the hot, humid Japanese summer. Housekeepers and housemaids, charwomen, cooks, and gardeners were provided without cost by the Japanese government, their number determined by rank. The authorised number of servants for officers without children was three, while for officers with children, it was four; for other ranks without children, it was two, and with children, three.[8]

In another of the exquisite paradoxes of an Occupation designed to display the virtues of democracy, *BCOF Bound* (1946), a guidebook provided to service families prior to departure, strongly recommends that close contact with the Japanese should be confined to the servants. Just as *Know Japan* begins with Northcott's instruction forbidding fraternisation, *BCOF Bound* concludes with it, quoted in full, along with prior warning that, although they were not subject to Japanese law, dependants had to comply with Occupation directives or be liable to arrest and prosecution by the provosts. The Japanese servants themselves were to be treated as humans like to think they treat dogs. BCOF housewives are told it is up to them 'to train them', and that one way of earning their loyalty is through their stomach. While the Japanese receive a food ration from civilian sources, the Australian women are advised that they may give them 'the unconsumed portions of their own meals'. Scraps, in other words. 'You will find this will act as a great incentive', the guidebook comments, having argued earlier that 'if you treat them well they will become devoted to you'. Yet, as with the Japanese people as a whole, the servants should be kept 'at a distance', though 'that should not be hard to do'.[9]

The guidebooks' implications are clear. Like the *memsahibs* (or 'lady masters') of the Raj, the BCOF women were to rule the roost in the domestic space as their men did in the hurly-burly outside the home. *BCOF Bound* provides tendentious historical and cultural information that must have influenced the way the women thought about the country as they sailed to Japan free of cost, irrespective of rank (though the wives of the other ranks were put in the lowest deck). Commander-in-chief Robertson's foreword invokes the usual inspiration of 'Western civilization' in exhorting a sense of mission in the newcomers, and attempts to placate fears by assuring them that 'European women and children have lived previously in Japan for many years and have lived comfortably'.

Unfortunately, Robertson's message is diluted on the first page of the following text, in which Japan is described as 'a primitive country populated by primitive people'. Where there is beauty in Japan, rank ugliness is never far away: the traditional gardens are 'spoiled by the pungent smell of the night soil' and, while there are temples and shrines to admire, there is 'much that is tawdry'. Kure itself is fairly aptly described as 'grimy', with none of 'the charm of the Orient'.[10] The language is too difficult to learn, and the people both repressed and contradictory. *BCOF Bound* did not promote a view of Japan that would make one want to venture too far beyond the settlement.

BCOF Bound's pages on Japan and its culture are the preamble to a long 'houses and house-keeping' section, along the lines of a commercial real estate brochure showing floor plans and sketch impressions of the range of housing on offer. This gives an indication of the lure of the Occupation. A brand new home with all mod cons was not to be underestimated. Due to long separations caused by the war, and housing shortages in Australia, Japan was to provide many couples with their first marital home. On the eve of the departure of one of the first batches of wives going to Japan, leaving Sydney in May 1947, the wife of an Australian officer remarked that she and her husband hadn't had a home together for seven years, 'so you can imagine what a perfectly good house of our own will mean to us. And it seems we'll have a home in Japan better than any we've had to date in Australia'.[11]

The new houses were variations on American plans, with modifications by Australian engineers to exteriors, such as porches. With hot-water systems, refrigerators, and electric stoves, they were equipped beyond the wildest imaginings of Australians back home. Nijimura's elegantly patterned, circular civic plan, with wide bitumen streets with names like 'Royal Avenue' and 'Dominion Circuit', a school, a cinema, tennis courts, a swimming pool, a theatre, and other amenities, was a model of desirable post-war suburban living. The settlement was dubbed the 'Rainbow Village' because of the multi-hued rooftops of its custom-built houses and duplexes – the sort of name that might have been dreamed up by a sharp modern marketer, albeit a name that sounds like a retirement village. One of the BCOF wives, perhaps unaware of possible irony, was reminded of 'a miniature Canberra'. While the Australian government charged a modest rent for the house and for utilities such as water, fuel, and electricity, the BCOF families were onto a good thing. There were no local rates or taxes; no charges for the telephone, or for medical and dental treatment; and there were benefits such as free accommodation at leave hostels, free transport, free entertainment and cinemas (with names like 'the Empire', 'the Rex', and 'the Royal'), and free schooling for the children. And, of course, the servants came 'free', as well.[12]

Yet the degree of emotional stress placed on the wives, restlessly pacing the floors in their brand new homes, is not to be underestimated. In *The Paper Chase* (1966), Hal Porter's autobiographical account, he refers darkly to 'the frequency of Occupation nervous breakdowns', and it has been suggested that what became known as 'culture shock', felt by American dependent wives, posed a major problem to US medical authorities.[13] But there is little documentation available to ascertain the extent of psychological disturbance experienced by the BCOF women compared with the men. It may be guessed that the latter, with a job to do and, in some cases, with a Japanese mistress, were less liable to be affected by ennui and what came to be called 'suburban neurosis'. Some housewives had a lot on their plates in Japan, with errant husbands and young vulnerable children to raise in an alien environment. There was also internecine bickering with neighbours to contend with. Although the Australian cantonments were based on democratic lines (in British garrisons, family areas were divided according to rank), inevitably, a certain amount of hierarchical squabbling occurred from time to time. In response to a call for dependants to recollect their experiences, I received this hair-raising email from a woman who had spent three years of her childhood in Nijimura:

> I started school in Japan. We were there three years. My mother had a fight with our neighbour and I believe this played a part in us coming home as he, the neighbour, was higher ranking than dad. I also had a bad experience with a house boy who tried to get into my bed. He was sacked and chased me one day in the Japanese sector. I escaped down a water drain ... We used to play in a high voltage area throwing stones at the transformers, so I guess it's lucky I got back in one piece. My mother was swimming at Nijimura and was stung by a stone fish; I believe she was pregnant at the time and I remember the ambulance taking her off ... My dad got a Japanese girl pregnant; she lost the baby but turned up on our doorstep ...[14]

At home, the *Australian Women's Weekly* gave a glowing report of the idyll in Japan, of communities of 'happy women and beaming youngsters', of days so full of pleasure and activity that they would 'just slip by'. For many women, the reality was different: at first,

Japan was a shock. After a month in the country, Mrs Gladys Cory, writing to a friend back home in Bellingen, New South Wales, says she 'hated every minute' of her first few days in Hiro, 'nauseated' by the smells and offended by some of the customs, such as men openly relieving themselves in the streets. 'Yes,' she writes confidently, 'one has to be broadminded to live in Japan'. Gladys Cory adapted to her new surroundings. She had to; her sojourn in Japan turned into an epic, lasting until February 1952.[15] However, for several of the wives, boredom, homesickness, and the physical and psychological effect of living in an enclave made life a struggle.

One example is Elsie Boyd, who lived in Nijimura for three years from August 1947 with her husband, the Warrant Officer Don Boyd, and her four children. Boyd's letters home reveal an intelligent woman, fundamentally well-disposed to Japan, fighting hard to combat what she calls feeling 'liverish', an eloquent synonym for unhappiness that was used by her generation. 'One day is the same as another here. They say we have plenty of time to write letters. I seem to do nothing but answer the door', she writes to her sister, of the endless number of local domestic staff lining up to perform some chore or other for her. 'I sit here for a while and work out the date', she writes at the beginning of another. 'One loses count of everything. I think I'm killed if I have to wash a few dishes … ' A sense of siege led to occasional outbursts against the Japanese. The inability to speak English and the ineptitude of her two maids irritate her, and sometimes she reacts against the Japanese for simply intruding into her domain. 'There are two Japanese sitting on the floor oiling the fans', she writes, in one letter. 'They drive me mad, always coming in and doing something.' Mrs Boyd relishes her brief forays into the Japanese countryside, picnicking on 'beautiful' Miyajima, or admiring the rice fields and local methods of cultivation ('we could take lots of lessons from the Japanese'). But, too often, the only respite from the domestic prison comes in the form of the social treadmill of parties and other engagements held in places like the 'Anzac Club' for soldiers and dependants. Of a BCOF holiday celebrating the Battle of Britain, she remarks: 'In this place the general rule seems to be any excuse for a holiday or a party.'[16]

Not all the wives suffered; many look back fondly on their Japanese sojourn. The Londoner Paddy Power, freshly married to her Australian lieutenant Tyrone Power – a contemporary of the Hollywood star, but named after the county in Northern Ireland – recalls 'one of the happiest times of my life'. To Power, who had a child in Kure delivered by an ear, nose, and throat surgeon from Melbourne, Japan seemed relaxing after the Blitz. The late Betty Comeadow spoke to me of having 'a good life' in Japan, despite the 'terrible social climbers' among the Nijimura community, and a serially philandering husband, the chief auditor of BCOF Canteens, whom she eventually left. Olga Stubbe, the wife of a brigadier (the deputy director of BCOF Medical Services) recalls 'nothing but extreme courtesy and friendliness', and considers herself 'extremely fortunate' to visit Japan under 'such favourable conditions' and live in an environment much 'safer' than her home town of Sydney. All these women revile the non-fraternisation edict as, in Paddy Power's contemptuous adjective, 'inhuman'.[17]

Determined to break out of the BCOF bubble, some of the women engaged constructively with Japan and its people. The RAAF wife Betty Page travelled as much as she could in the area around her Bofu house, often meeting local people, continually humbled by their hospitality. After taking tea at the home of a local artist, she comes away 'with a still higher regard for the individual Japanese who is putting such a good face on a no doubt unwelcome occupation'.[18] Other wives engaged in various forms of volunteer work of a charitable or educational nature, such as teaching English to Japanese people. Mary Bleechmore, also married to a senior officer, a lieutenant colonel who was commanding officer at Point Camp in Kure, was a singularly venturesome BCOF wife whose work in Japan is still remembered today. A law graduate of Sydney University, and the mother of the first

Australian BCOF baby born in Japan, Mary Bleechmore not only taught English but also ran YWCA classes on Australian culture and customs for Japanese women, realising that numbers of them would wind up in Australia as wives of BCOF servicemen. Engaging with Japan entailed a flagrant disregard for non-fraternisation:

> I also travelled around Japan a lot, often with a child on the back and one in the tummy. This was the most enlightening experience. I would put up overnight in little inns, swapping some Australian tinned food for the local product. I found the Japanese, in defeat, showed great dignity and rode over their great difficulties with courage and no self-pity.[19]

FRANK CLUNE thought the presence of the BCOF wives debilitating, but recognised that it was 'a great experience for the kids, who'll have something to blow about for the rest of their lives'. As the sons and daughters of an occupying power, the Occupation children enjoyed a life of rare privilege. Remembering his stint teaching the boys and girls of the BCOF community, Hal Porter lampooned 'the sort of luxury-cruise life Occupation armies seem always to bring into being'. Rosemary Jeanneret, the daughter of Keith Philp, an electrical engineer with the RAAF, takes up this idea. The 'special' experience of living in an enclave (at Iwakuni, in her case) with 'so many people from so many different backgrounds' could only be likened, she thinks, 'to living on board a ship'.[20] That the children who were aboard the SS *Taiping*, the first shipload of dependants entering Kure Harbour at the end of May 1947, now call themselves 'First Fleeters' extends the nautical metaphor.

The first civilian Australians in post-war Japan were entering a new world. The seasons, the vegetation, the food, the religion, the customs, and the people were all different from what they knew.

Some of them were apprehensive, and some were scared witless. This was the land populated by a race caricatured as bestial and unpredictably violent. The kids had heard the stories of Japanese wartime atrocities, and it was hard to dissociate the people from the propaganda. To Geoff Ockerby, who arrived in Japan as a 13-year-old aboard the *Westralia* on Christmas Eve 1947, the porters who came on board to take their luggage 'were attired as though they had just crawled out of the New Guinea jungle'; these were the creatures seen on the newsreels at home. Ockerby says, 'Nobody knew just what to expect. How will the Japanese treat us and furthermore how should we treat the Japanese?' For some youngsters, the experience verged on the traumatic. Jennifer Collier, one of Elsie Boyd's four children, was aged just five years and four months when the family settled into the house in Nijimura. She remembers being 'very frightened' of the Japanese people, often dreaming the family had returned home to Australia only to wake up still in Japan.[21]

In most cases, fear was quickly dispelled by the kindness of the domestic staff. The two house girls assigned to the Ockerby ménage on Etajima 'proved to be the most devoted people one could imagine'. Lyn (Lambert) Thompson, a major's daughter, was very frightened at first, hiding behind her mother when her ship docked at Kure. But, she says, 'as it turned out the Japanese were wonderful to us'. While the nature of the children's experience differed, the characteristic memory of Japan is of a 'wonderful time' and an 'idyllic', if 'artificial', way of life. The excitement began on the two-to-three week trip over from Australia, with the tearful send-off at Circular Quay, the dizzying array of shipboard activities, the occasional typhoon to contend with, and the exotic ports of call en route. In mid-1947, aboard the Burns Philp liner the SS *Merkur*, Gladys Cory and her five-year-old son Douglas stopped over at war-ravaged Rabaul, avoiding the sunken ships in the harbour, and gazing doubtfully at the active volcano overlooking the township. Entertained at an afternoon tea party, all the children were presented with chocolates and combs carved from bamboo. Later, the passengers were taken out on the water in canoes and serenaded by the natives, whose eclectic repertoire included 'Pistol Packin' Momma', after which they performed the 'Hokey Pokey', before sending them back to their waiting ship with the more dignified 'Maori Farewell'.[22]

A couple of months later, on its maiden voyage crossing the Equator, the HMAS *Duntroon* berthed at Port Moresby. Two young Kalgoorlie-born boys, George and Max Bazzica, were passengers, travelling with their mother to rejoin their father, a member of a BCAIR Engineering Unit helping to rehabilitate Hiroshima. They remember New Guineans greeting the vessel in dugout canoes laden with coconuts and fresh fruit, and the small children among them diving into the sea for pennies tossed from the ship. A common ritual of the several voyages throughout 1947 and into 1948 was a 'Crossing of the Equator' ceremony, in which a figure dressed as King Neptune pitchforked people into the swimming pool.[23] The big moment of the journey for many of the children was not so much arriving in Japan, but the sight of their fathers waiting for them at the Kure docks. The prospect of families reuniting after the dislocations of the war years had been a major motivation for the wives and their children to go to Japan. Absence had turned many a BCOF father into a stranger; getting to know him again was one of the most moving experiences of the Occupation. The father of the four Gratton Wilson children, the largest family aboard the First Fleet on the *Taiping*, had been a POW in Germany. Elaine Ladyga, the daughter of the noted army photographer Harry Dunkley, recalls him waiting for her in the sticky heat of the Japanese summer in August 1947. In her young life of ten years she had seen very little of him. 'I felt very special when I met him as we disembarked at Kure', she recalls, 'and he bought me a beautiful black silk fan with swans painted on it.'[24]

Japan itself meant adventure and licence. Recalling 'the three best years of my childhood', the RAAF dependant Wendy (Knight)

Barry nostalgically recalls 'the freedom to be able to go anywhere we wanted without supervision'. There were cherry blossom festivals, *sukiyaki* picnics, and teahouses; there was playing golf with her dad at the Kawana Hotel, staying at *ryokan* (traditional inns), going to glamorous Tokyo and glimpsing Fuji, seeing snow falling for the first time, and viewing the magnificent torii at Miyajima and the deer roaming its verdant countryside. The world – or Japan, at least – was their oyster. A common treat was a visit to Mikimoto's island near Nagoya to see the famous 'Ama', the nimble young girl divers used to reap the pearl harvest. The brigadier's daughter Prudence (Garrett) Keys remembers the venerable Mikimoto-san himself hosting an oyster lunch; in each shell was a pearl for the guests to take home. Japan was a place to enact fantasies. Riding horses in the vast grounds of the Kawana allowed the young teenager Geoff Ockerby to relive his childhood fantasies of being Hopalong Cassidy or some other Western hero he'd seen at the Saturday afternoon movies.[25]

Travel – either around the immediate locales of the Inland Sea or ranging more widely across mainly southern Japan – is the dominant motif in the recollections of the BCOF children. 'We always seemed to be going somewhere,' remembers Wendy Barry. Occupation-only trains were the main form of transit for long-distance journeys, though Wendy recalls one 'crazy ride' into Hiroshima with her father, sitting in the back of a weapon carrier. Contact with local Japanese kids was limited. John Coghlan, a 'First Fleeter', remarks that the children of BCOF families 'were never allowed to get very close to the Japanese people'. On occasions, he played with Japanese children of his own age, going fishing, and building little sailboats and having races with them. They lived not far from his Etajima home, an environment that may have been more conducive to intermingling than the more circumscribed enclave at Nijimura. Others have similar memories, but the divide separating the children of the Occupier from those of the Occupied tended to curtail close relationships.[26]

The contrast between BCOF living conditions and those of the Japanese was stark and did not go unremarked by the children. Nijimura resident Lyn Thompson recalls discovering a small Japanese boy living in a fruit box wedged in a heap of cobblestones down a path near the water's edge close to her home, and being desperately concerned for his welfare. Like many other BCOF women, Lyn's mother left food out for him, disobeying the strict official edict not to do so, just as she supplemented the rations of the house girls. Sometimes contact with their Japanese contemporaries served only as an embarrassing reminder of the gulf between them. Norman Hogg, the son of a warrant officer in the RAAF, recalls being selected as an eight- or nine-year-old to go and attend a dinner at a Japanese boy's home on the annual occasion of *tangu-no-sekku*, or 'Boy's Day', held in early May. 'We sat on the tatami mats,' says Norman, 'and I was treated like royalty'.[27]

Inevitably, much of the contact with the Japanese was limited to the domestic staff, the *mumma-sans*, and other servants. John Coghlan says he felt 'sorry and a bit ashamed that the Occupation forces were effectively treating them as though they were slaves', and it seems that occasionally the children themselves were the culprits. When questioned about his 'worst memory' of Japan, Barry Demmler cites his 'abominable behaviour' towards his family's house girls. Asked the same question, Bruce Fisher remembers the occasion when he swore at one of the young house girls and reduced her to tears. Yet the devotion of the servants, many of whom were mothers themselves, was largely reciprocated. Some parents made it their business to see that their offspring did not abuse their position in Occupied Japan, and that the Japanese people were generally treated with courtesy. 'I was never permitted to order them about or to be waited on', remarks Brenda (Hollis) Berry, who lived on Etajima. Another of Elsie Boyd's four children, Margery Sullivan, recalls that her father deliberately took his son and three daughters to 'out of the way places' and encouraged them to respect the local culture. After they giggled throughout a tea ceremony in Onomichi and deposited the rice cakes into their pockets, she remembers: '[He] tore strips off the four of us and left us in no doubt that we had behaved very badly'. This, she says, taught them 'a very valuable lesson'.[28]

This was the same Margery Sullivan who, in 1977, wrote to Hal Porter, taking him to task over his bilious portrayal of his charges at the Nijimura school in his autobiographical writings. As imaginatively reconstructed in *The Paper Chase*, Porter's Nijumura is populated by boozing, canasta-playing, souvenir-hoarding, black-marketeering BCOF women, who leave their idle, spoiled, arrogant, and precocious children – 'servants' children', 'gang children' – to run wild. Sullivan reminds Porter that many of the children had fathers in the other ranks; her own father was a warrant officer. Her 'marvellous' life at Nijimura was 'balanced by a sense of responsibility' and enjoyed under strict 'parental guidance and interest'. Admittedly, Margaret was a serious-minded girl: she was the school captain and president of the local junior YWCA. The dependants were sometimes nicknamed the 'BCOF Brats', which was not entirely undeserved. 'Looking back,' Rosemary Jeanneret believes, '[the Japanese] would have perceived us as uncivilised, boorish, undisciplined' and, as a result, may not have taken BCOF very seriously at all.[29]

Privileged as they were, the BCOF children and teenagers had to grow up fast in Japan. They saw some awful things. Daily exposure to the paraphernalia and consequences of war affected their lives. The physical ravages of Hiroshima were lodged dead centre in their childhood environment, as well as the sometimes suicidal despair of a population whose world had been turned upside down. Looking out their Iwakuni bedroom window one night, George and Max Bazzica noticed a Japanese family, consisting of mother, father, small child, and babe-in-arms, loitering near a playground before walking up to the adjacent rail lines, as if intending to wait for a train. As one came into sight, they lay down on the rails; the train blew its whistle but did not stop. After some minutes, ambulances arrived to clear away the bodies. [30] Both George and Max were under ten years old at the time.

John Hearnden, his brother Peter, and sister Carolyn were the only motherless children in BCOF. John's mother had passed away when he was just ten. His father, Jack Hearnden, a wing commander in the RAAF, went to Japan first, before arranging for his children's passage in August 1947 on the SS *Merkur*. At Bofu and Iwakuni, the numerous domestic staff looked after the children dotingly. But, one Sunday morning, John and his brother watched as three American aircraft took off from the Bofu airfield 'just a dropkick away' from where the Hearndens lived. It was a beautiful, clear day. The planes circled and circled again. Then came disaster. Their tails somehow clipped, and they went into a fatal spin. One aircraft spun off into the ocean, one crashed to the ground, and one tore into the side of one of the nearby hills. The two Hearnden boys ran to the wreckage of the latter, only to see the dead pilot still sitting in the cockpit. As John laconically says, this was 'something you don't see every day'.[31] The event had a shocking sequel some years later. Peter Hearnden followed his father into the airforce. He was a brilliant pilot and a member of the RAAF's 'Red Sales' aerobatic team, the antecedent of the famous 'Roulettes'. In August 1962, the team of four deHavilland Vampires was training at the RAAF base in Sale in eastern Victoria. Doing a very low-altitude barrel roll in diamond formation, all four planes hit the ground. Aged 28, Peter Hearnden was one of the six pilots killed. As a boy at Iwakuni, he had witnessed the manner of his own death.

For many BCOF dependants, the Occupation is now nostalgically equated with familial reconciliation and a fresh start after the upheavals of war. But for some, like Brenda Berry, it meant family disintegration. 'Japan does hold great sadness for me,' she says, 'because it is where my family ceased to exist'. Her father was a member of the BCOF Tourist Club, so the family enjoyed numerous outings, to the Mikimoto pearl farm, Miyajima, Hiroshima, and to more obscure places. But home life was volatile, and her father was not aboard the *Duntroon* when his wife and daughter sailed back to Australia after 11 months in Japan. His parents never saw one another again. After his discharge from the army, her father wandered around the world, meeting his daughter again only in his old age and, even then, not acknowledging her. Not surprisingly, Berry has no desire to ever return to Japan.[32]

Rosemary Jeanneret vividly recalls the drama of the dissolution of her own parents' marriage. She, her sister, and her mother were excited to be reunited with her father, Keith Philp, when the *Westralia* docked at Kure in April 1948. After handing his children 'presentos', the children were surprised when their father told them he needed to be alone with their mother. Only years later did they learn what must have been said. Philp had met Ruriko, a Japanese war widow with a daughter, who was working as an interpreter with BCOF, and he had openly formed a relationship with her. Over the entire period that the Philp family was stationed in Japan (well over two years), he would disappear on the weekends, carrying a dillybag containing canned foods, sugar, and other BCOF rations. Meanwhile, Mrs Philp, devastated by her husband's infidelity, began to drink 'rather much' at parties, while sympathetic young airmen began to pay her attention and service policemen questioned the family about his fraternising ways. It was a trying time. Upon the outbreak of the war in Korea the family left Japan, leaving Philp behind to serve in the conflict and, in time, to marry Ruriko. He and his Japanese wife, with whom Rosemary became friendly, eventually settled in Queensland. In the meantime, her mother had also remarried. After her mother's second husband died, Rosemary's father, long-estranged, started writing to her mother, and would sometimes visit her at her home in Tasmania, minus Ruriko. (Rosemary remembers her mother becoming 'starry-eyed'.)[33]

Now, all the major players in the drama are dead, but for Rosemary herself. It is a sad but uplifting story of rupture and reconciliation that somehow seems to typify BCOF.

CHAPTER ELEVEN

Honoured Tourists

Returning from Japan in 1946, John Morris criticised the Occupation forces for behaving more like 'a horde of honoured tourists' than a victorious army. The choice of collective noun is a calculated insult that reflects the almost-universal disdain in which tourists are held. They are vulgar, and they are vandals, moving ruinously across the landscape like marauding plagues of locusts. They are figures of fun, and they are always someone else. Australian Occupationnaires such as Allan Clifton and Hal Porter exploit the implicit distinction between themselves, as discerning *travellers* in Japan, and the lumpen tourist masses. Clifton mocks the acquisitive propensities of the Australians in Japan, which find their outlet in 'much publicised places' like Miyajima, with its 'gaudy' shops, street-corner photographers, and 'inartistic souvenirs'. But in the same paragraph, after lampooning the Miyajima tourists, he boasts about snaring 'some choice pieces of Japanese handcraft', purchased on the island with yen he had souvenired in Borneo just after the war.[1]

In the novel *A Handful of Pennies*, Hal Porter selects tourism as the most suitable critical metaphor for the Occupation. At the novel's end, a handful of Australian Occupationnaires, the central characters, board an airport bus for the long haul home. Their tour of duty in Japan is over. Two of them, Paula Groot and Padre Hamilton, are leaving under a cloud of sexual impropriety. Two more are departing in the china jars that contain their ashes, having committed suicide. Accompanied by some fellow Occupation personnel, including a War Crimes Commission interpreter, Paula and Padre decide to take one last look at a cele-brated local attraction, the 'Brocade Bridge' – what Porter calls a 'unique national poem of wooden engineering'. He is referring to Iwakuni's five-span undulating bridge, the Kintaikyo, originally built in 1673, which spans an occasionally turbulent, flood-prone river, the Nishiki-gawa. Often likened to a brocade sash, the Kintaikyo is an elegant icon of the Japanese aesthetic captured by the legendary Edo-era painter and printmaker Hiroshige, and appears on endless mass-produced fans, mugs, calendars, and other tourist paraphernalia. The Australians of BCOF remember it fondly, particularly those based at Iwakuni. Once, only samurai could cross it; but some Occupationnaires treated it like a toy. Rosemary Jeanneret still gets angry when she remembers American troops riding their jeeps over the five humps of the delicate wooden bridge. It was also the site of the rape of a Japanese woman, com-mitted by two members of BCAIR in June 1947. But in Japan, if war doesn't get you, nature probably will, and the bridge was vir-tually destroyed by a typhoon and flood in 1950. In Porter's novel, the departing Australians amuse themselves by purchasing 'before and after' photographs of the bridge from local vendors, which they slip into wallets and purses as the final 'pass-out tickets' of the Japanese sojourn, to impress their family and friends upon their return home.[2] Thus, the Occupation is condensed into tourism of the most voyeuristic and exploitative kind. Japan is aestheticised as a picturesque tragedy to be briefly enjoyed and blithely discarded.

Yet Porter's own experience of Occupied Japan, which ran from 1 September 1949 to 21 October 1950, was essentially that of a tourist. It was an opportunity for a man in his late 30s to indulge in a passion for Japan that he had nurtured through his childhood and adolescence. When he was growing up, his imagination had been excited by the Japanese bric-a-brac that decorated the family home; by many hours spent 'in a trance' in the National Gallery in Melbourne, poring over its collection of Japanese prints, looking at Hokusai and Hiroshige, and reading Hearn and *haiku*; and by the library of 19th-century books about Japan bequeathed to him by his grandfather. One of grandfather Porter's books to have most affected him was Isabella Bird's *Unbeaten Tracks in Japan* (1880), perhaps the first, and most influential, of the new wave of Western travel books about Japan to be published after the country's emergence from its long seclusion. But there were relatively few 'unbeaten tacks' in Occupied Japan. Porter trod well-worn paths, albeit occasionally in company with Japanese. He had himself photographed standing on the Kintaikyo, which he described brusquely as a '1673 job'. He also had himself framed in the classic *mise en scène* of Occupation tourism, at Miyajima, with the sea *torii* (which he called a 'shrine thing'), in the background.[3]

Looking back at his time in Japan from the vantage point of the late 1960s, Porter recalls 'the conqueror's privilege' of 'going anywhere and everywhere, and of being able freely to see places which would have been out-of-bounds to me, a foreigner, in normal times.' As a Nijimura schoolmaster, Porter had it good, with copious holidays and an officer's perks. He drank like a fish and avidly cruised the murky by-ways of 'society' in Occupied Japan. Major Arthur John remembers him adopting a gratingly superior attitude in conversation 'during which he had a habit of addressing all and sundry, from lance-corporal to brigadier, as "Old Boy"'.[4]

The common soldiery had fewer indulgences, but nonetheless revelled in their mobility. 'The right of way is ours', Clifton Pugh boasts to his mother. As we have already seen, it was a right the Australians were wont to assert. If Japanese traffic, or pedestrians for that matter, did not allow unobstructed passage to BCOF vehicles, they were liable to be mown down. Regulations forbade soldiers to travel on Japanese trains, except in carriages allotted to them exclusively. A self-consciously good traveller, Allan Clifton deliberately flouted the rule. Japanese themselves were forbidden to ride on the special military trains reserved for long runs. Some visitors to Occupied Japan, such as John Morris, were appalled by the sight of 'wretched Japanese waiting in pens like sheep' at railway platforms while luxury trains slid by. But by and large the average Australian Occupationnaire, while noting the contrast, at least affected not to be bothered by it. Who had won the bloody war? In a letter home Flight Lieutenant James Hawes articulates a commonplace attitude while comparing the commodious military trains with the rattling, jam-packed Japanese slowcoaches. 'Still,' Hawes writes, 'I suppose they have only themselves to blame for having lost the war – for having started it for that matter.'[5]

In the time-honoured manner of military tourists everywhere, the BCOF people were insatiable souvenir hunters and hoarders. In *A Handful of Pennies* the departing Australians had packed their cases of Japanese 'loot' which, too heavy for the plane, had already been sent on ahead or were to follow by the next available ship. 'Loot' is also the term invoked by L.H. Evers in *A Pattern of Conquest* to describe the booty acquired by the Occupationnaires. Describing Australians returning with cameras slung over their shoulders and trunks of souvenirs, Evers writes, with considered overstatement: 'The soldiers of Genghis Khan could hardly have carried more "loot" out of plundered Cathay than the Australian soldiers carried out of Japan.' Presumably Allan Clifton was able to transport the two 'magnificent' porcelain dolls and the 'royal purple' kimono he picked up for a song on Miyajima, though he is happy to end *Time of Fallen Blossoms* with a sneering reference to soldiers with strings of pearls hidden in boots or looped around gaitered ankles, nervously awaiting customs inspectors upon entering Sydney Harbour.

Most Australian servicemen preferred less fragile souvenirs than porcelain dolls, and items that signified their martial triumph more obviously. Samurai swords were an especially coveted item, and not only amongst the men of BCOF. In October 1945, there had been an American stampede in the lobby of a Tokyo Hotel when a sign was put up saying, 'war trophies issued here – men must be assigned to GHQ – one sword per man'. Someone had replaced 'men' with 'officers'. To the disgust of GI veterans of the Pacific campaign, a crowd of majors, lieutenants, and colonels reportedly trampled and jostled each other to pick up what turned out to be mere Japanese field sabres, 'the poor man's samurai sword'.[6]

Despite their often unedifying proclivities, many Occupationnaires made enthusiastic and often appreciative visitors to Japan. In his study of the New Zealand contribution to the Occupation, *Jayforce* (1997), Laurie Brocklebank comments on the 'division' in attitude among the Kiwi contingent, with some men 'wanting nothing to do with the local people, landscapes, and culture, while others were keen to interact with them'. He quotes the New Zealand army education booklet *Home was Never Like This* (1947), which comments with refreshing candour on the subject:

> After a month or two the crowd you go with usually splits up into two groups. There are those who retire within the shell of their camp life – as it is easy to do over here because we live in a little self-sufficient group – and these people never, except for special purposes, mix with the life of the Japanese people. The others do. They go out of the camp with their eyes open and find them opened still wider as they see more of Japan and learn about her people.[7]

The division was equally evident among the Australians. For every Jap-hating soldier who confined his interaction with the local people to playing the black market or torrid sexual encounters, there was the inquisitive young traveller keen to take a look at a country so different to his own. Much of this tourism was done independently, by small knots of friends. In May 1946, Captain J.T. Thorp of the Australian Army Education Service formed a BCOF Tourist Club and an offshoot, the Camera Club, both largely comprising officers and their spouses, as indicative of a semi-official initiative to give the impulse to travel some direction. The Tourist Club began life as the Readers', Writers' and Hikers' Club, and was intended to serve an 'educational' purpose. Even in its revised form, the club embraced a definition of tourism that was more than merely recreational. Its self-published history, *The Story of the B.C.O.F. Tourist Club* (1950), reprints a well-known *haiku* as a kind of motto about the solitary nature of real travel that runs counter to the group tourism engaged in by the club (to which at least 80 members belonged):

With the sky so vast and azure
When the rainbow vanished from my sight
A loneliness pervaded me – a traveller.[8]

The club's purpose was twofold: 'to enable members to tour Japan as a group, for the purpose of studying the habits and customs of the people of Japan, and to visit places of scenic, historical and/or general interest'. If the latter activity was engaged in rather more than the former, the group showed an admirable willingness to go beyond the usual Japanese itinerary. Mt Fuji was climbed, and Nara and the Himeji castle dutifully admired; but members also went on fact-finding trips to Hiroshima and distant Nagasaki, and visited shrines and temples in places as remote from Kure as Ise and Nikko. In racking up more than 43,000 kilometres by rail, road, and sea over a four-year period, spanning 200 separate outings, the members saw a lot of Japan. Admittedly, it was done, very largely, in extreme comfort – and was assisted by the good offices of the Japan Travel Bureau. Of the 30-odd members of the party who set out to scale Fujisan, an impressive 22 reached the summit. But they would have been fresh, having travelled to the foot of the mountain aboard the private Occupation-force train the 'Dixie Limited'. The front cover of the club history, an idealised view of the Inland Sea seen from the window of a splendidly equipped train compartment, with a Digger's hat with Rising Sun badge hanging casually from a hook, signifies that this was the travel of conquerors who were luxuriating in what Maida Coaldrake has described as a 'feeling of ownership of Japan'.⁹

Studded with tourist snapshots of 'exotic' Japan and anecdotes about the strange and surprising aspects of Japanese life, personal narratives by Australian Occupationnaires look, and often read, like travel books. Norm 'Bluey' White's account, *How Bluey and Friends Occupied Japan* (1991), describes a hectic round of sightseeing. White is apologetic about this, telling the reader that he wouldn't like to give the impression 'that it was all rest and recreation'; but he astutely thinks that his touristic impressions 'are of more interest than everyday work stories'. In fact, White's role as a driver took him to far-flung parts of BCOF's little empire, trips augmented by periods of leave at *onsens* such as Beppu, exploring the gardens and temples of Kyoto, and, as a matter of course, having his photo taken on Miyajima. These were augmented by regular weekend excursions to the countryside around Kure, occasionally participating in community events such as folk dances, going fishing with local people, and illegally visiting their homes to share their meals. *How Bluey and Friends Occupied Japan* is relentlessly jaunty. A photograph of a disfigured victim of the bombing of Hiroshima, a young woman working as a housemaid in the Beppu R&R hotel in which White stays, is accompanied by the caption 'Hiroko Nakamoto – Atomic Bomb Victim But Still Smiling'.¹⁰

Photographs are an important element of the published narratives of Australian Occupationnaires. Phillip M. Green's *Memories of Occupied Japan* (1987) provides an extensive potpourri of Japanese experiences. An officer in the RAAF, Green ranges across episodes as diverse as encountering the *eta*, Japan's underclass of 'untouchables'; attending a *matsuri* (festival) at the ornate Tenjin Shrine at Bofu; and, while on leave in Tokyo, visiting Sengaku-ji, the shrine of the 47 *ronin*, masterless samurai who in 1703 committed *hara-kiri* en masse, atoning for the death of their lord. The self-sacrifice of the 47 *ronin* is a Japanese story that fascinated and appalled the Australians. Green admires their 'fierce loyalty', but is so perplexed by their purported disregard for life that he is moved to quote Kipling's hackneyed lines about East being East and West being West. The book's photographs, many drawn from his large personal collection, suggest as much as the text. Miyajima's floating cliché is predictably there, but so too is a shot of the dapper, moustachioed Green smirking at the camera, while at his feet, two small Japanese boys shine his shoes. ('Price one cigarette each.') The photograph of a bare-breasted 'Ama', one of the female pearl divers who reaped the pearl harvest, is not out of place, as Green did pay the obligatory visit to the Mikimoto establishment. But it also gives a voyeuristic, anthropological quality to the text, like the titillating shots of naked natives that once dominated the pages of the *National Geographic*.[11]

The beauty of the Japanese countryside deeply impressed Green, and the majority of the BCOF cohort felt much the same way. As Allan Clifton noted, Kure was 'hardly the place from which to begin a pilgrimage to the shrine of beauty', but its very ugliness made the military tourists all the more receptive to the rural wonders that lay within easy distance. The war diary of Private Malcolm Guppy, from Nowra, on the south coast of New South Wales, is full of grumbling about Japan. Like everyone, Guppy loathed the local use of human excreta as fertiliser. When eventually he left Japan, after almost three years in the country, it is with a sense of olfactory relief: 'As we left Kure I said farewell to the land of Nippon, land of smells.' Japanese living standards are laughably low, and its buildings ramshackle; but the landscape, Guppy readily agrees, is magnificent. Lunching in the park by the Kintaikyo Bridge in Iwakuni, the Australian is moved to describe his appreciation, which is made all the more eloquent for being so simply and colloquially expressed. 'The autumn tints were in full bloom at the time. Gee they looked beautiful.' Clifton Pugh thinks Japanese men 'revolting', but he is gushing in his praise of its mountain landscape, which he appreciates with a keen painterly eye. He tells his mother, in a letter, that the scenery encountered in a motoring trip was 'bloody marvellous'. Japan is 'the prettiest part of the world. Everything is as it was thousands of years ago.'[12]

The BCOF reaction against the eyesore of war-wrecked urban Japan was to recoil from modernity itself. It was a reaction that seemed to affect everybody, from common soldiers like Pugh to VIPs like Macmahon Ball. On his visit to Ito to assess potential real estate for BCOF, Ball and his party wandered down to the wharves to observe the local fishermen – or 'fisher folk', as he calls them – unloading their immense catch. Their arrival caused a stir. The whole scene, Ball observes, 'had a genuine primitive animation and made you feel you were amongst real people in a real Japan'.[13]

'Real Japan' is a phrase that occurs again and again in the writing of the Australians. Staying in the beautiful house of one of his Japanese parishioners, a two-storied traditional house surrounded by pines and overlooking the sea in a remote part of the Izu peninsula, the Anglican missionary Reverend Frank Coaldrake feels he had 'discovered the real Japan for the first time'. Actually, Coaldrake had had an epiphany of 'Japaneseness' sometime earlier, during an alpine hiking holiday in central Honshu in the summer of 1948. On the road, travelling through 'God's handful of mountains' and 'God's bucketful of water', Coaldrake finds the essential Japan he has been searching for. Significantly, it is a bucolic, 'traditional' Japan that exists outside the net not only of encroaching modernity but also of the Occupation presence itself, though not its control. Near the town of Takayama, nestled deep in the Hida Valley, Coaldrake talks with a local farmer who tells him that many of the people newly resident in the region had fled there at the war's end 'because they were afraid of the coming of the conquering army'. This was the kind of place, Coaldrake pointedly observes, in which three-quarters of Japan's people lived and worked.[14]

Lamenting Japan's industrialisation and the spoiling of its voluptuous landscape is a dominant motif of modern Western travel writing. Works such as Richie's *The Inland Sea* and Alex Kerr's *Lost Japan* (1996) are elegiac accounts of the damage Japan has inflicted upon itself since the ravages exacted on the country by the war. One of the first writers to register this theme of loss was none other than Hal Porter in *The Actors* (1968), the product of a return visit to the country in 1967. The local landscape he once knew was unrecognisable. Making a nostalgic short road trip back to Nijimura, Porter notes that the rustic villages, whose inhabitants had once cultivated orchards of persimmons and loquats, had become the hideous factory suburbs of Kure. Tokyo had turned into a horrifying dystopia, a place where 'progress has become a pestilence'.[15]

In fact, Porter's estrangement from modern Japan was first expressed in the passages dealing with his Occupation experiences in *The Paper Chase*. After flying into Japan at Iwakuni, Porter takes a nautical route along the Inland Sea to Kure to begin his duties, after being offered a ride in the launch of a whisky-sodden brigadier. It is a fortuitous trip, for to have taken the customary means of travel from Iwakuni to Kure – by train, car, or jeep – would have taken him through Hiroshima. By 1949, Hiroshima was quickly re-emerging from its obliteration, but in the helter-skelter manner of much post-war Japanese redevelopment. En route, the vessel keeps close enough to the shore for Porter to view an idyllic Old Japan tenaciously outliving the depredations of modernity. The Hiroshige and Hokusai landscapes anticipated since his youth seemed to have survived – but only temporarily, Porter thinks, for the 'beast' of 'progress' was on the march. As the launch cuts through the choppy waters of the Inland Sea, he is conscious that Hiroshima lies a short swallow's flight away from the place 'where science celebrated itself with a sumptuous bang and bonfire'.[16] It is the aesthetic, rather than human, cost of the atomic bomb that bothers him.

In Porter's defence, at least he had an historical perspective on the bomb, seeing it as a portent of the awful paradox of techno-logical progress. Mankind had developed the means to cause self-annihilation. Other Australians had a more heedless view of Hiroshima. When John Morris toured the 'vast ruined china shop' of Hiroshima in 1946, his Australian driver complained about what a dull place it was, and how he couldn't get a drink while Morris visited the offices of the local newspaper, the *Chugoku Shimbun*. There was simply nothing to see. His irritated passenger asked him if he realised that the scene of desolation all around them was the result of the dropping of just one bomb. '"Hadn't thought of that,"' the Australian said. '"Pity we didn't drop a few hundred," he added as an afterthought.'[17]

CHAPTER TWELVE

By Ground Zero

That there was 'nothing' to see in Hiroshima was also the very reason the Occupationnaires felt compelled to go there. The bomb had turned Hiroshima into a tourist attraction. The first thing T.B. Millar did upon setting foot on Japanese soil in February 1946 was to borrow a jeep from the Americans and make the short journey to Hiroshima in the company of a few comrades. In the kind of admission that has come to haunt the BCOF veterans, Millar says he had never heard of radiation, and could not remember 'ever being given any information about it, then or later'. *Know Japan,* the official guidebook provided to the military tourists to help prepare them for the tour of duty, can't have been any help. Forthcoming on the diseases endemic to the Japanese landscape, and those lurking in the bloodstreams of the women, *Know Japan* never mentions the word 'radiation'. Not once.

By the time of the Australian arrival, a great deal of clearing up had taken place, and temporary structures had begun appearing.

But Hiroshima still provided a vista of mass destruction very like that seen by Wilfred Burchett less than a month after the bombing, when it looked 'as though a monster steamroller had passed over and squashed it out of existence'. The visual impact of the devastation was staggering. 'Nothing could have prepared us for the experience,' Miller has recalled. 'The devastation was enormous and appalling', he wrote, 'rubble, rubble, as far as the eye could see, with the occasional concrete building standing, burnt out and cracked, with trams thrown yards from the tramlines, twisted and burnt'.[1]

In 1946, John Morris observed in Hiroshima a determination to recover such as he had sensed nowhere else in Japan.[2] Recovery entailed restoring city services, getting the tramcars running again, and building new housing, primitive though much of it was. It also meant planning Hiroshima's rebirth as a city dedicated to 'peace'. This began virtually straight away, with the Hiroshima Reconstruction Bureau forming in January 1946 under the auspices of the municipal authorities and the city assembly, and with input from the citizens. At first there was talk of preserving the ruined landscape around Ground Zero, leaving it untouched as an eloquent monument to the bomb's destructiveness. However, on 6 August 1949, after a public competition won by Tokyo University's Kenzo Tange, the 'Hiroshima Peace Memorial City Construction Law' was put into effect, and what we now know as Peace Park came into being. Tange's masterplan envisioned a vast public space that included not merely an exhibition hall and various symbolic structures but also 'Heiwa Dori', or 'Peace Boulevard', a 100-metre-wide avenue at the southern end of the park. Securing the site proved to be difficult. The soldiers had to clear some 400 illegal shacks on the site, mostly housing *hibakusha*, and they had to move the residents on. During the excavation for the construction, workers unearthed human bones, moving them to tears.[3]

While most of the impetus for rebuilding the city stemmed from the residents themselves, the process was aided first by the

Americans and then the Australians, who became unofficial reconstruction advisors. The latter sought hands-on involvement. At
one point, before the competition to come up with a design for
the proposed museum, BCOF's Major S.A. Jervie, an Australian
architect involved in the domestic design of the Nijimura project,
demanded that Hiroshima's planning authorities accept his reconstruction, which was something along the lines of a Buddhist
pagoda. An acolyte of Le Corbusier, Kenzo Tange produced a more
modernist concept.[4] In August 1946, commander-in-chief
Robertson corresponded with SCAP on the matter of providing
BCOF engineers to assist with the 'replanning' and 'rebuilding' of
Hiroshima. Upon finding that the force had insufficient engineers
to divert to this purpose, he offered to send town-planning experts
to help with the massive task. The offer drew a curt response from
Colonel Bunker, MacArthur's aide-de-camp, saying that the provision of town-planning experts would provide an unwelcome and
unwise 'precedent' leading to other requests and demands from
the Japanese community. A prior memo from the American army
GHQ – headed 'Rehabilitation of Hiroshima' – elaborated, saying
that other Japanese cities would make similar requests, and that
the Occupation forces 'would be subject to unfavorable comment
because of the preferable treatment accorded Hiroshima'.[5]

Nonetheless, as Lisa Yoneyama points out in her study of the
memorialisation of the city, *Hiroshima Traces* (1999), Allied GHQ
'enthusiastically supported the idea of spatially rearranging
Hiroshima so as to turn it into an international showcase for
exhibiting the link between the atomic bomb and postwar peace'.
Given the stringent Occupation censorship of public debate about
the bomb, this enthusiasm may seem surprising. But there was a
calculated logic to Occupation thinking. If the idea and the actual
fact of 'peace' was concretely associated with the bomb, and the
two became interchangeable in public memory, it would be
established that without the timely intervention of an atomic
weapon, the Allied forces would never have achieved peace in the

Pacific. It was used to save lives, in other words. The identification of peace with the bomb also provided a rationale for a build-up of offensive force and for the US policy of nuclear deterrence itself. Hiroshima's rebirth as a centre of international pacifism ironically confirmed the view that world peace was to be produced and maintained by menacing military force and technological mastery. Hiroshima's design, in Yoneyama's words, 'thus spatially represented the master narrative of the post-World War II order in the Asia Pacific region'.⁶

It is very doubtful if, back in Tokyo, MacArthur would have viewed the new Hiroshima in quite such theoretical terms. He never bothered to visit this vastly significant place, though emperor Hirohito toured the city in December 1947, attired in clothes, according to an Australian observer, 'deliberately chosen so as not to be too much on the smart side', where he was greeted by a quarter of the city's population, some of them shouting *banzais* at the tops of their voices. But MacArthur would surely have been pleased to see the bomb's horrors camouflaged by a pleasant park, and the physical and psychological suffering it caused turned into such a nice idea as 'peace'. Many *hibakusha* themselves had misgivings about what one of them, the novelist Yoko Ota, sarcastically called the 'new Hiroshima'. This was a city, she observed in the 1960s, 'for sightseeing … made to be shown to visitors'. While tourists admire grandiose public spaces such as Peace Boulevard, the Hundred-Meter Road 'built by order of MacArthur', the survivors huddle together in cramped poverty. The people 'who are really suffering are hidden … they are less than people'.⁷

GHQ may have liked the idea of a formal site but, over the time it exercised power, it exerted strict control over commemorative practice and utterance. In 1950, the Occupation banned the Hiroshima Peace Festival, the annual ritual of local government-sponsored events, which was inaugurated on the second anniversary of the bombing. The Korean War had just broken out, and the popularity of the ideal of 'peace' and the widespread revulsion against the use of nuclear weapons were suddenly unwelcome developments. Peace was an irritating concept when there was a war to be won.

On the first anniversary of the bombing, the citizens held a rally at what was once the Gotoku Shrine, now the site of the home stadium of Hiroshima's famous baseball team 'the Carp', followed by a Peace Restoration Festival. There were 7000 attendees, some carrying banners with messages such as 'World peace begins from Hiroshima'. But it was an unofficial occasion, allowed only after SCAP, in Tokyo, and BCOF, in Kure, granted their permission. The occasion took place under surveillance, and no anti-Occupation speeches were permitted. The national broadcaster NHK recorded the event, though the broadcast was delayed until 11 August, due to censorship niceties. In 1947, the first of the official festivals took place, in an open area later integrated into the formal park, during which the Hiroshima mayor Shinzo Hamai read the first of the anti-war, anti-nuclear 'Peace Declarations', along with a goodwill message from MacArthur. The message was drowned out the following year when Robertson delivered his famous broadside at the assembled citizens telling them the disaster was their own fault. Frank Clune, for one, believed that the BCOF commander's 'soldierly' words 'cleared the air of hypocrisy' and provided 'a douche of reality' – as if the black rain of 6 August 1945 hadn't done that already.[8]

The legacy of the atomic bombing was easy to ignore from Tokyo, nearly 900 kilometres away, and even from BCOF HQ in Kure; but it was more difficult to turn a blind eye when one was confronted by it daily. The horrors of the place stayed with some of the Australians for years afterward. In the hot summer of 1946, when the Intelligence officer John Coffman's unit was detached to the repatriation depot at the city's port at Ujina, the unit detected an awful smell beneath one of the wharves. Investigations found numerous corpses 'in a congealed mass of flesh and bones falling apart'. In the extremity of their last pitiful hours, Coffman wrote in 1992, people caught in the firestorm had crawled towards the water to salve their wounds and to seek the cold privacy of death. Along with ex-Japanese soldiers and workmen, Coffman (vomiting into his gas mask) helped Buddhist priests clear up the ghastly remains. It was, he says, 'the nearest thing to hell I wish to experience ...'[9]

Despite Robertson's bluster, the BCOF leadership and many of its men were acutely aware of the morally compromising position in which the Commonwealth force found itself. As Shirley Hazzard observes in her award-winning novel *The Great Fire* (2003), partly set in Japan during the Occupation, the Australians exhibited 'the unease of conquerors: the unseemliness of finding themselves a few miles from Hiroshima'. En route to Hong Kong, where her father was taking up a government posting, Hazzard had herself disembarked at Kure in 1946, having sailed from Sydney on a ship containing a collection of BCOF wives. Twelve months after the 'Big Drop', as Frank Clune charmingly called the bombing, the centre of Hiroshima was still 'like a gray lake'. The attitude of Hazzard's own family and that of the officers was the conventional one of the times. The bomb was 'the inevitable and justified – and even merciful – outcome' of total war. 'Yet among these generally unreflective people,' Hazzard remarks, 'there was some uneasiness in discussing it.'[10]

An incident involving Major Arthur John on the occasion of the first anniversary of the bombing illustrates this touchiness. A Japanese language teacher attached part-time to the service, and who also worked for the daily evening newspaper, the *Yukan Hiroshima*, asked John, as BCOF's senior education officer, if he would contribute a short message for the paper's special commemorative issue on 6 August 1946. John duly provided an article 'to the effect that anyone who had seen the beauty of Japan before the war must be saddened to contemplate the devastation caused through the area, especially of Hiroshima itself; the lesson of the atomic bomb was for the whole of mankind and it was up to the whole world to make the United Nations Organisation a complete success'.

Unimpeachable sentiments, it might be thought. But when it appeared on the paper's front page, the article created a furore within the army hierarchy. John was dressed down by both the BCOF HQ director of public relations and the brigadier, and narrowly avoided being cashiered. Within days, a local routine order appeared prohibiting communication of any kind with the Japanese press.[11]

BCOF Intelligence in February 1947 noted a general 'lack of feeling' among the troops for the wartime sufferings of the Japanese. Even in Hiroshima, a philosophy that 'they brought it on themselves' seemed to predominate.[12] Decades on, some veterans still express little pity for the people of the city. Reg Adkins, an airman based in Bofu and then Iwakuni, visited Hiroshima to participate in sports events against the army (the levelled devastation of Ground Zero provided a superb venue for football matches). He holds a common view in firmly believing 'to this day' that 'the Japanese deserved what they got': the rapists of Nanking, the executioners of New Guinea, and the bestial torturers of POWs had to be punished.[13]

In this argument, a whole race – women, children, and the aged and infirm – is lumped into an anonymous mass deserving retribution. C.G. Jones, who served in a Field Ambulance unit stationed in Kaitaichi from February 1946, resorts to a brusque, colloquial metaphor in recalling his response to the damage wrought by the bomb. The city, he remembers, was 'flattened like a cow turd'. Maurice Anderson, an infantryman based at Fukuyama, visited Hiroshima several times on duty. He retains impressions of the massive effects of the bomb, and remembers feeling 'gratitude to divine providence' that the Kirin brewery, on the outskirts of the city, survived more or less unscathed and was soon restored to full production, to the joy of the Australian soldiery. 'It was certainly needed during the humid and oppressive heat of the Japanese summer', Anderson remarks. Indifferent to the hell endured by the *hibakusha*, some Australians concentrated on slaking their thirsts. The brewery 'was the centre round which the lives of most Australians revolved', Allan Clifton writes with sarcasm. A 'requisition' written on an army form was enough to secure a crate of beer. Often these bore the signatures – meaningless to uncomprehending Japanese eyes – of 'Ned Kelly', 'Ben Hall', and even, in fastidious deference to stating rank, one 'Captain Thunderbolt'.[14]

It is easy for those who didn't live through the war and go through the ordeal of battle to criticise the seeming callousness of elderly veterans. As Paul Fussell challengingly comments in his essay 'Thank God for the Atom Bomb' (1981), the degree to which people now register shock and shame about Hiroshima 'correlates closely' with their ignorance of Japanese wartime savagery and of the logic of war and survival. As a 21-year-old American GI based in Europe whose division was slated to take part in any Allied invasion of Honshu, Fussell broke down with tears of joy when he heard that the *Enola Gay* had 'dropped its package'. He was going to live; and 'the killing was going to be all over'.[15]

Many of the Australian soldiers who went on to serve in Japan, including those intensely sympathetic to the sufferings of the Japanese victims and politically opposed to nuclear weapons, could only agree. The bomb was awful, and awfully indiscriminate, but it saved their lives – and, they believe, those of many thousands, perhaps millions, of others. 'My attitude to nuclear warfare is that it should never again be used,' comments Don Nancarrow, an infantryman who left for Japan on the HMAS *Manoora* on his 19th birthday. 'Ironically, however … the bomb might well have saved my life.' Living in New York in the early 1980s, Shirley Hazzard recounts the visit of an old Australian friend, 'a poet and an entirely gentle person'. American President Ronald Reagan had just announced an intention to upgrade the US nuclear arsenal to counter the Soviet 'evil empire'. Despair was in the air. Then the poet mentioned his first memory of the atomic bomb. He was a badly wounded soldier on a remote Pacific island, his unit hopelessly outnumbered by Japanese troops. News of the bomb came through; he and his comrades were saved. He said, 'I never knew how to handle this is my mind; I wish the bomb had never been invented let alone dropped. But if it had not been, I would be a rotting skeleton these thirty-odd years.'[16]

The hard-headed pleasure at a measure of historical justice being served up to the Japanese ('it served them right') derived from an unwillingness to appear to be 'going soft'. The BCOF Intelligence's aforementioned noting of a 'defensive indifference' among the men was an accurate description of the way Australians in general reacted to Hiroshima. Nonetheless, meeting the *hibakusha*, especially the physically and psychologically maimed, moved many men to compassion. A teenage Occupationnaire, John Allen recalls that personal contact with a young lad who had lost his entire family in the blast, and whose only English was 'B29-Boom', turned him against nuclear weapons and softened his attitude towards the Japanese. Emotionally vulnerable young soldiers were forced to qualify their attitudes toward the Japanese by what they saw in Hiroshima. Even Frank Clune feels some sympathy when interviewing the survivors, especially if they happen to be young, female, and attractive. But it was the sight of the children, proverbial orphans of the storm, that most forces Clune to moderate his gleeful sense of vengeance. 'No man could see the ashes of Hiroshima and fail to feel qualms', he writes. Driving along the narrow coastal road back to Kure, he sees Japanese children playing at the water's edge, or swimming like amphibians. 'They at any rate had no war guilt,' he remarks, 'We couldn't honestly say it served them right.'[17]

Even the POWs, those with the most reason to relish the retributive justice of the atomic bombing, were affected. Originally captured in Malaya in 1942 and a survivor of the Death Railway in Thailand, Kenneth Harrison was mining coal in a POW camp in northern Kyushu when the Allies unleashed the atomic bombs. In company with a few mates, he celebrated his freedom rather oddly, by making a tortuous sightseeing trip to Hiroshima. Harrison boasts that his party consisted of the 'first' non-Japanese to enter Hiroshima after the bomb, which enables him to heighten the sense of drama at the beginning of the narrative as he enters a 'wasteland of desolation and ashes' pervaded by the smell and the silence of mass death. The place and its pitiably dispirited population shock him, and he records 'no sense of either history or triumph … Our brother Man went by crippled and burned and we knew only shame and guilt'.

Harrison's war story was originally called *The Brave Japanese* when first published in 1966 – not a title likely to win over the public at a time when the wartime enemy was still widely loathed. It was republished in the 1980s as *The Road to Hiroshima*, which accurately maps the Australian POW travail that effectively ended at the atom-bombed city. The encounter with Hiroshima also brought about a form of closure in Harrison's own attitudes. Leaving the city, his hatred of the Japanese had been 'swept away' by 'the enormity' of what he had witnessed. Harrison calculatedly uses the loaded term 'holocaust' to describe what he saw in Hiroshima – a reminder of how sensitive the American administration was after the war to comparisons between the atomic bombings and Hitler's 'Final Solution', and how these fears, in part, compelled the strict censorship of ghastly images and details of ground-level horrors.[18]

Albert Tucker also refers to the Jewish Holocaust in one of his Japanese works, the watercolour 'Hiroshima 1947'. In a Stygian scene of abject desolation, what appears to be a homeless child stands near a blasted tree, whose bare branches form the unmistakable shape of a swastika.[19] Tucker, who spent three months in early 1947 as an illustrator and correspondent attached to BCOF, found it difficult to document Hiroshima aesthetically. Hiroshima's unpaintability was matched by an intimidating sense of its indescribability. 'Indescribable' is a common adjective applied by observers to the atomic damage. It is used by the *hibakusha* themselves, who continually complain that they lack the means to describe what they saw and endured.

The bombings seemed beyond representation as well as comprehension. Echoing Theodor Adorno's aphorism, 'No poetry after Auschwitz', the Hiroshima poet and activist Sadako Kurihara observed that 'all the literary arts created by the human race, all the bittersweet romances of men and women, all the babies sleeping in their cradles, all our species – all were destroyed in an instant by that evil energy'. There was no military, historical, or literary precedent for what had taken place. The event defeated language itself. For some years following the bomb, the local newspaper the *Chugoku Shimbun* did not even possess the moveable type for 'atomic bomb' or 'radioactivity'. This resulted in a strange kind of public ignorance which, as the Nobel laureate Kenzaburo Oe observes in *Hiroshima Notes* (1965), suited the American Occupation authorities – the US Army Surgeons Investigations Team had issued a derisory public statement in the autumn of 1945 to the effect that all people expected to die from the radiation effects of the bomb had already died.[20]

The first sight of Hiroshima reduced visitors to stupefied silence. The journalist Eric Thornton, who went into the city with an advance party of Australians in February 1946, remarks that the men 'had no word to describe it, which is unusual for Australian soldiers'. Hiroshima even muted Lorraine Stumm, which was no mean feat. Six weeks after the bombing, she toured the city with a party of journalists, which made her, she boasts, the first Australian woman to view the devastation. Stumm was prepared for the sea of rubble, but 'nothing prepared' her for the piles of bodies, still visible then, she says, and for 'the bitter desolation of a once prosperous community'. The sight quelled the usual journalist banter: 'We were all so silent.' A stunned silence, followed by the tentative beginning of empathy and compassion, was a common reaction of the soldiers. Based south of Kure, the young Occupationnaire Frank Hayter went into Hiroshima with his mates for some sightseeing. They made a beeline for the brewery, but upon finding it inconveniently surrounded by military police, went to look at the bombsite instead. They were 'silenced' by what they saw. Having made the trip to snare some free beer, they made the journey back to camp 'very sober indeed' because of what they had witnessed.[21]

Years later, Albert Tucker looked back at his attempt to render Hiroshima with a sense of failure, derived from the fact that he was 'too young and inexperienced' to capture the immensity of the tragedy, and his 'empathic abilities weren't developed as fully' as he would have wished. This is a strange comment, since he was well into his 30s and had already produced some of his best work, including the 'Images of Modern Evil' series depicting sordid urban life in wartime Australia. The city moved other, less gifted, Australians to poetry, astounded as many of them were by the destruction. Norm Craig was an 18-year-old infantryman on his first trip away from home when he arrived in Japan in 1946. Looking back, he thinks the bombing was unnecessary and an 'absolute atrocity', and he draws a tenuous link between it and the 'butchery' going on in Iraq. Craig's poem 'The Ashes of Hiroshima' articulates a young man's impressions of the atomic ruins, with the 'scorched branches of leafless trees' raised 'like appealing arms, to a pitiless sky', and how the sight of them drained away 'the very last dregs of hatred' from his heart.[22]

Others empathised in the best way they knew how, by responding associatively to Hiroshima as Australians. In 'Reverie in Hiroshima', published in the Australian War Memorial's series *As You Were* in 1948, G.M. Hollis contemplates a badly mutilated but reviving eucalypt, a blue gum, standing by the moat encircling the ruins of Hiroshima Castle. Hollis is moved by the sight of this 'solitary Australian' standing like 'a sentinel', a survivor of a horrible past, and a symbol of hope for both Japan and the new

Hiroshima. (Having also survived being torn into two by a typhoon in 1971, the 'A-bombed tree' is still there today, an object of curiosity to visitors to the rebuilt castle.) Another Occupationnaire, a member of the Readers', Writers' and Tourers' Club, similarly sought to draw Hiroshima into the Australian orbit, in an impression of a visit to the city published in the first issue of the Education Service's magazine *The Gen*. The 'green' Japanese idyll of towering hills, paddies, and trellised grapevines is starkly juxtaposed with 'dead' Hiroshima. Yet the weeds sprouting in the atomic rubble indicate a sure sign of life. Cold science was being defeated; nature was fighting back. By the razed castle, one of the city's several broad rivers, the Ota, flows strongly to the sea. To the BCOF observer, this was 'a breath of Australia in Japan'. In another life, he had fished and lazed in that very spot. An identical spit of sand; a broad, creeping river shaded by trees. 'This was the Snowy River at the Jindabine [sic].'[23]

The empathy of soldiers was more than matched by that of the dependent children, who were less able to rationalise the tragedy as a justifiable means to an end. Most BCOF children seem to have reacted to Hiroshima with restraint and dignity, and vividly recall the sobering effect of visiting bomb victims in hospital. Concerned at the effect the place and its people might have on their children, especially the very young ones, some families tried to protect them from the very sight of it. Christine (Newlands) Cheetham remembers her father pulling down the blind as their train went through the city.[24]

But in general, the dependants got to know about the tragedy on their doorstep. Then well into her teens, Mary (Raymond) Bros went on a guided tour of the city with other senior pupils of Nijimura School. The itinerary included the famous 'shadow', the image of an irradiated body on the granite step of a bank, and culminated in a visit to a hospital where survivors were being studied by American specialists of the Atomic Bomb Casualty Commission. 'One was urged to place a hand beneath the raised cobweb of skin tissue on the back of a hideously scarred survivor,' Bros remarks: 'the memory remains today after all these years.' Rosemary Jeanneret visited Hiroshima many times and recalls seeing 'a beggar pushing a wooden trolley with all his possessions on it ... he looked as if his entire body was covered with shiny purple grape blisters'. As a 15-year-old, Margery Sullivan was selected to attend an International Moral Leadership conference on Miyajima – one of two chosen to represent Australia. The conference heard a Japanese girl speak of the day the bomb was dropped over Hiroshima: 'You could hear a pin drop as she spoke, and we realised the terror and devastation these people had suffered through.' Afterwards, the delegates caught a ferry back to Hiroshima, and were put on a bus to visit a hospital that housed radiation victims.[25]

HIROSHIMA WAS A RAW PLACE when the Australians were there, a far cry from the accommodating urban showpiece it is today. When Frank Clune visited the city in 1948, he was annoyed by the lack of facilities on offer. But he noted its 'tourist potential' as a 'place of pilgrimage for pacifists', and correctly foresaw a range of commemorative structures at the 'Centre of Impact'. The fledgling beginnings of a tourism industry were already in evidence, and the Australians were willing clients, literally buying (or looting) bits of Ground Zero to take back home. In 1946, the Occupationnaire Stephen Kelen befriended a local resident who had opened a bookshop called 'Atom' and was selling debris to tourists. These were usually humdrum household items remoulded in the tremendous heat caused by the explosion: holy relics of martyred Hiroshima. The magic word 'Atom', Kelen wryly observes, had earned the entrepreneur 'fame and fortune'.[26]

Others dabbled in the tourist trade for mere survival. As even Hal Porter acknowledges, 'the rake-off from the sale of fused gobbets of atom-bomb aftermath' fed families who were desperate to survive and to then get their lives back into some kind of order. As tourist hunter-gatherers, the Australians reacted and behaved in different ways. Annetta Chisholm's 'bonza trip' to Hiroshima included rummaging through ruined temples for religious relics. One of her Australian travelling companions snares a case full. Chisholm makes do with a small vase that is given to her. 'But if I ever get there again,' swears this young Australian woman of her day at the city of mass death and destroyed lives, 'I will buy more as they would make good gifts and be truly Japanese'. Kenneth Harrison claims he resisted the temptation to scavenge a souvenir when he visited the city soon after the bombing. 'One does not rob a tomb', he wrote. Similarly, Murray Elliott felt as though he was 'desecrating a massive cemetery' as he and his peers hunted for souvenirs of fused ceramics and glass to show folks back home that he'd been to the infamous Hiroshima.[27]

Few Australians failed to recognise the irony of sightseeing in this place of horror. And if they did, there was usually someone or something on hand to remind them forcibly of it. The *Quiberon*, on which Gordon Leed served, docked at Nagasaki twice on pirate patrol, but its centre of operations was Kure. One of the ship's officers had 'liberated' a jeep from the US army, for the cost of a bottle of Scotch it seems, and Leed was assigned the job of the ship's driver. This was a more appealing prospect than working in the boiler room stoking the *Quiberon*'s engines. But he soon tired of being pressed into taking naval officers to 'gawk' at the ruins of Hiroshima. Leed loathed what his messmates jokingly called his 'Hiroshima taxi run' and resented being used as a tour guide for idle, rubbernecking officers. One day he decided to show his day-trippers something that was not on their itinerary. He pulled up outside a shelter housing some badly disfigured survivors of the bomb whom he had befriended, and to whom he occasionally gave a 'presento' of BCOF rations. He blew the horn, and out came his friends, with faces 'scarred almost beyond belief'. His passengers were appalled. 'I say Leed,' one of the officers exclaimed, 'we came to see the ruins not to be made ill.' Leed could not contain his anger:

> Here were these bloody tourists who wanted to see the wreckage of war but not the suffering that went with it. For the first time in my naval life I was openly insubordinate, replying, 'Those people are the ruins mate.'[28]

PART FOUR

Embracing Japan: conquest and contact

CHAPTER THIRTEEN

Sleeping with the Enemy

'What are the women like?' Making his famous pilgrimage to Mecca in 1853, the same year as Commodore Perry's Black Ships entered the harbour at Shimoda, Sir Richard Burton thought this was 'the first question of mankind to the wanderer'.[1] Traveller and soldier, linguist and Orientalist, 'Dirty Dick' Burton had a remarkable knowledge of Eastern and African cultures and languages. But he was also a connoisseur of Eastern sexual practices: along with his numerous travel books, he collaborated on the translation of *The Kama Sutra*, as well as translating *The Perfumed Garden* and *The Arabian Nights*. Knowing the East, for Burton, meant knowing the women sexually (and perhaps the men, too; pederasty was a special scholarly interest). It meant understanding their sexual routines as a means of coming to grips with their cultures. His question reverberates today: in the Western imagination, 'the East' is still associated with female sexuality. Male travellers still venture to Asian locales, driven by their erotic potential as spheres of unbridled lasciviousness.

Fantasies of Japanese womanhood kept many of the Australians going as they cooled their heels in Morotai and the training camps in Australia, prior to embarking for Japan, and during the long voyage itself. As Allan Clifton observes, most of the men of the first shipments of Occupationnaires had been in the tropics, cut off from female society for long periods, 'and made no secret of what they wanted, or of their readiness, willingness and ability to recover lost ground'. The men's indiscriminate desires are suggested by the generic name given to the available women in and around the Kure encampments. They were called 'moose', a bastardisation of the Japanese *musume*, or girl. The women, Clifton writes, were 'quarry in a great game hunt'.[2] As the metaphor implies, this mating ritual was essentially a predatory form of human exchange, even when coercion or outright assault were not involved. The ranks of the professional prostitutes in the port city were swollen by uprooted women, some of them from poverty-stricken towns and villages elsewhere in Hiroshima Prefecture, who had to survive by any means at their disposal. Many were war widows with children and elderly relatives to support, and they grasped any opportunity. The young Sydneysider Bede Wall discovered that the fields of Occupied Japan were thick with 'moose'. The country was a veritable free-for-all. In his exhaustingly ribald memoir of a 'gauche' young Australian's sexual education, he recalls the advances of a middle-aged Japanese woman whose husband had been the captain of a freighter sunk during the war. She had invited him into her house as he was casually passing by one day. Over a cup of green tea, she told him her pitiable story and cuddled up close. A fumbled sexual encounter transpired, after which a panicky Wall fled the house, leaving her 'probably thinking, "what kind of breed were these Aussies?"'[3]

Japan was a revelation. To Wall, Japan's relatively 'relaxed' ideas about sex and unselfconscious attitudes toward public nudity made 'prudish' Australia look backward. Writing to his mother in the summer of 1947 about an afternoon spent swimming naked off Miyajima in company with local men and women, all similarly nude, Clifton Pugh asks, 'Could you imagine that in Australia?' M.D. Guppy struggles to articulate his amazement at the Japanese custom of communal bathing. 'They have bath houses where men and women bathe together in the raw', he remarks in his diary. For some of the youngsters, this was their first-ever sight of a naked woman, and it was a gobsmacking experience. Even a sophisti-cated and mature Australian military traveller such as Arthur John, a married man, found the mixed bathhouse a challenge. Staying at an inn at the *onsen* in Yamaguchi, he was enjoying a morning soak in a 'big Roman bath' when an attractive young woman entered, disrobed, and daintily stepped in. 'I had read somewhere "The nude is seen in Japan, but not looked at," John remarks. 'A glance was enough to see she had a pretty good figure. It was a little dis-turbing, so I decided it was time to leave.'[4]

Actually, the Australian servicemen did do a great deal of looking at Japanese women, and descriptions of their physical allure are a staple of male Occupation discourse. Australian travel-lers in Japan have been debating the merits of the Japanese female form since at least the 1870s, when James Hingston described 'a buxom little round lump of a thing that one mistakes for twelve years old until told she is eighteen or twenty ... Figure, to speak of, the female Japanese does not possess'. An Australian contem-porary of Hingston's, the journalist, traveller, and wheeler-dealer G.E. ('Chinese') Morrison is even less kind in comparing 'the Japanese lady' with her sisters in China, brutally portraying her as a 'misshapen cackling little dot with black teeth'. During the Occupation, Hal Porter (an admittedly unsympathetic observer) provides a typically harsh assessment. 'Japanese girls are very plain', he writes in a story about his house girl. Others were slightly more appreciative. In a discussion of the Japanese published in the Australian War Memorial's *As You Were* compilation in 1947, the army photographer Alan Queale admires the shop girls of Ginza as 'very feminine, exotic little creatures', and grudgingly remarks of Japanese women in general that 'some are tolerably good-looking'. But Queale feels it necessary to bemoan their lack of grace, their 'knobby knees and ugly legs', and their 'moon-like faces'. The subtext is that the women were unattractive to the Australians, who were chastely keeping themselves nice for the lady folk back home. Nothing was further from the truth. Many Australians, such as Clifton Pugh, were inclined to agree with the common Western observation, articulated by Lafcadio Hearn and many others, that the most wonderful aesthetic objects of Japan were not its ivories, its swords, or its lacquer ware, but its women. Pugh's painterly eye was impressed by what he saw while skinny-dipping at Miyajima. 'The women can afford to go naked here', he informs his mother:

> I have never seen a fat unsightly body yet and never will for they don't get fat. Quite a lot of the women have really beautiful figures – there is no denying they are very attractive but the men revolting ... Japan has two races – the men and the women ...[5]

Another admirer of Japanese womanhood, Murray Elliott, who was to become one of Brisbane's leading gynaecologists, provides a disarmingly thorough survey of them, as fastidiously detailed in its way as the ethnographic analyses of native races that graced the publications of the Royal Society in the 19th century. Observing a collection of Japanese women of varying ages employed at the convalescent depot he commanded on Miyajima, he makes a finding of an average height of 61 inches and weight of 93 pounds, and goes on to describe their faces, foreheads, eyes and eye sockets, noses, necks, hairlines ('Fuji-shaped'), waists, trunks ('elongated in proportion to their total height'), breasts ('round with well-defined areola and nipples'), hips, pubic hair ('short sparse straight'), buttocks ('taut'), legs, and feet. He even notes the unwelcome presence of halitosis – all that raw fish and seaweed – but has the grace to wonder how *they* viewed foreign males like *him*, with their 'grossness and hirsutism'. In general, the women pass muster. 'Not all were classically beautiful', Elliott claims, 'but most were attractive'. Less professional observers were equally impressed. M.D. Guppy is frankly admiring of the Japanese female form. 'To say there are no decent looking Japanese would be telling a lie,' he writes. 'Because I have seen some with really good figures. The curves have been in the right places.' From a long historical distance, some BCOF veterans sentimentalise the raw sexuality of those Japan days in lyrical, almost romantic terms. It is a task that proved beyond some of them. In his poem 'The Occupation', published in 1996, Les Denton's refrain is that 'we fell in love with the kimono and stole those geisha hearts'. Unfortunately, he struggles to find an apt rhyme, coupling 'geisha hearts' with 'honey carts' (the vehicles that transported human excrement around rural Japan) and, right the end of the poem, 'vegie marts'.[6]

The easy association in Denton's panegyric between desirable and available Japanese women and geisha is indicative of the Occupationnaires' habit of rationalising prostitution as an exalted female profession in Japan. The men were told often enough that the 'geisha' was not a common prostitute, but they liked to use the emotive term to dignify their street or brothel dealings with Japanese women. Their guidebook *Know Japan* is ambiguous on the subject of geishas, remarking: 'such is the nature of their organisation, their long studies in music and dancing and the art of repartee, that it is incorrect to name them mere prostitutes'.[7] Even Murray Elliott, one of the more discerning and culturally engaged members of BCOF, succumbs to the ready sexualisation of the geisha, albeit comically and at his own expense. During his stint on Miyajima as commanding officer of the convalescent depot, Elliott was asked to many parties attended by 'true geisha' at the famous Iwaso Inn, evenings enlivened by bottles of potent Australian whisky, which rendered some of the Japanese 'legless'. Aware that 'geisha' did not mean 'prostitute', he nonetheless harboured hopes that one might invite him to share her futon. On one of these occasions, while unbuttoning his trousers to urinate, two dainty female hands appeared from behind to help him perform the task. To his dismay, they then shook, wiped, and tucked him away. Another time, a geisha seated alongside him drew his attention to her lap and to the startling fact that she was not wearing underwear. She then proceeded to perform tricks with a cigarette inserted in her vulva, exercising her pelvic muscles to make it jerk up and down in a series of sudden and suggestive movements. Again, nothing eventuated, and Elliott was left to ponder the miserable irony of the performance. He quotes a well-known *senryu* to suggest a Japanese female view of gendered exchange during the Occupation:

> How she must loathe him
> To smile at him
> So brilliantly.[8]

Like many Australians, Elliott formed dignified platonic relationships with Japanese women. But the pervasiveness of sexual opportunity could weaken the resolve of even the most chaste men.

The chance of picking up an infection was an insufficient deterrent. Bede Wall was terrified of contracting a disease and appalled by grisly stories of the treatments. One of the landmarks of the Kure area was the Venereal Diseases Hospital, situated on one of the steep hills behind the city, surrounded by barbed-wire and lit at night by arc lamps. It was Kure's answer to the 'Hollywood' sign. The hospital's colloquial name was 'the House that Jack Built', after one of the slang terms ('the jack') for VD. But its notoriety did not stop Wall from continually putting himself at risk during chance encounters or sorties to one of the local 'butterfly houses'. Despite the pleas of some mid-ranking officers who advocated controlled prostitution in the form of semi-official red-light districts where the women could be given regular medical check-ups, the BCOF leadership intransigently opposed regulated prostitution, and efforts to control venereal disease were clumsy and heavy-handed.

Major Arthur John writes critically of the campaign of September 1946, which involved appointing 'Anti-VD Officers' who interviewed men who had contracted the disease, and then identified and rounded up the women who had infected them. 'Something in the nature of a panic was occurring', John writes, 'almost as though there were an outbreak of plague'. A BCOF wife recalled her house girls being systematically harassed, and one being removed from her service. The men themselves remained largely indifferent to the physical and social consequences of their promiscuity and antagonistic to the strictures of authority. The fraternisation ban was unjust as well as ineffective; the men felt that it forced them into the brothels. Moreover, they were fed inconsistent information by the BCOF authorities, who banned brothels on the one hand, while suggesting, on the other, that local prostitutes were performing a cultural function to which no stigma was attached.[9]

Some remarkably clumsy strategies were devised by both the Americans and the Australians to curb sexual activity. It was the shameless public canoodling of GIs and their Japanese sweethearts, rather than prostitution itself, which particularly bothered the US authorities. In March 1946, General Eichelberger observed: 'The sight of our soldiers ... with their arms around Japanese girls is equally repugnant to Americans at home ... as well as to most Japanese.' Public displays of affection were henceforth regarded as disorderly conduct. But SCAP refused to issue an unequivocal non-fraternisation order. 'They keep trying to get me to stop all this Madame Butterflying around', MacArthur complained. 'I won't do it ... for all the tea in China'. Instead, other ways of limiting contact with Japanese women were devised. One strategy, dreamed up by a general called Joseph Swing, involved military police being instructed to insert a calibrated measure between US servicemen and their Japanese dancing partners, in cabarets and dance halls. Oblivious to its suggestiveness, this bizarre edict was called the 'six inch rule'.[10]

The Australians opted for a more conventional approach. To stifle their urges, troops were officially advised to consult with the chaplains attached to the services. This was a proposal that smacked of desperation. One of the penalties for contracting VD was the loss of the beer ration for 15 days. If that dire prospect didn't act as a deterrent, a chat about God was hardly likely to have the desired effect. The visiting army chaplains-general who reported on the welfare of the force in 1947 had commented chastisingly that 'irreligion is widespread'. As Arthur John remarked, their expectations were unrealistic. Clearly, they visualised 'an idealistic army, like Cromwell's Roundheads', he jokes. The padres were manically active in opposing efforts to regulate the sex business. In Kaitaichi, the battalion padre took it upon himself to have an unofficial brothel near the infantry barracks burned down. It was Christmas Eve, 1946. A spectacular exhibition of impending hell-fire and damnation might serve as a warning. Or it may simply have been that he wanted to keep the men's thoughts focused purely on loved ones back home. That was the line often taken by the force's religious cohort.

The previous month, *The Church Chronicle*, the official BCOF Church of England magazine approved by the Kure Parochial Church Council, trenchantly advocated chastity and denounced the evils of 'loose morals'. The men were implored not to consider 'fornication with a harlot', because she is a 'fallen woman'. Being 'proud defenders of the women Empire [sic]' entailed being true to 'your mother, wives [sic] sweethearts, and sisters' back home. 'Remember God meant married love to be a fine, clean thing, so don't spoil it.'[11]

God obviously didn't consider marriage with a Japanese woman 'a fine, clean thing' at all. It was the men themselves who were spoiled, though not in the way that the padres thought of it. 'The

Japanese pussy got us all in the long run', Bede Wall quips.[12] The reference is crudely sexual, of course. But, in fact, Wall is inadvertently suggesting an attraction that, in hundreds and even thousands of cases, made Australians seek the sustaining emotional, as well as physical, 'comfort' of Japanese women. Many Australian servicemen wanted something more substantial and enduring than the brief, hectic exchange of the brothel and back alleys. In a sense, it was a small step from a casual transaction in a squalid brothel like 'The Cemetery', on the slope behind Point Camp, to a ménage 'up the yama', the generic location for the scattered community of kept women living on the mountain sides behind Kure. But it was one that often led all the way back to Australia, to shared lives that have lasted throughout the long decades since.

CHAPTER FOURTEEN

Brides of Japan

T he Western-male stereotype of the Japanese woman has always differed slightly from her eroticised counterparts in other parts of Asia. Added to her allure as Oriental forbidden fruit has been the appreciation of her sense of loyalty and obedience to her husband and 'lord'. This is not simply a Western male fantasy. The precepts set down in the neo-Confucian, late-17th-century ethical treatise the *Onna Daigaku*, or 'Great Learning for Women', have never been totally discarded in Japan. They provide a kind of code of domestic practice that makes acquiring a Japanese wife a beguiling prospect. 'If unvarying obedience, acquiescence, submission, the utter absorption of her personality into that of her husband, constitute the ideal of the perfect woman, then the Japanese married women approach so near that ideal as to be practically perfect,' observes the American Orientalist William Elliot Griffis in his influential book *The Mikado's Empire* (1876).[1]

The Mikado's Empire appeared not long before the invention of a myth of Japanese womanhood that has proved almost impossibly seductive for writers seeking to define the Western relationship with Japan. Drawing on Pierre Loti's *Madame Chrysanthemème* (1887), Puccini's 1904 opera *Madama Butterfly* has become a popular metaphor for the US–Japanese encounter. It depicts the relationship of the dashing US naval officer Benjamin Franklin Pinkerton and the fragile 15-year-old ex-geisha Cho Cho San, who falsely believes that her fake 'marriage' with a philandering American will endure. That the famous opera, like Loti's novel, was set in Nagasaki has made it all the more appealing as a narrative that dramatises the self-destructiveness of Japan's post-war embrace of an insouciant America.

The British filmmaker Ken Russell's staging of *Madame Butterfly* in 1983 picked up on this, rejigging and updating the Puccini original by setting it just prior to Pearl Harbour, turning Cho Cho San into a prostitute working in Nagasaki's red-light district, turning Pinkerton into an American opportunist, and ending the opera with a spectacular simulation of the atomic bomb 'Fat Man' falling on the city. The Cho Cho San story is recycled in various Occupation fictions, from the Australian BCOF novels *Sowers of the Wind* and *Pattern of Conquest*, to James Michener's tale of the romance of an American officer and a Japanese woman, *Sayonara: a novel of forbidden love* (1954), to the Australian Steven Carroll's sharply ironic contemporary take on the paradigm in his novel *Momoko* (1994). In Michener's novel, the American officer Gruver admires his Japanese lover Hana-ogi in terms which precisely define the appeal of Japanese womanhood to many Occupationnaires. He sees her as 'the radiant symbol of all that was best in Japanese womanhood: the patient accepter, the tender companion, the rich lover'. Despite the 'cruel privations' of their lives, Japanese women 'remained the most feminine women in the world'.[2]

There was no shortage of Japanese women to fulfil the role of 'tender companion'. John Dower reports that, in the borrowed

English of the day, women who 'flitted indiscriminately from customer to customer' were known as *batafurai*, or 'butterfly'. But there were those – the *onrii*, short for *onrii wan*, or 'only one' – who committed loyally to a single patron, for complex reasons that often included simple pragmatism.[3] To Michi Law, the subject of Keiko Tamura's study of the Japanese war-bride phenomenon *Michi's Memories* (2001), committing to an Australian soldier was 'a show of the feeling in the defeated nation to those of the victorious nation'. Of course she felt strong feelings for her husband-to-be; but she also 'did not want to worry about where the next food and clothes would be coming from'. On occasions, deeper cultural factors compelled the relationships. Just as Cho Cho San proclaimed herself 'an American woman' through her liaison with Pinkerton, many Japanese women identified themselves with the Occupier through intimate relationships. Such is one pernicious effect of Occupation – a conquered people trading their identity for that of the conqueror. In *Pattern of Conquest*, L.H. Evers embodies this state of mind in the manipulative person of Tohana, who enters into multiple relationships with Australians in order to fulfil her dream of escaping Japan. Having lived in Canada with her parents before the war, Tohana convinces herself that she is not, in fact, Japanese at all. 'You don't think I'm a Jap, do you?' she asks her Australian lover.[4]

It is a sure bet that most of the Australians in BCOF had not heard of the *Onna Daigaku* or *The Mikado's Empire*, or even of *Madame Butterfly*. However, many of them came to the conclusion that Japanese women made marvellous wives, whether legal or not. Dependent on the food and other luxuries that the men could secrete for them from service stores, the women displayed a gratifying sense of obligation. Helpfully, the service guidebook *BCOF Bound* conflates what it calls 'commercial love' and marriage in the Japanese context, stating that, commonly, the 'professional' prostitute comes 'from a farmer's or fisherman's family and remains until she accumulates a small dowry, when she returns home, marries, and becomes a good wife'. Douglas Mancktelow, who wound up marrying one of his Japanese girlfriends and eventually emigrating to Canada with her, writes with some exaggeration in his autobiography *Atsuko and the Aussie* (1991) that 'nearly everyone' had what was called a 'set-up'. This was often no more than a room in a rough shack somewhere, where the soldier would venture to nightly, under cover of darkness, returning to camp by daybreak, with the aid of a friendly sentry.[5]

For some Australians, the paragon of obliging Japanese womanhood was represented by the female servants prodigally provided by the military. House girls, sometimes called 'bat girls', were allotted to all officers in the Occupation forces, usually in some form of shared arrangement, as well as to the families of dependants. Civilian employees with officer status and privileges, like the teacher Hal Porter, were also entitled to 'help'. Working in the domestic service of the Occupation was an alternative to walking the streets or working in a brothel – though, inevitably, many servants did sleep with their bosses, either through coercion or compliance.

In early 1947, BCOF Intelligence commented on local scuttlebutt about the house girls, many of whom were married women and mothers, and the 'degrading remarks' (threats, too) made by Japanese men. Yet many of their relationships were decorous. Steve Macaulay has remembered his house girl Masako Yamada as 'less a servant, than a mother figure'. She scolded the men for their untidiness and their drinking, and would tolerate no funny business: 'Masako was not a servile, ever-bowing slave to a man', he writes. It took a while for the RAAF officer James Hawes to become accustomed to the female servants' lack of embarrassment at the proximity of male nudity, but he was appreciative of the constant attention. Writing home, Hawes is brusque and circumspect about the house girls, whom he calls an 'unnecessary luxury' arising from the presence of British and Indians in the Commonwealth contingent. However, upon his return to Australia after 15 months in Japan, his personal girl Hisako (describing herself as his 'wayward servant') wrote him a long and emotional letter bidding farewell to her 'beloved master'.[6]

The complex intensity of the relationship between house girl and Occupationnaire is captured in Hal Porter's short story 'House Girl' (1954), in which Porter describes his servant, Ikuko. A fuller treatment of their transient intimacy, living almost as man and wife, appears in *The Paper Chase*. As his biographer Mary Lord notes, Ikuko was 'the only woman Porter wrote about with genuine tenderness', though the relationship was certainly non-sexual. 'I have loved few people as much,' he writes in *The Paper Chase*, 'and none in the same way.' The depiction of Ikuko oscillates between Porter's characteristic cruelty and the mawkishly sentimental: 'Too ugly to engage the interest of brothel-suppliers', he says in 'House Girl', she had passed through various Occupation hands before landing in his service. But her 'coarse shell' was lit up by the beauty of her 'inner self', reflected by her unaffected charm and, not least, by her selfless dedication to his comfort and happiness.

Porter soon sees her as the embodiment of the classical virtues of Japanese womanhood, which he lists as 'obedience, grace, sweetness, femininity, domestic wisdom'. Conversely, his off-hand and complacent treatment of her reveals some 'unpleasant truths' about himself, as a reflection of the master–servant, Occupier–Occupied relationship generally. Their agonising sayonaras are described with some sensitivity in *The Paper Chase*. Porter was returning to Australia; thus, Ikuko was soon to be out of work, 'back on the market'. Dressed in her best kimono, she hands him a present, which he opens on the aeroplane home. It contains a piece of silk that had been her first going-out sash as a little girl, and two letters written on paper provided by the Australian Comforts Fund. One is a letter of thanks from her father, thanking Porter for his kindness to his daughter (her mother had been killed by the Hiroshima bomb); the other, also a letter of thanks from her brother, signed 'Chihiro Sakamoto'. To his shame, Porter realises that he had never bothered to find out Ikuko's family name.[7]

The semi-permanent and permanent sexual and emotional liaisons were much more problematic and, predictably, provide compelling subject matter for the BCOF novelists. Many of them were initiated out of a combination of chivalry and pragmatism. In Hungerford's *Sowers of the Wind*, the central character, the officer Rod McNaughton, buys his love-interest Fumie out of her contract in one of the dance halls in Kure, and 'shacks up' with her in a room 'up the hill'.

The dance halls, as Hungerford recalls in his Occupation memoir 'Tourist with Haiku', were worked by destitute girls, many from Hiroshima or the surrounding villages, who were staked to bed-and-board by the management, sleeping in large dormitories. The girls were proud not to have become prostitutes, but they were trapped in a form of enslavement that often resulted in sexual relations with their clients, anyway. McNaughton is genuinely fond of Fumie, thinks her a 'nice little thing', and had been hankering for something more than 'someone for the night'. But his interests were also mercenary. Fumie was happier in a place of her own, but it was an arrangement that was 'cheaper' for him, as he was 'paying out dough at the dance-hall, and that swine was getting most of it'. According to his biographer, the fictional relationship was based on Hungerford's own experience. Hungerford had moved in with a Japanese woman he had met in a Kure dance hall, an upper middle-class girl from a naval family, whose husband, also in the navy, had been lost in a submarine somewhere off Singapore. He enjoyed 'the most sexually fulfilling period' of his life, though marriage was never on the cards: 'He made his position plain at the start of his relationship'.[8]

In *Sowers of the Wind*, the experienced Digger Norm Craigie, who counsels the younger McNaughton on his relationship, sees it as 'loneliness and hunger masquerading as love', only made possible by the Occupation. 'God almighty, in ordinary circumstances, they wouldn't have given each other a second look, but now Fumie wanted food and Rod wanted Fumie, and no question of moral consideration entered into it'. Many of the liaisons were simply expedient. The attitude, put bluntly and colloquially in *Pattern of Conquest*, was 'love 'em and leave 'em'. Captain Truscott, an Australian on leave in Tokyo in Porter's *A Handful of Pennies*, meets a cabaret dancer called Imiko and, together, they enjoy the proverbial whirlwind romance. Within a few hours of first meeting, 'they had assessed their feelings as love, for both were romantics'. The arrangement is mutually convenient. Imiko, his first sexual conquest, relieves the Australian's 'homesickness of the spirit', and she is given a leave-pass from quasi-prostitution. But when Truscott receives a telegram informing him of his promotion and imminent return home, he unhesitatingly abandons her. Porter draws a laboured parallel between Imiko and the legendary Okichi, Townsend Harris's concubine who, rejected by her foreign lover and shunned by her community, eventually drowns herself.[9]

But it is the Madam Butterfly analogy that is most consistently appealing to the novelists. *Sowers of the Wind* ends with McNaughton sailing 'Pinkerton-like' out of Kure Bay, leaving behind his broken-hearted Japanese girl. Aboard ship is the Jap-hater Weisman, who had himself left behind a Japanese woman and their baby. Weisman informs McNaughton what everyone but the complacent father-to-be knows: Fumie was pregnant. The novel concludes with the appalled McNaughton's mind being invaded by nightmarish images of his hybrid progeny held hostage to a Japanese future, of his son dragging a toy boat 'in an open Kure sewer, sucking on a bit of boiled sweet-potato', or his daughter 'living and dying in the filth of a Jap fisherman's bed'. That was the great taboo – not the fact of mating with, or even marrying, a Japanese, but of breeding with them. 'There must be no children', Norm Craigie had told McNaughton; Fumie was 'a nice girl, but yellow'.[10]

The reference to 'yellow', with its echo of the Yellow Peril, is culturally loaded. On the Australian cultural colour chart, 'whiteness' is a signifier of like humanity. In Larry Lacey's compilation of reminiscences, *BCOF: an unofficial history* (1995), an Australian veteran measures the time taken for an Occupationnaire to enter into a sexual alliance with a Japanese woman according to how 'white' the woman looked. 'I had been in Japan long enough for Japanese girls to be very white', he remarks. 'In an extreme case girls would be white in less than a day. Normally, the effect was total within three months.' Colonial-Australian phobias of inter-mixing with the Asian hordes were still prevalent in the post-war period. *Sowers of the Wind* dramatises a racial trauma in evidence at least as far back as Carlton Dawe's novel *A Bride of Japan*, published in 1898, when Australian racial anxieties were at their most feverish. In *A Bride of Japan*, interbreeding is treated through the disgraceful marriage of a Japanese temptress – alternately described as 'a delicately dainty morsel of orientalism' and 'a piece of tinseled heathenism' – and a Britisher (in colonial fiction, most Australian heroes became identified as 'British' as soon as they left their native shores), who saw himself as 'a white man who had sold his birth-right' by fathering a 'mongrel' child. The child dies, and the woman does too, but not before this deathless rewording of Kipling: 'Yellow is yellow and white is white, and between the two flows a river of conflicting currents.'[11]

Many Australians had a cavalier attitude to the consequences of their relationships with Japanese women. T.B. Millar's Intelligence duties with the 67th Battalion often had him dealing with the irate fathers of young Japanese women who had become pregnant to Australian soldiers. Oddly enough, they would storm into his office demanding to see the same man, a 'Private Ned Kelly'.[12] The large numbers of abandoned mixed-race children is one of the saddest, yet most symbolic, aspects of the Occupation. In June 1946, SCAP took offence when, barely ten months after the coming of the American troops, Japanese radio announced the birth of the first child of mixed Japanese-American parentage as 'the first Occupation present'.

According to Yukiko Koshiro, the presence of illegitimate (or even legitimate) mixed-race children became a consensual taboo subject on both Japanese and American sides as a product of the shared racism that lay behind the diplomatic veneer of the US–Japan friendship. Very few stories on the mixed-race babies appeared in the local press during the Occupation – a silence that was lifted after SCAP eased censorship policies in 1949, though there was still no official census taken. Estimates of their numbers vary wildly. The Japanese Division of Health and Welfare Statistics cited a figure of around 3500 as of February 1953; however, Miki Sawada, who in 1948 established an orphanage (the Elizabeth Sanders Home) for racially mixed children near the town of Oiso in Kanagawa Prefecture, believed that there were up to 200,000 children fathered by American servicemen alone.[13]

Definitive numbers of Japanese children fathered out of wed-lock by BCOF servicemen are difficult to come by. A report in 1960 gave the figure of those effectively abandoned by Australian servicemen as 'at least 103', along with a number of infants sired by British, New Zealanders, and Indians. The year before, a survey undertaken by the Japanese branch of the ISS, the International Social Service, identified 52 Australian-fathered children actually living in the Kure area. But in a documentary on the 'Kure Kids', screened on Australian television in August 2005, Walter Hamilton speaks of 'more than 100 mixed-race children of Australian paternity'. The ISS Kure case file, he remarks, 'remains full to overflowing'. 'Disowned by White Australia and scorned in the land of their birth', these mixed-race people, now deep into middle age, constitute what Hamilton calls the 'hidden legacy' of the Occupation.[14]

For hundreds, perhaps thousands, of Japanese women left liter-ally holding the baby, the Madame Butterfly analogy was no joke. In 1947, the YWCA welfare worker Joan Haigh visited a Christian orphanage mostly run by European nuns, located in Beppu in Kyushu. She was moved by the sight of such 'poor little scraps of flotsam and jetsam', some of them 'entirely Western in appearance', including an Australian, as well as 'a bull headed Yank if ever there was one', and 'one little negroid fellow'. 'It is bad enough to be an orphan in Japan,' Haigh writes, 'but much more so to be an "occupation baby"'. They are 'the lowest rung on the ladder'. Nonetheless, Haigh's sympathies lie rather more with the 'angelic women' who look after them than with the infants themselves. The attitude of the Australian government was one of indifference, both at the time and for years afterwards. When in 1960 an international church organisation sought financial help from the Menzies government for a support fund for the half-Australian children left behind, the request was denied. The government then relented in 1962, and some money filtered through for several years thereafter, augmented by the Ferguson Fund, a private, charitable fund named for a Melbourne businessman moved by the plight of the mixed-race children on a private visit to Japan in the 1950s.[15]

Stigmatised by their communities, many of the mothers endured a very hard time. Yet some Japanese women who entered into liaisons with the Australian Occupationnaires did so with their eyes open. There was a shortage of Japanese men, and those who were around seemed to Michi Law to be 'dragging dark shadows with them'. By contrast, the Australians were open, happy, and enjoying themselves. They also had money. Michi knew her relationship with her Australian husband Gus was tenuous. He was young and footloose, had casual affairs with other women, and sometimes 'made it clear that he did not want to be tied down with a wife and children'. She had heard of Australian soldiers leaving their women behind in Japan and never seeing them again. However, she wanted children, as they would give her 'something to live for'. In her late 20s, she was getting on, and the prospects of marrying a Japanese man and having children with him were becoming dim. After he left for Australia in December 1951, Gus made good on his promise to have their relationship formally recognised in his homeland. Reunited with his wife and two children, they sailed as a family from Kure to Sydney in March 1953.[16] Others were not so fortunate. Some young women entered into secret marriages performed by sympathetic Shinto priests, which were regarded as expedient rather than binding by the men themselves, who went along for the ride because it was the only way they could be guaranteed a sexual relationship with their girlfriends.

In early 1948, immigration minister Arthur Calwell had reasserted the government's position that no Japanese woman would be permitted to enter Australia, irrespective of whether or not she was the wife or fiancée of an Australian serviceman. The bar applied also to Nisei or Japanese women (of even 'partial descent') holding an American passport or other national papers.[17] The men knew where they stood, and BCOF made it as hard as possible for men to validate their marriages. Couples with a serious mutual commitment had almost insurmountable obstacles placed in their way. Military authorities deemed the Shinto weddings a punishable breach of discipline. Neither the chaplains nor even the Australian consul could marry the couples, as the Australian government had not passed a Foreign Marriages Act.

Civil marriage performed by the British consul in Japan was possible under British law, but army regulations compelled a soldier to apply to his commanding officer for permission. This was the mistake made by a young Australian signalman, John Henderson, in early 1948. Henderson had married a young university graduate, Mary Kasahi Abe, by Shinto rites. With his wife pregnant, and worried about the legality of the Shinto ceremony, he sought to be married by the battalion chaplain, the well-known BCOF identity Padre Laing. Laing's duty was to inform military command, and Henderson was peremptorily repatriated. The officer given the task of putting the order into effect related, 40 years later, that someone at BCOF HQ had decided to make an example of him. This was easily achieved, as he was a low-ranking, demoralised youngster of no consequence. A 'thin, frail-looking lad', Henderson was reduced to tears upon hearing the news. Accompanied by the padre and two MPs, he was put on the *Kanimbla* and locked in the brig to be returned to Australia, the father of a baby daughter whom he never got to see.[18]

Henderson's treatment illustrates the bloody-mindedness of post-war Australia. During the debacle, and while his family was receiving abusive anonymous mail for supporting their son, the papers were full of photographs of radiantly smiling British migrant families arriving in Sydney. These were the kinds of people Calwell wanted to boost Australia's population at a time when Japan was getting back on its feet. Its population had risen by 1.5 million in 1947, he noted anxiously. (Some of these new-born were half-Australian, but never mind.) Calwell played to the crowd, stating that, while there were living relatives of the men who suffered at the hands of the Japanese, 'it would be the grossest act of public indecency to permit a Japanese of either sex to pollute Australian or Australian-controlled shores'.[19] What an irony: John Henderson had himself suffered, directly and not vicariously, from Japanese wartime brutality. He had laboured on the Burma–Thailand Railway, no less, and later in the coalmines in Japan. There, he had been befriended by a guard who handed him food, including small gifts from his sister, treats such as sweets, and rice cakes. The very reason Henderson decided to volunteer for BCOF after the war was that he wanted to meet his benefactress. He did, they became strongly attached, and they married – and now, his own government had decided that her presence would 'pollute' Australia.

There is a sad postscript to this story. Despite his promises, Henderson never returned to his Japanese family. He had asked a couple of his army mates remaining in Japan to keep a friendly eye on his wife in his absence; in the meantime, his parcels and letters stopped after some months. Years later, in late 1953 or early 1954, one of them returned to Kure after completing his service in Korea, and met the woman, by chance, downtown near the railway. She was with her pimp, having been reduced to prostitution, with a mixed-race child, in order to survive.[20]

In March 1952, with a belated but imminent peace treaty with Japan, and with patchy but intensifying public sympathy, Harold Holt, the immigration minister in the Menzies Liberal government, lifted the blanket Australian ban on the Japanese wives – after police screening to weed out any prostitutes, communists, criminals, and psychiatric cases that might be lurking among them. But several lives had already been wrecked. BCOF memoirists and novelists relate the distressing sight of handcuffed Australian soldiers being led onto ships at the Kure wharf, shouting promises to women. There was the notorious case of the forcibly repatriated Frank Loyal Weaver, who lived up to his middle name by smuggling himself back to Japan no less than seven times (and serving time in prison for it) in order to be with his wife, whom he wedded in a Shinto ceremony. Weaver had even sought to renounce his Australian citizenship and take a Japanese name, but to no avail. Eventually, his wife gave up on him and found someone else. Unfortunately, Weaver was a dodgy character, a known miscreant and mischief-maker who had spent much of his time absent without leave in Japan. Arthur John, a tolerant man, had no time for him – one of Weaver's exploits included burgling his office and stealing his library on Japan.[21]

Other cases were more tragic. Two days before his enforced repatriation, Douglas Mancktelow's best mate Bill and Bill's pregnant girlfriend Toshiko threw themselves in front of a train. The Australian government changed its policy on the Occupation marriages just four months later. Evidently, this was not an isolated case. In May 1948, a Japanese woman committed suicide by being run over by a train at Kaitaichi. At the time, she was in the company of an Australian soldier with whom she had been living and who had been absent without leave for a week. According to the official report, he had made a 'death pact' with her, but changed his mind at the last minute. After being taken into custody, the Australian was admitted, hysterical (but very alive), to the local military hospital.[22]

A few Australians stayed on with their Japanese wives. The best known of these is James Beard, largely because Hal Porter used him as the eponymous 'Mr Butterfry' in a short story of that name published in 1970. (Porter found it impossible to resist making a joke out of the Japanese difficulty pronouncing the letter 'l'.) In 'Mr Butterfry', Porter's surrogate narrator meets an old friend from the Occupation, nicknamed 'Blue', in a Tokyo beer hall that had become a famous haunt for expatriate Australians. They haven't seen each other for 18 years, from the days when Porter was living in the officers' mess in Kure and Blue was a corporal wooing his major's house girl (when he wasn't dealing in the black market). Now, Blue is a sales representative for a foreign-commodities company. He has married the house girl, fathered two girls, and made money in real estate. Blue invites Porter back to his home to meet his wife and the two 'half-caste' daughters, whose exotic appearances have earned them fame on television as photographic models. But Blue is a pathetic figure, a con-man who has conned himself into believing in some faux dream of Japanese prosperity, an outsider in a country that despises him, a man desperately seeking the companionship of a compatriot. As the Australian academic and long-time Japan resident Gregory Clark has commented, 'Blue' Beard bears little resemblance to Porter's 'obscure anti-hero'. His marriage to Sadako was a success, and one of his model daughters had married the grandson of Japanese prime minister Ichiro Hatoyama, while the other had married into the family that controlled Japan's biggest tyre company. Both young women were 'completely bicultural', and Beard was comfortably and harmoniously integrated into Japanese society.[23]

Newcastle-born Reg Clancy was another Australian to make a life in Japan. His is one of those stranger-than-fiction stories of the Occupation that provide a stirring reminder of what a singular historical event it was. In mid-1942, Clancy had managed to enlist in the army at the age of 15. While serving in New Guinea from 1943 to 1944, he was wounded, which led to the discovery that he was under-age, after which he was immediately discharged. After a stint in the merchant navy (serving for a time with the US Army Transportation Services), he rejoined the army and ended up in Japan with BCOF in October 1946, working in Canteens – first in Kure and later, from July 1947, at the large issue point at the Ebisu Camp in Tokyo.

In Tokyo, he met his future wife Kimie Ono, who was employed at the camp as a copy typist. Their relationship blossomed, and they started going to the movies or, sometimes, merely travelling around and around the city on the Yamanote line encircling central Tokyo, just to be together. After Kimie transferred to Yokohama to work for the Americans, their meetings become harder to arrange. Worried about the dreadful possibility of a foreign boyfriend, her family had determined that she must marry a Japanese. A go-between was engaged to have her meet prospective husbands. Sometimes Reg and Kimie would meet at a suburban station on her way back from Yokohama and would sit and talk in the grounds of a local temple. It was a bittersweet time. The family pressure for her to choose a Japanese husband grew.

Then, in the summer of 1948, they went on a day trip to the cool mountains outside Tokyo. At a Buddhist temple, they told their troubles to a monk, who turned out to be an American-born Nisei who had been interned in the US during the war and later deported to Japan. Moved by the young couple's story, the monk married them on the spot. Not surprisingly, her family was outraged after she summoned the courage to tell them she had been betrothed to an Australian corporal whom they had never met. However, they accepted him into the family, and he lived secretly with them until his discharge came through in June 1950. A meeting with the Australian businessman Roy Bowen, one of the many Western wheeler-dealers who gravitated to Occupied Japan, led Reg and his wife to move to Kobe, where he managed a trading-company store for Bowen during the day and a club called the 'Morocco' at night.

In 1957, Reg set up his own establishment, 'Clancy's Bar', in Kobe, mainly serving the foreign tourist and expatriate communities. He became a local celebrity, known as 'the big man with the little bar'. In the meantime, their two sons were educated at the Marist Brothers International School in Kobe. Eventually, the family returned to Australia in 1973, 27 years after Clancy's arrival in Kure, and after a long battle with the government to have their children recognised as Australian citizens. But Japan still beckoned. In 2005, around the time that Reg sent me his highly detailed typescript of his life, he told me that he and his wife had revisited there on 14 occasions since.[24] Reg Clancy and his wife made the exemplary Australian–Japanese BCOF marriage. Indeed, they were wedded to each other exhaustively. Their spontaneous wedding in the temple on the hot summer's afternoon outside Tokyo was followed by a Japanese civil marriage at the Hyogo Prefecture Office in Kobe, then again at the British consulate and, finally, after Kimie's conversion to Catholicism, by a wedding in Kobe's Sacred Heart Church. Four times! In the end, they were so thoroughly and comprehensively wedded that no one, not even the Australian government, could complain.

CHAPTER FIFTEEN

Coming to Terms

It is fair to say that BCOF contained few multitalented men of the ilk of Sir Richard Burton, scholar and sexologist. Sexual knowledge was the customary way for Australians to come to terms with Japan; language was the path less chosen. Of course, knowing some rudimentary Japanese was a means to a highly desired end. To Andy Waller in *Sowers of the Wind*, the only Japanese words worth knowing were those pertaining to sex and the black market. Conversely, the desire of Japanese girls to increase their English proficiency was merely a prelude to a fling. As one veteran remembered in 1993, the request 'will you teach me English?' was 'rapidly consummated with teaching and bedding'. Even the geisha deigned to use some English to communicate with the foreigners. In an Australian newspaper article designed to clear up the misapprehension that she was 'a lady of easy virtue', Peter Russo observed, in March 1948, that the geisha had adapted to the Occupation by 'learning to smatter English for the benefit of the lonely GIs'. Courting in Occupied Japan was a clumsy business, involving a great deal of rummaging through dictionaries. But language proved no barrier to desire. As T.A.G. Hungerford recalls in 'Tourist with Haiku', it was 'astonishing how much could be managed with a few words of Japanese on one side, a few words of English on the other, and a phrase-book in between'. What the girls he met in the dance halls couldn't express verbally, 'they'd make clear with eyes, hands and expressions,' he says. 'Which made for very lively times under [sic] the *futon*.'[1]

Allan Clifton's capabilities as a Japanese speaker were often called upon by the men to facilitate their couplings, which became a matter of some dissention, as the women ignored the clumsy advances of their suitors in favour of this rare Australian who fluently spoke in their own tongue. Douglas Mancktelow says he had 'the time of his life' being 'worshipped' by the girls because he had 'mastered' the language. There is an element of cocksure big-noting here, though Michi Law has recalled that one of the reasons she fell for her future husband Gus was his smattering of Japanese. Soldiers involved in ongoing liaisons with local girls would bring Clifton their love letters to translate, some of which were 'pure poetry' – literally so, for several would contain quotations of romantic clichés from anthologised Japanese verse. Their suitors' responses, wearily converted into Japanese by Clifton, were 'pretty crude efforts by comparison': the men's protestations of undying love were not as constant as they would have had their girlfriends believe; similarly, some of the passionate outpourings of the women were not reserved for one man alone.[2]

Clearly, proficiency in Japanese helped facilitate a committed relationship. The BCOF linguist Les Oates met his wife Tsuyako in his line of work in early 1949, and they were eventually wedded in a Japanese Christian church in Kure, following a marriage at the British consulate in Kobe. But several successful marriages managed to scale the language barrier. Reg Clancy never learned much Japanese, despite residing in the country with his wife for nearly 30 years; and after well over 20 years of marriage, James

Beard, Porter's 'Mr Butterfry', still relied on his bilingual daughters and a set of simple phrases to communicate with his family.[3]

During the Occupation, all servicemen acquired a few of the common Japanese idioms, often deliberately butchered for comic effect. *Arigato* ('thank you') became "Arry's garters', and *do itashimashite* ('don't mention it') turned into 'don't touch the moustache'. The Army Education Service assiduously publicised its Japanese conversation classes at its headquarters, Kure House, and tried to convince the men that the legendary difficulty of the language was 'greatly exaggerated'. But the majority remained intimidated by its seemingly unfathomable strangeness, and most resisted a serious attempt to learn it. This had more deleterious consequences than simply making it harder to pick up women. A 1947 intelligence report observing the force's 'indifference towards Japanese institutions and people as a whole' determined that this was at least partly due to the 'unusual complexity' of the Japanese language, which formed 'a barrier to all but superficial contacts'. Les Oates recalls that the extensive pidgin Japanese used by the Occupationnaires usually involved no more than adding 'o' to an English word.[4] This habit placed them in distinguished company: legend has it that, stationed in Italy late in World War II, the English novelist Evelyn Waugh comically used the same tactic to communicate with Italians.

Yet many of the Australians had a serious go at learning Japanese. Major Arthur John notes more than 250 enrolments in the language classes run by army education as early as April 1946.[5] Some of the translators and interpreters who were assigned to CSDIC contained some formidable linguists, such as Allan Clifton, D.C.S. Sissons, and Les Oates, who had all studied in the army's Japanese language school in Melbourne before their overseas postings. But others had learned the language by themselves, on the job. Keith Boothroyd was a member of a training battalion in the Cowra area at the time of the infamous prison breakout by Japanese POWs in August 1944. Boothroyd believed that the tragedy could have been averted if the Australian guards had been able to communicate with a prison informer. From that moment, he developed a 'desperate urge to learn the Japanese language', which he later commenced in Rabaul. After further training in Australia, he served with CSDIC in Japan, helping process the masses of repatriated Japanese soldiers returning from the theatres of war on mainland Asia.[6]

In Japan, one of Boothroyd's CSDIC colleagues was the Berlin-born Alex Weaver, one of the more exotic, resourceful, and durable characters to serve in BCOF. Weaver was in Kenya with his parents at the outbreak of World War II. At the time, this was not a good place for a German to be. Posing as a German-speaking Pole, he made his way to New Zealand by ship and, eventually, managed to get himself into the AIF, aged 19, in 1942. He served in New Britain in the final months of the war, enlisted in BCOF, then remained in the professional army after the Occupation, serving as a platoon commander in Korea. He was still touring as a 'soldier of fortune', as he sardonically calls himself (albeit a decorated one), in Vietnam in the later 1960s.

Like Boothroyd, Weaver availed himself of the services of Japanese-language teachers in Rabaul and Morotai while waiting to embark for Japan, studies that he says he pursued 'on a constant and concentrated basis without any respite'. Weaver's linguistic ability helped him not merely to get by in Japan, but also to capitalise on the opportunities for cultural contact that came his way. On an Intelligence assignment in Miyoshi, north of Hiroshima, working in close cooperation with the municipal police and officials, Weaver found himself 'lavishly entertained' by local families and bonding with the community 'in a most pleasing manner', going cormorant fishing, partaking in the tea ceremony, and learning about Japanese culture at what he calls 'grass root level'. The ability to speak the language assisted in connecting with the people. Ralph Perrott, who arrived in Japan a postal clerk attached to 34th Brigade HQ before moving into the education service, reflects that learning the language made it easier to link with Japanese 'in all walks of life', and helped them accept him more easily.[7]

Ultimately, of course, coming to terms with the recent enemy was more about being receptive and bearing goodwill than about having language skills or cultural acumen. It was always going to be harder to achieve rapprochement with Japanese men than with the women. Writing in the *Sydney Morning Herald* in April 1952, just after the decision to permit the war brides to enter Australia, Stephen Kelen dissociated these female 'New Australians' from Japan from the warmongers and brutes who had terrorised the region for years. 'After all,' he wrote, 'it is never women who wage wars – they only suffer, and pay for man's folly no matter to what race or country they belong'.[8] Relationships with Japanese males were wary, bristling with subdued, but potentially volatile, antagonisms. If nothing else, the Occupation drove home the point about who won the war, and many of the repatriated Japanese soldiery, defeated in all manner of ways, remained sullen and resentful. 'The returning troops hated us,' asserts Keith Lobb, a driver with 123 Transport Platoon, though his memories may be coloured by his own undying animosity. Lobb's most cherished memory of Japan remains the amount of damage done to the country – 'they deserved it'.[9]

Many Australians were able to work off their animosity, often in the most literal sense. The Commonwealth forces employed thousands of Japanese, around 40,000 by some estimates, or at least as many as the force itself. They performed a range of jobs: the women in mainly domestic or clerical tasks, the men as manual labourers and in various kinds of semi-skilled and skilled work. The workers formed themselves into unions, such as the Kure District Union of Occupation Workers, and sometimes went on strike for better wages, to the consternation of BCOF authorities who, as Christine de Matos has noted, were acutely concerned, right though the Occupation, about the power and pervasiveness of communist influence. But working cohesively with the Japanese had a remarkably beneficent effect on some individual servicemen. B.L. Robinson went to Japan in the winter of 1947 as a 19-year-old instrument fitter who associated the Japanese with atrocities, and who expected hostility. Though maintaining the view that the women were 'a different species to the men', he changed his mind about the males, impressed by the technical ability and 'general friendliness' of the tradesmen.[10]

Australian soldiers, like the rifleman Halton Stewart, started seeing 'through non-military eyes'. This took time. At first, Les Semken remembers, 'we were frightened of them and they were frightened of us'. Through the helpful use of an interpreter, the Australians in his work unit got to know a bit more about the men they were working with. One of the Japanese crew had flown in the Pacific: 'here was a bloke who had been trying to kill us … [but] I was never threatened'. Semken's dangerous work in bomb disposal brought him into contact with a Japanese technician who he knew simply as 'Joe'. One day, sprinting to safety after setting up a detonation on one of the biggest repositories of explosive ordnance remaining in Japan, at Okunoshima, Semken fell and sprained his ankle. Joe dragged him to safety around a promontory. Without his intervention, he recalled, he would have been 'history'. Semken and his workmate 'came to accept each other as people … a couple of fellows doing a job', he says. 'Joe was my friend.' What had divided the Australians and the Japanese also united them. 'We couldn't forget the war,' remembers Keith Reeves, 'but I guess neither could they'.[11]

The altruism of many of the BCOF servicemen is striking. 'We learned to co-operate with our old enemy and they learned to co-operate with us,' observes Richard Hines. For Hines, it had been a long road to Japan from Broken Hill, where he was living upon his enlistment in the Second AIF in 1942. Hines was in Balikpapan in Borneo at the cessation of hostilities, where he had learned a smattering of Japanese from members of the defeated army. Curious to know more about them, he volunteered for BCOF duty in the Royal Australian Engineers. In Kure, he met and married his wife of over 40 years. Looking back today, he recalls: '[It was] a great experience. I was young, I wanted to make things better and I think we did.'[12]

Japanese employed by BCOF tend to give glowing, even slightly skewed accounts of the Occupation, for it threw them a lifeline. Like many Japanese, Shizuo Inoue was facing the bleak prospect of penury, and was grateful for the job as a labourer that BCOF provided, first at the depot in Kaitaichi and then at the 165 Radar Station in Hiroshima, where he fatefully met Gordon Edwards. In the words of Reverend Frank Coaldrake, the employees were 'Occupation-conscious' or, even, 'Occupation-happy!' Just the sort of people, in other words, that the authorities liked visitors from Australia to see. When T. Inglis Moore went to Japan in early 1948 to lecture to BCOF personnel, Coaldrake took him around his Odawara parish to meet the locals. In Moore's six weeks in Japan, these were the first 'truly' Japanese people that he had come across. These people – the 'real Japan' – had never given a thought to even meeting one of the interlopers and, Coaldrake implies, harboured rather less sanguine feelings about the Occupation.[13]

Yet many Australian–Japanese relationships, such as the mateship formed by Gordon Edwards and Shizuo Inoue while working together in Hiroshima in 1947 and 1948, were built on a basis of mutual respect. One of the most affecting partnerships involved the Townsville-born Foster Barton, a corporal in the British Commonwealth Movements Group, and Fujikane Noboru. In March 1948, as a 21-year-old corporal, Barton was posted as a railway officer at the village of Mitajari, the railway station servicing the Bofu airfield, home to the RAAF's 81 Fighter Wing. The airfield being some kilometres away, Barton lived in a substantial Japanese mansion just outside the town, looked after by a cook, a housemaid, and a yardman. Several Japanese, including interpreters and baggage boys, worked around the clock at the railway office. Fujikane Noboru, or 'Fuji', as Barton called him, acted as the Australian's liaison officer. In his mid-20s, he had served as a sergeant with the Japanese army in China for four years before returning to Japan and joining the railways. Abandoned by his wife, he lived with his young son and a woman (whom he later married) in some stables nearby. Foster and Fuji were almost inseparable, working and socialising, going swimming in a local river, and communicating in their own language, a pidgin that no-one else could fathom.

The two lost contact after Barton returned home in March 1949. When he eventually revisited Japan in 1985, he headed straight for Mitajiri, by then absorbed into the industrial sprawl of greater Bofu. Miraculously, he was able to track Fuji and his wife down, and the intervening years instantly fell away. Local newspapers recorded the reunion. Numerous reciprocal visits ensued, the families seemingly shuttling between Japan and Australia, before Fuji died of a stroke on Christmas Day 1990. On the final day of Foster's last trip to Japan, in 1994, he sat in the rain by Fuji's memorial, saying goodbye. At virtually that very moment, their old Mitajiri railway station received its last train; a new station had been built. 'Fuji was the brother I never had and his soul will be with me forever,' Barton says.[14]

THE WOMEN were abundant in number, and abundantly charming; even some of the men were okay, once you got to know them. But it was the children, swarming throughout the BCOF areas, who most encouraged Australian empathy. They were dirty and bedraggled, perpetually hungry, snotty-nosed, and carrying all manner of infections, but the soldiers found them irresistibly likeable, and they were instrumental in softening attitudes to the Japanese and Japan. The sight of starving kids scrounging in the food bins and slop buckets placed outside the mess halls is one of the most insistently recorded memories of the Occupation. So too is the image of the mute terror with which many of these traumatised infants first confronted the conqueror, and the memory of the slow process of winning their trust. 'We had blokes with us who were good linguists,' remembers one veteran. 'Any attempt to talk to the children was met with the same blank stare.' As late as the 1990s, he was still haunted by mental pictures of them.[15]

Personal encounters with the children could have a mutually therapeutic counter-effect, providing an antidote to the pervasive squalor of post-war Japan. M.D. Guppy recalls visiting an orphanage, armed with sweets. 'You should have seen their eyes light up,' he remarks in his diary. 'I know we regretted leaving the place.' Dan Hart recounts the story of a Christmas party thrown by the 65th Battalion for the children of one of Onomichi's main schools. High on a hill above a local park where the kids had gathered and a band played, three Santa Clauses bearing great boxes appeared down a steep track. They were not as sober as Santa Clauses are supposed to be. One of the red-robed trio, which included the ex-POW Allan 'Bluey' Chick, teetered, and fell headlong down the slope. The snowflakes fell, the 'presentos' were distributed, and Hart was 'nearly crushed to death' by a happy mob of kids.[16]

Getting on with the children, it must be said, made highly emotive propaganda. At the end of *Watch Over Japan* (1947), one of two Occupation documentaries directed by Geoffrey Collings for the Australian National Film Board, the narrator intones that 'children are the real rays of the Japanese rising sun'. Guided by the Occupation, it is they who would forge a democratic New Japan, 'so that one day, perhaps, she will walk hand-in-hand with the peace-loving nations of the world'. The final scene shows the men of BCOF walking hand-in-hand with children through a sunlit village street.[17]

But individual Australians sought constructive, as well as rhetorical, engagement with the often piteous plight of local children, especially the orphans. After more than 20 infants were discovered living in a bombed-out shelter in Kure, Shirley Garrett, the wife of one of BCOF's most senior officers, helped find a building to house them, women to look after them, and teachers to school them. Instances of such practical charity abound. In December 1947, through the good offices of an Australian stationed in Kaitaichi, a Warrant Officer named Biggins, BCOF provided the materials to build five classrooms at a primary school in a Hiroshima district, Senda, which had been burnt to the ground by the bomb. The children had been forced to study in the open air, braving the biting winds. A monument to the efforts of the Australian Occupation forces and Biggins, as 'a bond of goodwill between Japan and Australia', was dedicated at the school in March 1985.[18]

Throughout the Occupation, many Australians visited local schools in their area. The CSDIC operative Eric Saxon recalls how the children loved to speak with a foreigner in their own language; others, like the teenage infantryman C.F. Jarrett, taught English to schoolchildren in return for them teaching him some Japanese.[19] Major Arthur John was a frequent visitor to schools, providing guidance on such issues as coeducation, and factual accuracy in instruction on history and political institutions. The SCAP directive about the dismantling of the old militaristic curriculum was being met, but John recognised the shaky ground the Occupation was on when it sought to erase patriotic sentiment from the Japanese school ground. The national anthems and songs chanted at home and in Britain were hardly pacific. John quotes from 'Land of Hope and Glory': Wider still and wider shall thy bounds be set, God who made thee mighty, make thee mightier yet.[20]

Much of the attention to making amends was focused on Hiroshima, partly through guilt, and partly because the material and moral need was so compelling. This took some surprising forms. Arthur John recalls a benefit concert in a Hiroshima theatre in October 1946, with a visiting Australian soprano and other artists performing to a packed audience. An Australian Occupationnaire gave a speech in Japanese arguing for 'the propagation of culture as a means of forging a peaceful world'; a teenage orphan thanked the performers in English, and some young Japanese dancers dressed in red and black drapes performed a dance representing the burning of Hiroshima.[21] In the aftermath of the catastrophe, an orphanage had been established on the little off-shore island of Ninoshima. Right next door to the orphanage was a detention centre for BCOF miscreants. A director of the children's home, Yukata Kikkawa, has recalled that when the soldiers exercised, the children on the other side of the fence mimicked their movements and called out to them. The prisoners enjoyed their cheeky mockery, passing on some of their modest rations to them, and even buying them sweets. In the early 1950s, Kikkawa-san and an Australian teacher established an Australian–Japanese Friendship Association. The children's home was still going in the 1980s, and several of its graduates had visited Australia.[22]

In a few cases, the Australian commitment to the orphaned children extended beyond Occupation service. Warrant Officer Frank Fisher knew something about being parentless, and about war. Born in 1898, both his parents were dead by the time he was four. He put his age up to serve in the Great War, where he was gassed and wounded in the fighting at Mouquet Farm. A generation later, he put his age down to serve in World War II. In April 1946, he left for Japan aboard the *Manoora*, and served there for three years, living with his wife and three children at Etajima and then Nijimura. Fisher gave practical, as well as financial, assistance to the children at a Hiroshima orphanage while he was in Japan and for some time afterward. His son Bruce retains a letter written in 1952 by the orphanage's founder thanking him for the donation of money and other kindnesses. Fisher corresponded with one orphan, a young girl called Shigeko Akiyama, for several years. Her letters of thanks make affecting reading. In one of them, she appreciatively recounts the day he departed Japan for Australia: 'you patted my head and told me not to cry but stay in good health and study hard'.[23]

CHAPTER SIXTEEN

Cultural Penetrations

I n her history of Australian cultural engagement with Asia, *The Yellow Lady* (1992), Alison Broinowski describes the Occupation of Japan as a lost opportunity. Compared with their more adept and adventurous American counterparts, the Australians refused to explore Japan on its own terms, and so, in her words, 'lost the peace'. 'The Allied Occupation was like a repetition of Commander Perry's arrival in 1853,' she writes:

> Once again Americans were quick to exploit peacetime opportunities by becoming the new Japan experts, in business, education, and culture. Few Australians in the occupation spoke enough to compete with them, and few thought of learning it.

To prove her point, Broinowki makes an unflattering comparison of Tom Hungerford with his 'American double', the American Japanologist Oliver Statler. They were direct contemporaries: both were born in 1915; both served in New Guinea, fighting the

Japanese; and both then joined the Occupation. However, while Statler immersed himself in the country and its traditions for years, eventually penning the classic *Japanese Inn* (1982), Hungerford did his year in Japan, moaned about the place, and went home to write a novel, *Sowers of the Wind*, 'littered in errors in Japanese'. Hungerford is turned into a sadly representative figure; a victim of the 'culturally impoverished inheritance' that Broinowski claims limits the Australian experience of Japan.[1]

It is axiomatic that, at least until the Vietnam War era, Australians were Eurocentric and resistant to Asia, though Broinowski herself unearths a crowd of Asia-literate individuals to confound the generalisation. As the poet Les Murray wrote in 1978, the Asian countries to the north formed 'a band of mysterious darkness' to most antipodean travellers, a twilight zone 'lying between their safe colonial world and the cool green ancestral spaces of ancestral Europe'. Educationally, Asia was the proverbial black hole. 'History' was something that happened in Britain and Europe, where 'civilisation' was also to be found. Barbara Hogg, then a 16-year-old daughter of an RAAF serviceman studying for her Leaving Certificate by correspondence at the Iwakuni dependants' school, laboured over a question on the British Corn Laws that the Victorian Department of Education had set on the examination. She still shudders at the memory. Her experience was typical of generations of Australian students. Even 'Australia' only obtained meaning through its kinship with the Mother Country, which crossed the vast geographical distances. As for Asia, it was off the radar entirely, other than those bits (India, in particular) that were dragooned into the British Empire.[2]

In an article published in the *Argus* in 1940, Peter Russo remarked that ten years' effort interpreting Japan to Australians had impressed on him their lack of interest in Asian peoples and cultures. 'Any man who wants to go to the East to study is regarded as a bit of a freak,' he complained. There is the echo of the cultural martyr here, the contempt of the self-conscious expert who had lost patience with the unappreciative hoi polloi. But it is true that the Australian Occupationnaires went to Japan with a stack of acquired suspicions in their baggage, antagonisms boosted by the recent war. Their view of the world was shaped by a very familiar duality. As Clifton Pugh wrote to his mother in September 1946, 'the longer one is in Japan the more you realise the great gulf between East and West. They can never mix – the minds are so utterly different'. Those who sought to bridge that gulf were seen almost as traitors, not merely to their country, but to an entire ideology of difference. In one of Stephen Kelen's recollections of Japan, an Australian talks caustically of the Occupation equivalent of 'going troppo' in the islands. He calls it going 'Nippo', a madness that overtakes those Australians who are so impressed by the superior cultural virtues of Japan that they aspire to remain behind. 'Nothing Aussie is good enough for them any more,' he sneers.[3]

Yet Broinowski's argument is unfair to Hungerford. To dismiss him as a cultural pauper because he measures lower on some notional barometer of Japanophilia than the obsessive Statler, who ended up living in Hawaii on the basis that it was closer to Japan, seems prescriptive. *Sowers of the Wind* is a no-holds-barred exposé of Australian prejudice. Moreover, Hungerford's autobiographical 'Tourist with Haiku' is directed squarely at the inculcation of cultural learning in Japan, as Hungerford enjoys an enriching friendship with a male Japanese schoolteacher. (Though the friendship is consummated by Hungerford's 'shouting' of a girl for the teacher when they visit a local brothel, which rather confirms suspicions that Australian interests in Japan and the Japanese essentially lay below the waist rather than above the shoulders.) There is no Australian to rival Donald Richie or Faubion Bowers, the one-time interpreter for the forces in New Guinea who used his influence in MacArthur's court in Tokyo to almost single-handedly save the classical repertoire of *kabuki* from the depredations of SCAP censorship. But BCOF was not bereft of individuals able to engage with the Japanese at sophisticated levels, both culturally and linguistically. Of the CSDIC cohort, for example, D. C.S. Sissons went on to become a pioneer in the scholarly field of Japanese/Australian relationships, and he and his colleague Les Oates played constructive roles in the infant, but burgeoning, academic field of Asian Studies in Australia in the post-war period.

Then there is Allan Clifton, one of the most singular individuals of the Occupation from any national branch of the Allied Forces. If *Time of Fallen Blossoms* attacks the cultural ineptitude of Australians in Occupied Japan, it is also a register of his own love affair with the country. Clifton's infatuation with Japan had begun during a family holiday in western Victoria 12 years earlier, when the local village schoolmaster, an Englishman, had scratched some Japanese ideograms on the dirt of a rough, earthen tennis court. Clifton became hooked on the idea of Japan. The country itself had confirmed the attraction. Leaving it by ship at the end of his tour, and returning to what he calls 'spiritual exile', Clifton likens himself to two of the biggest names in the history of the West's dealings with Japan, the early-17th-century English sailor, shipbuilder, and confidante of the shogun, Will Adams, and Japan's great lover and interpreter, Lafcadio Hearn.

The initial Australian arrival in Occupied Japan, disembarking on Kure in the cold of a February morning, had been a reversal of Hearn's famously ecstatic first impressions of Japan, 'seen in the white sunshine of a perfect spring day'. Clifton's arrival home in Sydney was similarly anticlimactic. The moment is registered by his observation of the 'pale-faced painted women' awaiting their menfolk at the dock, women with 'hairy legs, and thin ankles' who shouted to the men on the incoming vessel 'in loud, harsh voices'. The comparison with their decorous, decorative Japanese counterparts is unspoken, but deafening. Clifton spent much of the rest of his life back in Melbourne, working as a proofreader with the daily evening newspaper the *Herald,* married to the artist Nancy Clifton. But his feeling for Japan never left him. Like Adams and Hearn, he died there, after suffering a stroke in Fukuoka in June

A first glimpse of Japan: Australians arrive at Kure port, c. 1946.
(*The Argus* Newspaper Collection of Photographs, State Library of Victoria)

Atomic tourists: Australian soldiers by the 'A-bomb Dome', Hiroshima, c. 1947.
(*The Argus* Newspaper Collection of Photographs, State Library of Victoria)

Security patrol in the Inland Sea: members of the 66th Battalion on Ninoshima, May 1946. (Australian War Memorial, negative number 129959)

Souvenir hunting in Hiroshima, c. 1946. (Argus Newspaper Collection of Photographs, State Library of Victoria)

Shirley Garrett, wife of Brigadier A.R. Garrett, with Kure orphans, c. 1946–47.
(Photograph courtesy of Prudence Garrett Keys)

BCOF on parade: outside the Imperial Palace, Tokyo, May 1950.
(Australian War Memorial, negative number DUKJ3137)

Toasting the birth of Prince Charles: BCOF Commander Lieutenant General Horace Robertson at the Kawana Hotel, with Bruce Fisher and his father, Warrant Officer Frank Fisher, to his immediate right, November 1948.
(Photograph courtesy of Bruce Fisher)

Sukiyaki party at the Kawana Hotel, c. 1947.
(Australian War Memorial, negative number 133189)

Happy days: Gordon Edwards (second from left) and Shizuo Inoue (at rear) with friends,
Hiroshima Prefecture, c. 1947.
(Photograph courtesy of Gordon Edwards)

Love among the ruins: Australian soldier Private Ian 'Robbie' Robertson and Japanese girlfriend, c. 1950.
(Australian War Memorial, negative number PO1813.417)

Hal Porter (fourth from left, front row) with students of the Nijimura School, c. 1949–1950. (Photograph courtesy of Rosemarie Carman)

Cherry-blossom time in Miyajima: BCOF dependants with Japanese domestic staff, undated. (Photograph courtesy of Rosemarie Carman)

Nuclear business: An Australian soldier visits a newly opened bookshop, Hiroshima, c.1947. (*The Argus* Newspaper Collection of Photographs, State Library of Victoria)

Japanese farewell: Major A.W. John, BCOF Education Officer, leaving his Nijimura house with his wife and two children, April 1952. (Australian War Memorial, negative number HOBJ28646)

Brides of Japan: Les Oates (left) with wife Tsuyako, and John Cook with wife Sasayo, aboard the SS *Taiping* bound for Australia, Dec. 1952.
(Australian War Memorial, negative number 148252)

Remembering BCOF: Shizuo Inoue by a BCOF monument, Yoshiura, Japan, Nov. 2006.
(Photograph taken by the author)

1995 while holidaying with Japanese friends. A traditional Buddhist cremation followed, vividly recalled by his son Tony, the well-known *Newsweek* reporter. Tony Clifton had covered a lot of conflicts all over the world and had witnessed some terrible things, but was unprepared, at the Fukuoka crematorium, to be invited to pick at the skeletal remains of his father with a set of chopsticks, in order to garner a few remnants as a memento.[4]

Time of Fallen Blossoms came out in 1950, the same year as the literary critic A.A. Philips coined the phrase 'the cultural cringe' to describe the internalised sense of inferiority that seemed to mark (and perhaps still marks) the Australian sense of national self. *Time of Fallen Blossoms* is full of the cringe, especially when Clifton witnesses Australian misbehaviour at its most embarrassing. When his countrymen ran amok, he wrote, 'no trace of culture, breeding, or restraint was discernible, and one wished that the side-upturned slouch hat did not so unequivocally distinguish' the culprits as Australians. Conversely, Clifton writes immodestly how he 'became known far and wide' in Japan for the justness of his own dealings with the people, and for his knowledge and linguistic skills. After the *Yukan Hiroshima*, the local evening newspaper, asked him to record his impressions of Japan and the atomic bomb, he began to receive fan mail, he says, some from young women. In Hiroshima, Clifton did have something to boast about. For a time, he acted as John Hersey's interpreter while the American journalist toured the city interviewing victims and collecting material for his book describing the horrors of 6 August 1945, which caused such a sensation when published in the *New Yorker* (as the entire issue) in August 1946. Clifton expresses some frustration that Hersey beat him to the punch.[5]

Presumably, Clifton would have concurred with the findings of a BCOF intelligence report stating that, compared with the lack of interest shown by most Occupationnaires, only a 'minority' of 'educated soldiers' appreciated Japan. With a hint of concern, the report noted that these tended to adopt 'a pro-Japanese bias'. It is true that most of the BCOF cohort was poorly educated. These were men whose schooling and youth had been ruinously disrupted by the upheavals of war. They were resistant to learning new languages, cultural as well as literal. It seems that many were really not that interested in learning anything. At the Army Education Service, Major Arthur John came to the rueful conclusion that 'less than half the troops were interested in any educational activity at all'.[6]

Army education did its best to disabuse BCOF troops of mindless prejudice in its weekly (then fortnightly, and finally, monthly) newspaper, which John edited, *The Gen*. From its first issue in August 1946 to its last in March 1951, *The Gen* ran articles on Japanese society, from calligraphy to *zaibatsu*, as well as pieces of topical interest, such as the peace-treaty negotiations, book reviews and theatre reviews (such as those by Hal Porter), along with information concerning the educational programmes being run at Kure House and Point Camp. One of John's colleagues John Thorp, a teacher in civil life who originally set up the Education Centre in Kure, inaugurated a series of articles called 'Know Japan', while also running sessions with the same name on the BCOF Radio Station. On the whole, the articles are much less tendentious than the guidebook *Know Japan*. While noting Japan's unique traits (some of them unpleasant, notably the repressive treatment of its women), they stress the common humanity of the Japanese, and offer a retort to those who scratch their heads at their apparent 'mixture of politeness and brutality'. The Japanese, it is suggested, 'are scarcely less inconsistent' than Christian Europeans, who 'have been known to burn each other alive, hang starving widows for stealing bread and deport young men for poaching rabbits'. One of the 'Know Japan' authors articulates a depth of personal response to Japan that some were too embarrassed to admit. 'Japan, to some, will have been just another stopping-off place on the road to demobilisation,' he states. 'To me, and I know to many others, it has been an invaluable experience: a revelation of a different world'.[7]

BCOF made a concerted attempt to engage in cultural exchange with the local communities. Some of this activity was remedial. The people of Kabe, a town near Hiroshima whose main attraction was a *sake* distillery had, not unreasonably, gained the impression that the Australian forces consisted solely of drunken soldiers being pursued by military police. A concert was held to build bridges. John Thorp gave the obligatory talk on democracy; Arthur John sang some songs, and the gifted Japanese-speaking sergeant John Hanson played piano. Not an awe-inspiring performance, but the audience listened politely and patiently. In return, the locals performed native dances and sang Japanese choral items. British Commonwealth Week, held in December 1948, was a bigger affair. Sponsored by the Hiroshima Prefectural Government, it staged a multitude of events and endless speeches, providing commander-in-chief Robertson with another opportunity to remind the Japanese of their weaknesses, and the need for them to learn from the shining example of the British. The audience was more diverted by an eloquent address given by the distinguished English poet and war writer Edmund Blunden, then a cultural advisor with the UK Mission in Tokyo. A few months earlier, not far from the Kawana Hotel, a monument had been erected to the seafaring Will Adams at Ito (the town with which he is associated), engraved with a limp Blunden verse celebrating 'that man/who first united England and Japan'.[8]

For individual Australians, the best opportunities to learn about, and from, the Japanese came outside these formal occasions, in unofficial (and unlawful) explorations. 'Last night I fraternised!' exclaims the YWCA worker Joan Haigh, as if admitting to an indecent act. Chaperoned by an Australian male friend, a Japanese speaker with a sound knowledge of native customs, her act of recklessness was to visit a Japanese home. Her hostess taught *ikebana*, dancing, and the tea ceremony. The elaborate ritual of the latter is impatiently dismissed as 'palaver'; but Haigh is entranced by her encounter with the Japanese on their private turf. At the other end of the spectrum, the schoolteacher Jean Westmore threw herself into the country's social and literal landscape with abandon. In Japan, she was known as Jean Eastman, an experienced teacher on two years' leave of absence from the NSW Education Department. She was in her late 20s, a divorcee alone in Japan, and a feminist even back then. Posted initially to the Ebisu School for dependants in Tokyo, where she lived at the Marunouchi Hotel, she then went on to the Nijimura dependants' school, whose ex-students vividly remember her today. In addition to her teaching duties at Nijimura, she attended regular Japanese classes, and voluntarily taught Japanese students one night a week. 'I didn't go to Japan to drink in bars with officers,' she told me when I met her in her Sydney apartment in March 2005, a razor-sharp 84-year-old.[9]

In a spirit of outrageous independence, Jean Westmore got out and explored the country. She had an Australian friend called Bill, an interpreter who had learned Japanese 'on the tatami', so to speak. 'I thought if that's the way you learn Japanese, I'll find a Japanese friend,' she said to me. 'I found a young man whose parents had a hotel up in the mountains outside Hiroshima. He was a very nice boy, who had been in the war'. On weekends, she and her friend would travel in Bill's jeep with his girlfriend up to the hotel. 'It was all very proper', she told me with a glint in her eye. Nonetheless, 'a woman on her own goes a long way,' she assured me. Jean also purchased a pushbike and cycled out into the country, staying at inns and with local families, attending festivals, and visiting shrines. Her independent encounters with the Japanese led her to admire 'a fantastic race of people, with character and ideals – a model for us all'.

Experience of the Occupation and her proximity to Hiroshima made her ferociously anti-nuclear and anti-war. She tells the story of her Nijimura house girl, Hiroko Matsumoto, the middle-aged wife of an army officer who had served in Manchuria with the Japanese Occupation, where she herself had unlimited domestic help. In Occupied Japan, Hiroko had been forced into domestic service to support the family. Jean recognised Hiroko's fate as an 'object lesson in the fortunes of war'; the Occupation taught her that 'they' are 'us'. After Japan, Jean Westmore met and married an Australian who had been a prison labourer on the Burma Railway, and went to live and teach in New Guinea for 25 years, where one of her students was the politician Michael Somare. At the age of 63, she ventured to Malaysia as a volunteer teacher, working in an Islamic secondary boarding school near Malacca.[10] Her story shows that genuine (and genuinely lasting) engagement came in ways that cannot be measured through an elitist account of Australian cultural penetrations of Japan.

Jean Westmore's exploits seem positively hell-raising in contrast with the BCOF experiences of Bruce Ruxton, the RSL spokesman whose anti-Japanese rhetoric scarcely softened over more than half a century. But even he succumbed. In Japan, Ruxton, whose epically long stint in BCOF from February 1946 to December 1948 was chiefly distinguished by a short course of instruction in the BCOF School of Cookery, acquired a taste for Japanese flower arrangements. It seems scarcely believable, though another veteran, Norm White, confirms that the men did indeed try their hand at *ikebana*. 'Can you imagine a group of rough-and-tumble young Australian soldiers attending flower arranging classes? Well, we did', he writes.[11]

Norm White, whose very name seems emblematic, provides a telling example of the surprising impact of Occupation service. Too young to have seen active service in the war, Norm had never been out of Sydney when he volunteered. His only brush with the Japanese had been the shocking spectacle of 'battered' Australian POWs returning on troopships from Singapore and Burma, seen during a stint working on the docks. A typical knockabout Australian of his time, Norm was surprisingly receptive to Japan. While in Japan, he attended Japanese language classes at Kure House. Learning the lingo, as he puts it, helped him to explore more of the country, venturing into places normally off limits to

Occupation troops, both personally and also professionally, as he was given a job driving visitors around the BCOF areas. On weekends, he drove his jeep deep into the countryside, where he befriended the local people, casting his net with theirs into the cold mountain rivers and sharing the catch. 'It was an ordeal to do the right thing by our hosts,' Norm readily admits, eating raw fish 'with their eyes staring at you'. But he lived to tell the tale.[12]

Direct encounters with the people could be more than merely recreational; these encounters not only changed the perception of the Japanese but also disturbed the settled and complacent attitudes Australians took to Japan. One evening Colin East, who commanded a company of the 65th Battalion based in Onomichi, east of Kure, took his medical officer, Dan Hart, to the house of a Japanese schoolmistress he had met. Northcott's absurd edict against fraternisation meant that this innocent meeting was illegal. A well-educated woman who spoke good English, their hostess took an iconoclastic view of the Occupation, mischievously suggesting that if the Japanese had won the war, it would have been the Allied leaders, including Churchill, who would have been tried for war crimes, not General Tojo and company. Hart was annoyed by the woman's thinking; at the same time, he was glad she did not bring up the merciless bombing of the German civilian population. To illustrate her cynicism, she sang the Australians a parody of the famous Japanese song 'Kago no Tori' ('Bird in the Cage'), an allegory of the Occupation that began with: 'All alone in the darkness, disregarding old Northcott ...'[13]

THE REBUILDING of Australian national relationships with Japan in the post-war period owes much to members of the BCOF community. The responsiveness of feisty feminists such as Jean Westmore and solid citizens like Norm White was as significant, in its own modest way, as the renewal of diplomatic ties and the clinching of trade deals in the 1950s, after the Occupationnaires had long packed up and gone home. Stephen Kelen was another such individual. Boosted by a body of highly significant writing about both Japan and the Occupation, Kelen's is an extraordinary story. One reason why he was so sympathetic to the Japanese war brides coming to Australia in the early 1950s was because he was a migrant himself.

Born in Hungary in 1912, Istvan (Stephen) Kelen was educated in Budapest and then at a university in Prague, and had travelled to every continent before the war, largely as an international table-tennis champion, of all things. He first lobbed into Australia in 1937, partnering his countryman Miklos Szabados in a series of exhibition matches and competitions with local stars around Australia and New Zealand, apparently captivating audiences wherever they played. In Melbourne, at the long-demolished Wirth's 'Olympia', the brilliant Hungarians played to a packed house of 5000. The Hungarians liked the country so much and were so well received that, after being rendered stateless by refusing to return to Hungary for military service, they both decided to settle in Sydney. Kelen displayed his commitment to his new homeland by enlisting in the army in 1945, belonging to an Intelligence unit in New Guinea and North Borneo before joining BCOF. He then served in Intelligence with the 66th Battalion before joining the newspaper *BCON*, working in Osaka, Kure, and Tokyo.[14] During and after the conflict, he wrote prolifically, first as a journalist writing for Australian newspapers (where his first-hand knowledge of Japan, visited as a ping-pong player, lent him a measure of credibility), and then as a playwright, a short story writer, a novelist, and a memoirist of local note and a certain international reputation. Kelen was a multi-talented man who was also multilingual, able to speak numerous languages including English, Japanese, and his native Hungarian, and other European languages including Czech, German, Dutch, and even Portuguese.

In a series of articles published in the *Sydney Morning Herald* and the Melbourne *Argus* during the war, Kelen had been one of the few Australian journalists who had made some kind of dispassionate attempt to analyse 'a strange, unscrupulous and, in many ways, a reckless enemy'. He did not completely succeed. He had originally gone to Japan before the war, believing that 'the differences between the Nipponese and the Occidentals were purely ideological', and that essentially 'they are just the same human beings as we are'. First-hand experience had taught him otherwise. In an article titled 'Japs Differ from Us in Many Little Things', such a substantial cumulative case is made for the inscrutability and strangeness of the Japanese – in everything from building habits and practices, eating, and writing, to gender relations – that they may as well have come from the moon. In fact, that is precisely the analogy Kelen resorts to in another article, called, 'What Sort of Person is the Japanese Soldier?' In appraising the considerable collective strengths and palpable weaknesses of the enemy, he concludes that the Australian needs to develop specially tailored tactics to deal with a people 'as strange to us as the inhabitants of the moon'. For all his good intentions, Kelen repeats the mantra of the battalions of Jap-haters in the armed forces and the urgers in the popular media. 'Fighting them,' he says, in one piece, 'is different from fighting any of the Occidental powers, including the Germans.'[15]

A very different people emerges from Kelen's writings on the Occupation, which were consummated by the publication of his memoir *I Remember Hiroshima* in 1983. For three years, Kelen lived and worked in close proximity to the atom-bombed city, walking its shattered streets, speaking to the survivors, and inscribing and photographing it. By the time of the first anniversary of the bomb, he had visited the city many times. Nothing was going to keep him from attending the Peace Restoration Festival on 6 August 1946. He set off from the camp of 66th Battalion at Kaitaichi expecting to find gloom and sorrow, and possibly some anger. Incredulous, he found acceptance and festivity. Girls were clad in their best kimonos, and young men were dressed in white shirts and shorts, with black sashes around their waists and white handkerchiefs around their heads, and they came bearing minia-ture shrines. People were singing, laughing, dancing. The first anniversary of the dropping of 'Little Boy' had coincided with the Festival of the Dead, the *Bon Odori*. Known simply as the *O-bon*, this annual dance ritual, held every August for over 500 years, has evolved into a Buddhist summer holiday honouring the departed spirits of one's ancestors. It is a kind of family reunion, during which people return to their hometowns to visit family and friends and pay respects at the gravesites of their deceased relatives. That the first anniversary of the bombing coincided with *O-Bon* was an irony not lost on Kelen. Predictably, the festivities in August 1946 had been arranged to honour those killed by the blast. In the flick-ering light of kerosene lamps, and to the monotonous sound of drums and the clapping of hands, the people of ruined Hiroshima danced the *Bon Odori*, 'forming a circle, moving round and round, greeting the dead whose souls had been liberated from their suffer-ings in the Buddhist hell and elevated to a state of celestial bliss'.[16]

Watching this, the only foreign observer, Kelen felt distinctly uncomfortable. 'How would we have reacted if the enemy had destroyed Sydney a year ago?' he asks himself. Then an amazing thing happened. The music and the movement suddenly stopped, and a man, perhaps the master of ceremonies, called to the Australian: 'Come and dance with us, honourable soldier'. Two grimy Hiroshima urchins, a boy and a girl, took him by the hands and led him into the circle. There on the bank of the Ota, Kelen writes, 'in front of a grotesque skeleton of a building, with the people of Hiroshima I too danced the *Bon Odori*'.[17] As an epiphany of cultural reconciliation, this is hard to beat. More in hope than in expectation, an editorial in the Sydney *Daily Telegraph* the day after Japan's signed surrender, 2 September 1945, asked for Australians to contribute to the shattered country's reconstruction in a spirit of humility, 'for we cannot hope to make others better than we are'. The editorial was headlined 'Let Us Re-educate the

Japanese – and Ourselves as Well'.[18] In the end, no one was more surprised than the members of BCOF that so many of them took this challenging message to heart.

Remembering the Occupation

Iraq catapulted the Occupation of Japan, historically distant and largely forgotten, back into the public consciousness. In the exultant days after the swift removal of Saddam Hussein in April 2003, and for some time afterward, the administration of the US president George W. Bush prematurely sought to impose favourable comparisons with Japan as the modern standard against which 'regime change' – and military occupation – might be measured and justified.[1]

Any comparisons between Japan and what became the bloody shambles of Iraq are tenuous in the extreme. In Japan, the Occupation's legitimacy was accepted on both sides. The nation's legendary cohesion was tested, but it did not disintegrate into convulsive internecine conflict. Bureaucratic and social structures remained in place and were cannily mobilised by the Occupier. Among the Japanese, there was bitterness at having their country taken over so completely. The occasional assault was reported, knives were brandished, but no death squads roamed the country.

There were no assassins. Some suicides took place, but no suicide bombings. The BCOF commander Robertson says he felt free to wander completely unarmed among the common people populating the villages near his HQ in Hiroshima Prefecture. The only hostility he ever encountered, over the more than five years he was in Japan, occurred soon after his arrival in June 1946, when a lump of coal the size of a fist shot through the open window of the train leaving Tokyo Station for Kure.[2]

Yet reading the self-congratulatory master narrative of the Occupation as unimpeachably benign and uniformly successful is questionable. Not all SCAP's grand plans came to fruition, at least partly because of a shift in Occupation policy, as the idealism of the Occupation's early months was gradually replaced by a Cold War *realpolitik* that situated Japan as a key regional conservative state in the global struggle against communism. The Americans, Macmahon Ball remarked in 1963, 'moved into the shadow of a Third World War while Australians were still lingering in the shadow of the Second'.[3] Inevitably, Australia followed the American lead.

By the end of 1949, when the Chifley government was swept from power, the reformist energy had evaporated from the Occupation, and Robert Menzies's incoming Liberal/Country Party coalition government supported SCAP's 'reverse course' of winding back, and even shelving, original policy priorities in Japan. As one of his first acts, MacArthur had legalised the Japanese Communist Party in Japan in October 1945 and encouraged the emergence of labour unions. These were decisions MacArthur came to regret. In mid-1948, he withdrew the right to strike from public employees, a troublesome source of industrial action; and, by 1950, many Japanese had been purged from public life for left-wing sympathies – a clearing-out extended, after the outbreak of the Korean War on 25 June 1950, to include the private sector. Disconcertingly, the 'Red Purge' was accompanied by a 'depurge', the reappearance on the scene of discredited individuals who had been banished from public life for serving the cause of ultra-nationalistic militarism. The 'reverse course' suited some American players in the Occupation more motivated by self-interest than by abiding concern for Japan. Among those basking in the atomic sunshine were businessmen directly or indirectly involved in the American administration, exploring opportunities for trade, making contacts, ingratiating themselves with the *zaibatsu*. Occupied Japan, according to Mark Gayn, a left-wing journalist targeted by MacArthur, was a 'carpetbagger's dream'.[4]

Of course, some real advances to the civil and political state of Japan were accomplished. The Occupation helped give Japan lasting stability and enviable economic prosperity. It also gave Japan democracy, albeit of a chronically compromised kind. The lot of Japanese women, a priority of the Occupation, was improved, although a 2006 global report on gender equality ranked the country a lowly 79th in the world in the areas of female economic, educational, and political empowerment and opportunity. As for MacArthur's ambition to Christianise the Oriental heathen, it literally went up in flames. Many of the Bibles issued to the Japanese were torn up and turned into cheap cigarette paper as a substitute for the genuine article, which had been priced out of common reach on the black market. The Christian population of Japan, inadvertently blasted almost out of existence by the American atomic bomb dropped over Nagasaki, has remained miniscule.[5] Nonetheless, the real post-war religion of Japan is one that the general might have approved of – capitalism. In the Kagurazaka district of Tokyo, there is a sign over a doorway, emblazoned with the famous acronym 'SCAP'. A rare relic of the Occupation, it might be thought. Closer inspection reveals that it advertises the premises of a municipal commercial organisation called the 'Shopping Center Association Project'. Yet that, in a way, is as appropriate a monument to the American mission in Japan as any statue or museum.

The Occupation, of course, has never really ended. More than

40,000 US military personnel and associated civilian staff remain there to this day, subsidised to the hilt by Japan. Many are still, contentiously, stationed in Okinawa, which the Americans did not officially hand back to Japan until 1972. Even then, they did so only after a secret pact allowing US nuclear weapons to be brought into Japan in a crisis, negotiated with the Japanese government by president Richard Nixon's national security advisor, Henry Kissinger. 'Whether under direct military rule or nominal Japanese constitutional rule', according to Gavan McCormack in *Client State: Japan in the American embrace* (2007), 'Okinawa remained essentially a "war state", serving as a major base for wars in Korea, Vietnam, the Persian Gulf, Afghanistan and Iraq'.[6] US Forces also occupy huge mainland bases, such as the Yokosuka naval facility in Kanagawa Prefecture, just south of Tokyo; the Camp Zama army base; and the Atsugi Naval Air facility, in the same prefecture. The old BCAIR stamping ground at Iwakuni became a springboard for American aircraft heading to and from the Korean conflict in 1950. Today, it is home to about 5000 US marines and family members, who share the base with members of Japan's 'Self-Defence Force', or SDF. Half a century on, the Occupation's project to demilitarise Japan has ended up with a brilliantly trained and equipped Japanese fighting machine, well over 200,000 strong. Ostensibly hamstrung by Article 9 of the pacifist constitution imposed on it by SCAP, the SDF remains a formidable factor in American strategic and tactical planning.[7]

Geopolitically, the country remains locked in a long 'embrace' with the US, as Gavan McCormack expresses it, suggestively reconfiguring the sexualised relations of the Occupation. Like the postwar Japanese prostitute who is loyally committed to a single GI patron, Japan sees the US as the *onrii wan*, the only other country that really matters. Meanwhile, it has cheerfully embraced nuclear energy, and accepted the rorting and cover-ups that have accompanied the colossal industry that produces it. Its tumultuous, earthquake-prone landscape is pockmarked by more than 50 occasionally malfunctioning nuclear reactors. Japan has a vociferous anti-nuclear movement that is pitted against an overwhelmingly pro-nuclear political and bureaucratic establishment. Still nurturing a sense of wartime nuclear victimhood, Japanese civil society is largely committed to the abolition of nuclear weapons. But real or inherited memories of the 'black rain' of August 1945 are cast aside by the reassurance, as a near neighbour of North Korea and the old bugbear China, of being able to shelter under the American nuclear umbrella.

For Australia, the Occupation is a more equivocal matter. By the time the Korean War broke out in June 1950, with the other national contingents long gone, BCOF consisted of fewer than 3000 men. The old Australian 65th and 66th battalions also having departed, it was down to a single grossly undermanned army battalion, the 67th (redesignated the 3rd Battalion Royal Australian Regiment when the three BCOF battalions were consolidated into a single regiment in 1949), one RAAF squadron, a naval party, and some administrative personnel. The Menzies government had decided it was time to pull out; BCOF was becoming an unnecessary drain on the limited manpower available to the regular forces. In late May, MacArthur accepted the withdrawal, praising BCOF for its 'splendid efficiency'.[8]

Almost immediately, fighting erupted on the Korean peninsula. BCOF was revitalised and redeployed to supply and administer the Commonwealth forces in Korea, though the military occupation, as such, formally ended on 28 April 1952 with the ratification of the Peace Treaty. Many of the old BCOF men grabbed the opportunity to fight in Korea as a chance to get back to Japan on R&R. The armourer Patrick Knowles had left the country reluctantly in 1948, after his tour of duty was over. When war broke out in Korea, he couldn't re-enlist quickly enough, though the new conflict was 'secondary'. Kure was again flooded with Commonwealth troops en route to the battlefields or on leave. They were on high-pleasure alert, and enterprising Japanese catered to their needs. The beer halls and brothels did a roaring trade. With the Korean ceasefire in 1953, the Australian presence began its terminal decline. By November 1956, the final remnants of the force departed Japan: Australian Kure was over. In Japan itself, Australian numbers quickly dwindled to virtually nothing. According to Immigration Bureau statistics cited in 1958, there were just 248 Australian registered residents in Japan, only 17 of whom lived in the Chugoku region that was once the hub of BCOF activity.[9]

In the post-Occupation era, the normalisation of Australian relations with Japan has been based on the twin economic and political imperatives of accessing the gargantuan Japanese market, and of recognising Japan's strategic importance as the US's principal and most acquiescent ally in the region. The cultural fallout from World War II is more problematic. The war has so poisoned attitudes towards the Japanese that many Australians still cannot view them as 'just' people at all. The bitterness has eased as the generation who fought them has slowly died off, but it has never disappeared, being channelled instead into a variety of cultural discourses. In particular, the contemporary folk-hero status of revered POWs such as Sir Edward 'Weary' Dunlop has disseminated the painful memory of Japanese captivity into the broader population and across generations, entrenching the automatic association of Japan with fanatical militarism. Australia's economic dependency, and the fact that Japan seems to have 'won' the peace, remains a lingering irritation. The fate of the old Sydney-built HMAS *Warramunga*, which had participated in the South-West Pacific landings during the conflict, and had been present in Tokyo Bay when the Japanese signed the surrender before patrolling the Inland Sea during the Occupation, tells a significant post-war story. The *Warramunga* was decommissioned and sold off for scrap in 1963 – to Kinishita and Company Limited, of Japan. As the Japanese say, *makeru ga kachi*. He who is defeated wins.

The purported lack of a genuine apology for wartime brutalities and the heavily publicised visits of obeisant Japanese leaders to Tokyo's Yasukuni shrine (housing the spirits of all Japanese war dead, including those of convicted war criminals) have exacerbated the problem of translating 'Japan' into something other than war and iniquity. No amount of contrition is ever enough. A thousand apologies, one suspects, would never suffice. An American veteran of the Occupation, Howard Schuler, now resident in Melbourne, told me he has been 'amazed' at the animosity toward Japan in Australia.[10] Anti-Japanese sentiment is endemic in the general community, and 'Jap-bashing' still makes good copy in the popular media.

Many Australians find it unsettling that their country now enjoys a defence relationship with Japan; it was galling, for instance, when Australian troops provided security for a Japanese engineering unit doing reconstruction work in Iraq during 2006. More closely cooperative bilateral military arrangements have been greeted with something approaching outrage. In August 2006, when the Howard government's foreign minister Alexander Downer foreshadowed a new security pact emerging from an official parley in Tokyo, the front page of the *Australian* accompanied the announcement with a cartoon of an emaciated Digger, tagged '1945 Changi', standing dolefully alongside the portly Downer, caricatured as a bloated Sumo wrestler and labelled '2006 Tokyo'. Downer's own father, also a leading politician, had been a POW incarcerated in Changi; the generational treachery of contemporary Australia is unambiguously implied. When the joint security declaration was eventually signed in Tokyo by prime minster Howard and his Japanese counterpart Shinzo Abe, a letter writer in the *Age* retorted: 'On behalf of my uncle, a POW on the Burma–Thailand Railway, I have just one thing to say: Prime Minister, how dare you?'[11] It is not hard to be sympathetic to people whose loved ones suffered at the hands of the Japanese, or to understand their lingering grievance. Yet it is true that those who most noisily relive the horrors of war do so vicariously.

The veterans themselves have been more accepting. Not all of them, it must be said. One Occupationnaire insists that his attitude now, as an old man, remains the same as when he went to Japan in 1946 as an 18-year-old – 'placid until I would hear or read of their atrocities … and then you'd feel no mercy toward them and would kill the lot if you had the chance'. In the questionnaire I prepared for BCOF veterans, I posed the question: 'What is your best memory of Japan?' I received some interesting replies. One respondent replied: 'its disappearing coastline seen from the deck of the HMAS *Kanimbla* as that vessel headed south to Australia in September 1947'.[12]

But for every implacably anti-Japanese veteran, there are people like the BCOF veteran Allan Chick. If anyone should have hated the Japanese, it was him. A cray fisherman from St Helens, on the east coast of Tasmania, Chick endured not only the prison camps of South-East Asia, but also the sinking of the vessel, the *Tamahoko Maru*, that was transporting him to the labour camps in Japan. Close to the Japanese coast and relative safety, the ship was torpedoed by the American submarine *Tang*. Some 560 of the 772 POWs aboard lost their lives. The archetypal survivor, Chick then somehow beat the atomic bomb, having been resident in a Nagasaki prison camp less than 2000 metres from Ground Zero on 9 August 1945. Miraculously outliving these calamities encouraged him, at the time and since, to take the long view. 'Haven't the least desire to bash Tojo or anyone else', he wrote reprovingly, in a letter to his mother from Occupied Japan, way back in July 1946. 'It's a funny thing but the people back home who never actually contacted the Nips are more hostile than the chaps who fought them'.[13]

During the Occupation itself, the continuing controversy over the Japanese war brides starkly revealed the cultural distance separating the civilian public and the BCOF community. 'No Australian mother whose devoted son, no Australian wife whose decent husband lies buried in some Pacific battlefield will have her feelings outraged by an Australian flaunting a Japanese wife before her', thundered Arthur Calwell, the incumbent immigration minister in March 1948.[14] It was rhetoric that annoyed many of the men serving in Occupied Japan. In his letters home, 'Bluey' Chick had teased and tormented his mother about his girlfriends, and the appalling possibility of her acquiring a Japanese daughter-in-law. Fearing a hostile response, he procrastinated for years over revealing the truth of his enduring commitment to his lover Haruko, and didn't inform his family of their wedding in a Hiroshima church in December 1951 until six months after the event.

In January 1952, just as the Occupation was being wound up, a member of a visiting Australian delegation of journalists wrote in Sydney's *Sunday Herald* that Australians 'must be prepared for some shocks' as the BCOF men return home. 'One of the cultural discoveries we made during our tour', he noted, 'was the degree of liking for the Japanese developed by Australians who have lived among them for any length of time. The longer their stay, the stronger this feeling has become'. The article's headline was designed to shock: 'Our Soldiers Like the Japanese'. As late as 1956, the travel writer Colin Simpson observed that most Australians 'still tasted bitterness' when they thought of Japan. Simpson notes that the average Australian serviceman of the Occupation 'had it pretty good in Japan', liked the country and the people, and was reluctant to leave. Yet when he returned to Australia, he learned that the caricature of the vicious prison guard had come to represent an entire race. Simpson cites an officer bemoaning the fact that 'you just can't talk to the people at home'.[15]

Simpson's observation points to one of the redeeming cultural truths about the Occupation. For all the individual cases of their boorish behaviour in Japan, BCOF personnel are far in advance of their countrymen and women in their attitudes to the country. Even the RSL has made its peace. On a six-member official RSL visit to Japan sponsored by the Japanese government in 2003, the group's only Occupationnaire Brian Rose writes of a tour of 'reconciliation'. Everywhere the group went, from Tokyo to Etajima, they were confronted by people apologising for the part Japan played in the war. 'They appreciated it when we said that the time for apologising was over and was not further necessary,' Rose recalls, 'agreeing with us when we said it was time to forgive, but not forget, and that it should never be allowed to happen again.' BCOF veterans like Norm White remain alert to Japanese malfeasance in the war, but haven't let that knowledge sour their responses to the country or its people. In recent years, he has played host to Japanese students studying in Australia, whom he has since visited in Japan, and he has become an active member of the 'Tomadachi [Friends] Club' in Katoomba, near his home in the Blue Mountains town of Wentworth Falls. In his backyard, he has constructed two small Japanese gardens, which he is proud to show guests, a testament to a memorable interlude in his personal history.[16]

The BCOF dependants are living evidence of how the Occupation placed its participants at a problematic distance from their homeland. In many individual cases, this distance was as much legal as cultural, as several of the more than 150 Australians born in Occupied Japan have had to struggle to establish their national identity, after the introduction of the Australian Citizenship Act in 1948 consigned them to what Christine de Matos has described as 'citizenship limbo'.[17] At the annual reunions of the 'BCOF Kids', as the dependants' organisation calls itself, men and women now in their late middle-age share a bond at being part of a unique event, and circulate nostalgic stories of a country reviled by their contemporaries. Marshalled by Rosemarie Carman, who arrived in Japan on Christmas Eve 1947 as one of six daughters of the career soldier Major Claude Raymond, the 'BCOF Kids' have met annually since 2003. Coming together gives them a chance to talk freely about their shared experience, after suppressing it in the face of widespread antagonism.

The dependants were confronted by local hostility upon their homecoming. Some of the children, in particular, suffered deeply. 'Japan was not a popular topic when we returned in 1950 – people still hated the Japanese and thought we were almost traitors for having lived there', remembers Gail (Fallon) Young, the daughter of an education officer with the RAAF who was stationed at the air force bases at Bofu and Iwakuni from 1947 to 1949. Her sister Kerry Seipolt remembers feeling isolated back at school in Australia: 'I found that many people hated the Japanese and I was called "slit eyes", etc. So I stopped talking of Japan or even admitting I'd been there'. Margery Sullivan was in Japan for well over three years from August 1947, and met her future husband on the way to a holiday at the Kawana Hotel. Sullivan says that she and many of her friends 'had the cultural journey of their young lives'. However, it was not a journey she felt she could share with others. 'There was still a lot of bitterness against the Japanese and I for one never spoke outside immediate family about my years in Japan'. The RAAF girl Wendy Barry, who spent three years of her childhood at Iwakuni, says that, upon her return to Australia, people 'seemed to want us to tell them tales of horror rather than stories about what fun we had and how well we got on with the Japanese'.[18]

Many of the dependants now reflect on how their experience of Japan at such an electrifying historical moment extended their sympathies, and how they now see themselves as internationalists, especially linked to the Asia-Pacific region. For some, the Japan effect has been subtle and almost uncanny. Born in Kure (the son of an Australian in military Intelligence), Dean Wells was less than four when he returned home, and has only a few flashes of significant memory. He retains images of visiting Hiroshima, of a pier beside a river, and of the awful shape of a human shadow on a stone, 'which my father told me he would explain to me when I grew up'. Now a senior Queensland politician, he has been an active anti-nuclear campaigner all his political life, participating in the 1995 International Parliamentary Protest in Tahiti against the

French nuclear testing in the Pacific.[19]

An Occupation child of another kind, Glenda Gauci provides a salutary BCOF biography. She was the daughter of the Melbourne waterside worker John Gauci, who met her Japanese mother in Kure. After staying on in the country for several years after the Occupation, the Gaucis settled in Australia. A brilliant young scholar, their daughter Glenda became Melbourne University's first exchange student to Tokyo's prestigious Keio University, before embarking on a diplomatic career in foreign affairs, which included a stint as trade counsellor in Tokyo, an ambassadorial appointment to Cambodia, and a term as senior political counsellor at the Washington embassy. She was struck down by an asbestos-related cancer in August 2006, at the age of 47. Glenda Gauci's 'Japaneseness' pervaded her life, and her career can be seen as the apotheosis of the Australian Occupation of Japan, as opening a new way forward for national responses to the Asia-Pacific. Her life also reminds us graphically of the effect of the BCOF marriages. When the Menzies government gave the go-ahead for the wives to enter Australia, it was thought that only a dozen or so would come. But they came in droves. By the time all Australian military remnants had vacated the region, 650 Japanese women had arrived in Australia as war brides. The Japanese war brides dealt a grievous blow to the fortress of White Australia, from which it has never recovered.[20]

THE PEOPLE OF BCOF were pioneers of a kind, a step ahead of their countrymen and women. But the moral courage it took to come to terms with Japan doesn't win medals, or even grudging recognition, in Australia. The negative reportage, especially the reports of immoral conduct and the prevalence of venereal disease, took an immediate toll. Some men removed their BCOF colour patches and badges upon their return. Frank Akhurst was pleased to join the force in 1946, as his father and uncle had fought in the

Great War and his older brothers had seen action in World War II. After a year in Japan, he returned to find himself shunned by the RSL, not having proved his mettle the culturally sanctioned way, on the field of battle. The civilian world also regarded him suspiciously. BCOF veterans, Akhurst ruefully recalls, 'found it took some time to be really socially accepted on arriving home – especially the girls!'[21]

Now old and ailing, they campaign for the rights routinely accorded Australian servicemen and women. A particular bone of contention has been the Australian government's continuing failure to accept the 2003 Clarke Report on BCOF entitlements, which recommended that those who served in Japan up to mid-1947 were involved in 'warlike activity' and, hence, should qualify for a service pension and the Gold Health Card. The politicians, one veteran caustically remarks, are 'waiting for us all to die'. Dying they surely are. The medical problems of the Occupation community dominate contemporary BCOF debate and dialogue. These include inordinately high rates of cancers (well above the national average; up to 80 per cent of veterans by some reckonings), and other mysterious maladies and genetic abnormalities that the veterans attribute to intimate exposure to atom-bombed Hiroshima. Of all the ugly Occupation narratives, this may be the ugliest one of all, and one which demands to be documented and told as a story all on its own.[22]

Murray Elliott now looks back with amazement that he and his medical colleagues went to Hiroshima as 'gawking tourists', and did not educate themselves about the significance of atomic fusion. He wonders why, as a doctor, he did not consider residual radiation a hazard, and drank so freely of the local water, as well as the beer and whisky produced by the brewery on the city's outskirts. Like others, Elliott and his friends spoke blithely of a 'clean bomb'. 'In those days we had no idea what radiation was', says the dependant Rosemary Jeanneret, whose father and sister both died prematurely of cancer. The ignorance of the participants was one thing; but the retrospective mockery of an outside observer, Frank Clune writing in *Ashes of Hiroshima*, was regrettably common. That Hiroshima rose from the ashes was enough for Clune to laugh at nuclear contamination. To his observation in 1948, the bomb had actually done the people good. Clune looks in vain for 'Atomic Freaks' in the crowded streets of 'Phoenix City', as he calls it, but sees only 'happy hordes' of healthy children, the progeny of fertile parents who appear to have been vitalised and energised by the 'uranium rays'.[23]

Clune's facetious refusal to contemplate the possibility of pernicious radioactivity might be put down to the naivety of his time, and to his own unwillingness to recognise the enormity of dropping the bomb. The Japs got what was coming to them; that was enough. More unforgivable has been the stonewalling of governmental authorities, who continue to refuse to countenance claims for compensation for purported radiation-induced disease. BCOF veterans such as John Collins and Syd Margetts have dedicated their lives to fighting for the cause of their comrades beset by inexplicable illnesses or cruelly cut down before their time. They have lobbied US presidents and Australian prime ministers, a series of sympathetic but unhelpful veterans affairs ministers, members of parliament, radio talkback hosts, and others, to little avail. Admittedly, the claims are hard to prove, and are disputed by a sceptical medico-scientific establishment which argues that residual radiation from the atomic bomb would have been at 'natural levels' by the time the Australians arrived. They might also point to Shizuo Inoue, fit as a fiddle and still scaling mountains at over 80, as living testimony to their scepticism. Yet the BCOF lament that the force 'served Australia far better than Australia served BCOF' rings true.[24] No formal and comprehensive health study of Occupation veterans or their dependants has ever been conducted by Australian authorities.

Inevitably, the claimants are now succumbing to the various afflictions of old age. But not, so far, John Collins. In *The War of the Veterans* (2001), Collins chronicles his battles, in league with the 'Atomic Ex-Serviceman's Association', with bureaucratic, political, and public indifference to the plight of radiation-affected servicemen from both Japan and the atomic testing in Australia in the 1950s. Collins drove a bulldozer in Hiroshima, cleaning up the 'dead inferno' of the city. Within months, he was passing blood, his hair began falling out, and he started suffering from a succession of chronic allergies and other infections. In 1986, he was diagnosed with a form of bone-marrow cancer, diagnosed as terminal, but from which he has managed to survive with the aid of serial transfusions. He has taken on the Department of Veterans Affairs in a series of hearings, appeals, and counter-appeals that have left him with little more than huge legal bills. Collins locates his plight deftly, with a sardonic reference to the travails of the Vietnam vet, much better known in Australia than those of the men of BCOF. 'Some folks take a long time to die,' he remarks. 'I was killed by the atom bomb at Hiroshima in 1947 when, like it says in the song, I was only nineteen'.[25]

The indifference to the plight of men like John Collins is symptomatic of a more general indifference to the Occupation that permeates the cultural, as well as literal, politics of the event. The Americans, never overly generous in recognising the contributions of their Allies (a charge that could also be levelled at Australians), have blithely overlooked BCOF. In his autobiography *Reminiscences* (1964), Douglas MacArthur allots a 60-page chapter of the story of his brilliant career to the Occupation. In a staggeringly immodest self-appraisal of his mastery of Japan, not a single reference is accorded the Australian commanders of BCOF, nor is there even any reference to the activities of the force itself, other than the quotation of his speech of thanks upon their withdrawal. This, of course, can be put down to MacArthur's ego. Yet even in his vast and otherwise inclusive study *Embracing Defeat*, John Dower dismisses BCOF as a 'token' force and never mentions it by name.[26]

For their own reasons, the British have also been inclined to belittle BCOF and to mock the ambitions with which Australia entered into the Occupation. A characteristic view is expressed in Macdonald Hull's documentary novel *Snow on the Pine* (1956). In the novel, Hull, a senior British army officer who was attached to the Australian HQ of the force, has his autobiographical protagonist describe BCOF (to an American friend) as a 'farce' that is risibly dependent on US directives. Its 'one really important duty' was to mount ceremonial guard outside the Imperial Palace in Tokyo, 'with the maximum of pomp, ceremony and general bull'.[27]

American heedlessness and British disdain are predictable enough; what is so remarkable is that the Occupation remains a relatively ignored episode in Australian history. This sits oddly with cultural practice. When it comes to military matters, Australia can hardly be accused of undue modesty. One might have thought that several thousand victorious Diggers sporting the famous 'rising sun' emblem in the Land of the Rising Sun was a beguiling iconic marriage that would have excited more interest among Australia's military historians, who are an enthusiastic bunch. In the wider community, if one asks people about the nation's contribution in post-war Japan, they will give you an uncomprehending stare. Occupied who? When? Usually, Australia venerates its servicemen to the point of exaggerating their contribution to momentous happenings. But, if they think of the event at all, Australians still tend to talk about the 'American occupation'. In the popular imagination, the Occupation is personified by the figure of the swaggering but big-hearted American GI, distributing bonhomie and largesse to awestruck Japanese children.

Not surprisingly, the BCOF veterans are insecure about their place in the Australian pantheon. Bob Christison was just 19 years old when he went to Japan. Trained by NCOs 'who had earned their stripes in the campaigns in the Pacific', he was chuffed to wear the slouch hat with the rising-sun badge. 'We would have taken on the world once we had that uniform on', he remembers.

Yet now, in his mid-70s, Christison wonders, 'What is wrong with the name BCOF?' Many thousands served in Japan and nearly 80 died there, 'and yet nobody ... wants to know us'. Many of their personal written accounts are marked by a special pleading that sometimes strains credulity, as in the claim that BCOF was 'the best disciplined' Australian force to serve overseas.[28]

The frustration of the veterans is understandable. They had to fight long and hard for a medal recognising their service, an Australian Service Medal with clasp 'Japan', which was only gazetted at the end of 1997. Blink and you'll miss the meagre presentation afforded the Occupation, hidden away among the copious documentation of national military endeavour in the Australian War Memorial in Canberra. The memorial's 'Conflicts 1945 to Today' gallery, opened in March 2008, extensively illustrates peacekeeping operations from Cambodia to Somalia to East Timor, as well as major battle engagements in Vietnam and the Middle East. But the long Occupation of Japan is given scant attention as an event in itself, and is contextualised, rather, as expediting quick action in Korea when war broke out on the peninsula. Those few artefacts selected as Occupation iconography include a suitcase, a leave pass, a booklet entitled *Japanese in 3 Weeks,* and (most telling of all) a box Brownie camera. The implication is clear: the BCOF tour was a kind of working holiday. Outside, in the memorial's gardens, a modest granite memorial, fringed by three cherry trees, was constructed in the late 1990s. But it is the nearby bronze of Simpson and his donkey that attracts the spectators.

Identified with the demeaning drudgery of garrison soldiering, BCOF scores just three passing references in *Diggers* (1994), a glossy two-volume paean to the Australian serviceman and woman 'endorsed by the Australian Defence Force'. In *The Oxford Companion to Australian Military History* (1995), a vastly more erudite text, the entire force attracts little more wordage than the entry for a single World War II general, the 9th Division leader Leslie Morshead. Admittedly, BCOF did nothing to compare with warding off Rommel's marauders in the cauldron of North Africa. If the 'Rats of Tobruk' that Morshead commanded wore their unlovely nickname with pride, the surviving members of BCOF continue to suffer the label 'the Forgotten Force'.

TODAY, THERE IS little left in the hills and valleys around Kure, let alone in the rebuilt city itself, to remind the visitor of BCOF. The location of the Australian camp at Hiro has become the grounds of the handsome campus of Hiroshima International University, whose monolithic redbrick structure suggests something of the vaulting aspirations of post-war Japan. Nijimura is long gone. Now, just the original street plan remains, occupied by a light-industrial complex that includes the Public Sanitation Office. When Beverley (Holland) Waldie, who had spent her early teenage years in Nijimura as the daughter of an Australian officer, revisited the area with her sister in the early 1990s, her requests to locate the cantonment were met by dumb looks. Nobody had heard of this little detached piece of Australia. Eventually, the two sisters stumbled upon their teenage stamping ground, locating it through topographical features and the old sea wall, adjacent to which the staked oyster gardens of the Inland Sea are still to be found. But the houses, the theatre, the little school, the shops, the canteen, and the pool had all vanished. Beverley eventually spotted a sign by a park where she estimated the centre of the Australian village had been located. Hoping that the sign might commemorate Nijimura – 'This was the site of the Rainbow Village, where … '– she took a photograph. Later she had the sign translated. It read, 'Keep Off the Grass!'[29]

Kure City's glossy tourist literature calls it 'a city of hidden history and stories'. But no mention is made of the Occupation. The home of the Australian Army Education Service, Kure House, now contains recruiting offices for Japan's Self-Defence Forces. In 2006, windows and boards were adorned with posters of photogenic young men and women engaged in various Japanese overseas peacekeeping ventures and military activities. One photograph showed a serviceman surrounded by a group of grateful Iraqis. Nearby, the mansion in which BCOF commander-in-chief Robertson lived and entertained while Australia ruled the roost in the late 1940s has been restored and redecorated in memory of its original occupant, the commander of the Kure Naval Base. The tiny childhood home of Admiral Togo, the 'Nelson of Nippon' and hero of Japan's destruction of the Russian armada at Tsushima in 1905, has been relocated to the residence's verdant grounds, as has the clock tower of the former Kure Naval Arsenal.

Today, Kure's major tourist attraction is the Yamato Museum, memorialising the 'world's biggest battleship', built in the local yard, which was sunk by American naval aircraft in April 1945 while on a mission to attack the US fleet near Okinawa. Nearly 2500 men perished. In the museum, the disaster is turned into a celebration of Japanese technological acumen. Contemporary Japan sails serenely on. Out in the Inland Sea, Etajima has resumed its original function as the Japanese Naval Academy. When the Australians were there, the YWCA served up afternoon teas in a grand Hellenic-style structure, built in 1936 from contributions by Imperial Naval Officers. The Australians christened it the 'Dew Drop Inn'. Now, it is a museum showcasing Japanese naval victories, kamikaze memorabilia, and (in oblique deference to Admiral Togo), a lock of Horatio Nelson's hair.

Up the coast at Hiroshima, things have changed dramatically since the days of BCOF. Yet, in a sense, they have stayed the same. Today's Hiroshima is a paradox, an outgoing, progressive city that is obsessed with its historical destruction. So successfully have the municipal authorities packaged its status as the original 'Ground Zero' (efforts to purloin the term for New York City's obliterated World Trade Center notwithstanding) that its very identity is fixed by the fact of 6 August 1945. Other cities in Japan have moved on from the war, even atom-bombed Nagasaki. Neighbouring

Fukuyama was burned to the ground by a massive air raid on 8 August, two days *after* the bomb. (The US wasn't resting on its laurels.) These days, it runs an annual rose festival. Nothing so trivial preoccupies Hiroshima. Central Hiroshima is one vast memorial to its nuclear devastation. The expanses of Peace Park, across the river from the World Heritage-listed A-bomb Dome, have become so crowded with statues and monuments that new structures have spilled out onto the surrounding streets. 'Peace', like religion in the Vatican, bombards the visitor from all sides. The analogy seems even more appropriate during the commemorative rituals held each year on 6 August, when the park fills up with oppressively penitent Americans, pilgrims of peace, each looking as if he or she has made the journey purely to accept personal responsibility for the tragedy. Robertson must be turning in his grave.

My research in Japan ended with Shizuo Inoue driving me from Hiroshima to Kure along the serpentine coastal road that skirts the Inland Sea between the two cities. It is a testing-enough drive now, but it was much more hazardous during the Occupation – even narrower, treacherously potholed, and choked with Japanese bicyclists and BCOF motorists, not all of whom were sober. Our objective was to view a roadside monument constructed to commemorate the death of an Australian officer, Captain J.P. Smith, who was killed when the small BCOF bus carrying him and others ran off the road and down a steep embankment into the sea, in the early hours of the morning of 25 June 1949. Smith was a mason and had been returning from Lodge business. I had seen the pencil-shaped stone monument, located on the coastal side of the road, in an old photograph. As BCOF is short of such tributes, I felt it was my duty to see it. On the way to Kure, I could not find it; the apparent widening of the road and development must have swallowed it up. But on the way back to Hiroshima, near the town of Yoshiura, I caught sight of it, standing in a parking bay on the other side of the road. It had been moved. We swerved into the bay, and got out to take a look. It is a simple obelisk, about six feet high, with an inscription that recognises BCOF and also Captain Smith's membership of the Lodge:

He
Deserved and Obtained
The Esteem
Of All Good and Worthy
Brethren

To get up close to read the inscription, we had to wade through a sea of garbage that swelled to a disgusting mound around the base of the monument itself. This stretch of the Inland Sea now aspires to be Japan's Côte d'Azur. The day-trippers at the manufactured *plage* across the road must have driven up to the parking bay, dumped their rubbish, and moved on. There were cigarette butts, mouldering *bento* boxes, soft-drink cans, and what looked like a discarded condom. It didn't pay to look too closely. Shizuo was horrified and apologetic. It was as if his nation had committed a disgraceful offence against Australia. I told him not to worry, thinking awhile that this trashed BCOF memorial said something about the general neglect that Australia itself had dished out to the Occupation and its veterans.

Back home in Australia, I received an email from Shizuo. From old newspaper clippings, he had discovered that the memorial had been moved as early as 1950, when the road was widened, and that, in 2000, an errant truck had knocked it down. Distraught, the driver had contacted police to seek whom he should compensate. No one had any knowledge of it; the city authorities had to investigate their files to find its provenance. It was just *there*, as it had been for half a century. Shizuo had attached a few photographs to his email. They revealed the monument scrubbed and cleaned, and sitting in a neat space bereft of rubbish. He had cleared it himself. One photograph shows him standing by the monument. It is as fitting a closing image of the Occupation as any – a proud Japanese man and a memorial to an obscure Australian death, on the road to Hiroshima.

Afterword

nniversaries of its nuclear destruction are major events in Hiroshima, days when the city remembers its tragic past and reinforces its status as an international centre of anti-nuclear activism. Among the thousands cramming the commemorative spaces within and adjacent to Peace Park, I was there to observe the proceedings on 6 August 2015, the 70th anniversary of the bombing. In high summer, the wooded park was buzzing with cicadas, while all around was a cacophony of chanting Buddhist monks and megaphone-wielding protesters berating the Japanese government for its recommitment to nuclear energy after the post-Fukushima hiatus. Above the hubbub could be detected the strains of John Lennon's 'Imagine', a signature tune at these events. Pilgrims of peace from all over the world were seeking the miracle of global amity: I was reminded of Ian Buruma's analogy of Hiroshima and Lourdes.[1]

Numerous Australian tourists mingled among the crowd. Most of them were young, in their twenties. Generationally, at least, they were the granddaughters and grandsons of the men and women who had served in Occupied Japan. In the past two decades, Australians have gravitated en masse to Japan; tourist numbers have risen by almost 1,000 per cent, while Japanese travellers to Australia have halved. If one recent observer is to be believed, not all of these youthful antipodean visitors have been well behaved – instead, treating Japan as a playground, a kind of Bali of Northeast Asia.[2] It was not surprising that Hiroshima's nuclear notoriety drew them to the place. Most would have travelled to the city with a clear image in their minds of the A-bomb Dome, picturesquely preserved in its state of ruination, the Nuclear Age's most recognisable icon. Certainly, they had their photographs taken in front of it, making sure not to smile for the camera. Yet they were patiently respectful that day, standing in the blistering sun, listening to the customarily impassioned speech by Hiroshima's mayor as doves were cast into the cloudless sky.

But did any of them know about the Occupation, and that thousands of Australians had laboured and lived it up in this very neighbourhood some years before? Were they aware of their nation's involvement in the remaking of post-war Japan, including the reconstruction of Hiroshima itself? Of course, Hiroshima's significance is universal rather than parochial, as what John Whittier Treat calls a 'trope' of 'a new fact within the human condition': mankind's ability to commit omnicide. But in its own way Hiroshima – as the principal location of a national endeavour that signalled a reorientation of the Australian global perspective away from ancestral Europe toward the Asia-Pacific – is as significant a place in Australia's national story as mythic sites of battlefield striving such as Gallipoli or Kokoda.[3] Yet Australia's involvement in the Occupation has disappeared from public view into a black hole of ignorance.

In 2008, the year that *Travels in Atomic Sunshine* was first published, the Australian prime minister, Kevin Rudd, visited Hiroshima, touring the Peace Museum and laying a wreath at the

Cenotaph before announcing, in Kyoto, the establishment of a commission to propose the tightening of the Nuclear Non-Proliferation Treaty, by then 40 years old. Eight years before the US president Barack Obama's historic visit in 2016, this was perhaps the first time a serving Western leader had paid an official trip to the city. Not even the RSL could any summon any opposition. None of the usual calls for an apology from the Japanese for its wartime iniquities were uttered, although Peter Ryan, the author of the notable New Guinea memoir *Fear Drive My Feet* (1959), responded to the occasion by reminding Australians of Japan's whitewashed version of its conduct, before quoting Paul Fussell's confronting catch-cry, 'Thank God for the atom bomb'.[4] In Hiroshima, Rudd's rhetoric diplomatically supported 'the common mission for peace' in a nuclear-free world. But it is strange that, in the reportage of this symbolic visit, no mention – at all – was made of the substantial post-war Australian presence in the city.[5]

Military occupations have acquired a bad name in recent years, especially after the quagmires of Iraq and Afghanistan, against which Occupied Japan looks like a beacon of constructive benevolence. Nonetheless, the Occupation was rife with the institutionalised and random injustice that ensues when one group of empowered people assume armed control of another – in the other's own country. Reminiscing about his trip to Japan with the painter Albert Tucker, Harry Roskolenko remarks that military occupation encroaches upon and corrupts all manner of human exchange. 'When troops occupy', he wrote in *Meanjin* in 1947, 'they also regulate, as exchange, the nature of an economy, of love and sex; as well as the disproportions of time, war and man.'[6] In *Travels in Atomic Sunshine*, I detailed the particular nexus of racial antagonism and sexual transgression that marked the Allied takeover of post-war Japan. This attracted the annoyance of one or two reviewers, who opined that I was too hard on the Australians and too easy on the Japanese. The good name of the Australian military remains sacrosanct, and Jap-bashing is not quite extinct.

Clearly, my invocation of Kipling's 'white man's burden' to define the neo-colonialism of the Occupation as a Western justification for redeeming the barbaric East was not exactly intended to dignify the event. However, it is important to recognise, again, the background to the Australian deployment and its political, economic and cultural legacies. It is also necessary to acknowledge the vast network of intimate individual connections between the two peoples that it produced. Uplifting friendships and enduring influences – even mere fond memories of a unique moment in the national life – tend to confound the reductive assimilation of the Occupation into the long and unedifying tradition of Western penetrations of Asia.

In her account of Australian engagement with the Asia-Pacific in the past few decades, *Visiting the Neighbours* (2014), Agnieszka Sobocinska writes that the BCOF deployment 'embodied the view that Australia should work to restore – and even extend – European imperialism in postwar Asia'.[7] If 'European' can be taken to include 'Western', or specifically American, this is very true, for Australia's involvement helped advance the US project to turn Japan into a reliable political and military ally in a highly combustible region – and a convenient base for its military forces, of which around 50,000 are still stationed around the country, most contentiously in the tropical prefecture of Okinawa.

Yet the Australian government's intentions went beyond re-entrenching old hegemonies, at least until Robert Menzies's incoming Liberal-Country Party coalition supported MacArthur's 'reverse course' of stabilising Japan, and halting communism rather than democratisation became the priority. As Christine de Matos has observed, the Australian commitment to Japan represented a vision of the future rather than a nostalgic nod to the past. In encouraging the process of Japan's material, political, and social renewal, the Chifley government sent a message of active regional engagement to the developing nations of the Asia-Pacific struggling to emerge from the yoke of Western (and Japanese) control.[8] As I sought to show in *Travels in Atomic Sunshine*, Australia's determination to speak with an assertive independent voice on issues of social justice and labour reform in newly democratic Japan put Britain off-side, and irritated not merely the Americans but large sections of the Australian public as well, who wanted retribution, not rapprochement. Writing in 2013, the renowned British Japanese Studies specialist Ian Nish commented that Australia had 'taken on a new post-imperial approach' toward Japan, revealing itself as 'a power with an Asian connection and an Asian conscience'.[9]

Menzies himself became an advocate of reconciliation, reminding Australians in a public broadcast in March 1954 that 'the war is over'.[10] Holding Japan back was not good for Australia either. Rapidly rejuvenating, the former enemy seemed to be winning the peace after losing the war; bilateralism made good economic as well as political sense. But economic self-interest was not the be-all and end-all. By December 1957, Menzies was extending a handshake of friendship to Japanese prime minister Sato upon the latter's arrival at Essendon airport in Melbourne; at an official luncheon in Canberra, he spoke of the commonality of Australia and Japan's 'destiny in the Pacific'.[11] A few months earlier, Menzies had followed in BCOF's footsteps by himself journeying to Japan. Giving his all for the bilateral good, he was photographed heroically tackling sushi, tentatively transferred from plate to mouth with a pair of clumsily handled chopsticks. In between the prime ministerial visits, the Australia-Japan Commerce Agreement was signed, which was to become integral to Australia's prosperity in the 1950s and throughout the 1960s. Sixty years later, it was singled out for its historical importance in a meeting of Australian and Japanese prime ministers, the former (Tony Abbott) declaiming that the once-bitter adversaries had now become (for diplomacy's sake, at least) 'best friends'.[12]

It is impossible to imagine these developments without the cultural as well political groundwork laid by the Occupation, of which perhaps the most fundamental outcome was the Australians' realisation that the Japanese were people much like themselves, and not just an anonymous mass of military sadists and social automata. For all their foibles and occasional follies, and for all the ambivalence with which it approached Japan, the BCOF community was before its time, making its way in a country that has been *terra incognita* to most Australians until relatively recently. Over the years, much has been made of the gusto with which the Japanese throw themselves into the serious business of living. This, notoriously, can give the appearance of fanaticism, even neurosis. The great Meiji-era novelist Natsume Soseki called his countrymen and women 'an unfortunate people beset by the fierce appetites of life'.[13] To me, that description can equally be applied to the Australians who occupied their country after the war, many of whom enthusiastically savoured the cultural experience, and many of whom were morally overwhelmed by the power they had temporarily been granted.

Writing history is about striking a balance between opposing points of view and tallying the documentary evidence. This is especially so when that history concerns an event that combines so many co-existing contradictions as the Australian Occupation of Japan, in which attraction jostled with repulsion, welling sympathy with implacable vindictiveness, and entrenched parochialism with increasing worldliness. It was not too difficult to unearth material that illustrated the Japanese historian Eiji Takemae's perception of Australian 'supremacist attitudes' in Japan.[14] But that was not the whole story.

A recent work, Neil C. Smith's *Disarming the Menace* (2012), goes a little too far in attempting to retrieve the BCOF's reputation as a force for good. Smith's emphasis is on Australian kindness and compassion, and on the undying gratitude of the Japanese. Robertson, the BCOF commander – he who refused to shake a Japanese hand, and he who publicly admonished the citizens of Hiroshima for creating their own mess – is described as 'firm but fair'. Apparently the locals were bereft with sadness when he departed the country.[15] But the author does convey some delightfully revealing details, such as the fact that Robertson's driver, George Schneider, married a Japanese – a reminder of the astonishing number of BCOF servicemen men who wed Japanese women, bringing them home to an Australia slowly beginning the process of becoming less White. *Disarming the Menace* provides the first complete nominal roll of the BCOF fraternity, listing who was there and the units in which they served. That such a roll took until 2012 to appear, and then only through exhaustive independent research, is telling.

Meanwhile, the fight of the 'forgotten force' for official recognition continues. In 2018, the Australian War Memorial announced plans to expand its exhibitions, including galleries dedicated to modern veterans, those who served in Afghanistan, Iraq, the Solomons and East Timor, and in peacekeeping and humanitarian operations. However, it appears the BCOF will have to continue to make do with its little collection of relics and tourist paraphernalia. Occupation veterans finally received the coveted 'Gold Card' in 2017, covering their treatment for all health conditions, regardless of service. Nevertheless, the Department of Veterans' Affairs remains opposed to granting them a service pension, on the grounds they did not face danger from hostile enemy forces.[16] For an increasing percentage of BCOF vets, it is now too little, too late.

If the surviving BCOF servicemen, women, and children were upset at some of the censorious judgments of the force I made in *Travels in Atomic Sunshine*, they were too much too polite to say so. To enliven the documentary record, I drew deeply from the well of their goodwill and their preparedness to share their recollections. Usually, I met these people in their homes, from Brisbane to rural Victoria, going through their photo albums and admiring their carefully preserved memorabilia.

Talking about the war and its aftermath in Japan was a memorable experience. I felt like I had entered the world of my father, John Gerster, an artilleryman with the AIF who did two tours of duty to New Guinea and Bougainville from 1943 to 1945. This was to be his only travel abroad, ever; I remember this every time I touch down in Japan, to enjoy anew that extraordinary country. Tom Brokaw's *The Greatest Generation* (1998), on the generation of Americans who endured the Depression and then the armed conflict of the 1940s, could well be applied to their Australian contemporaries. Like others of my fortunate post-war generation, I have been the beneficiary of their travails.

Acknowledgements

This project was supported by a Discovery Grant from the Australian Research Council, which enabled me to conduct extensive research in Australia and abroad. In Japan, the hospitality of my good friends Bill Gater and Teruaki Fujishiro has been inexhaustible; I am also grateful to Akemi and Koichi Sato for their fine company and practical help over many years, first as neighbours in Tokyo and, more recently, as hosts in Yamaguchi. Shizuo Inoue, a citizen of Hiroshima and one-time BCOF employee, was of enormous assistance and is a remarkable figure in his own right. The curators at the Kure History Office were patiently obliging, and I thank Professor Takeshi Chida of Hiroshima International University for his guided tour of Occupation sites in Kure and Hiro. In the United States, James Zobel, the archivist at the MacArthur Memorial Library in Norfolk, Virginia, knew exactly where to find the material I was looking for. Thanks also to the librarians working with the Occupation holdings in the Butler Library at Columbia

University in New York City, and with the Prange Collection at the University of Maryland.

In Australia, the people at the Australian War Memorial Research Centre were always helpful, as were the staff at the National Archives. At Monash University, thanks to Carlin Payne and Louella d'Costa for their administrative support, and to Dunya Lindsey for her research assistance. Barbara Zion's proof reading of the manuscript was both discerning and rigorous; and Christine de Matos, Peter Eckersall, Kevin Foster, Peter Gerster, Peter Pierce, Lindsay Van Jager, and Margaret and John Wyenberg were sources of support and useful advice. The editorial and production staff at Scribe Publications were a pleasure to work with; I must particularly thank Henry Rosenbloom for his incisive comments on the book's early drafts. At home, Deborah, Benjamin, and Rafael patiently indulged my many absences during the four years I was immersed in this research.

The BCOF community in Australia was endlessly accommodating. I owe a debt of gratitude to Rosemarie Carman, the indefatigable spokesperson for the BCOF dependants. Rosemarie was always generous in sharing her intimate knowledge of, and research into, the lives of Australian families in Occupied Japan. Her meticulously detailed emails alone would make a book. Among the dependants, special thanks also to Bruce Fisher. Of the veterans, I want to acknowledge the goodwill of John Collins, Gordon Edwards, Murray Elliott, Dan Hart, Syd Margetts, and Les Oates. To all the BCOF people, I offer my apologies for any inaccuracies or ill judgments in the text.

Notes

Full citations are provided for sources the first time they appear in each chapter; thereafter they appear in abridged form. The following abbreviations signify major archival collections:

AWM: Australian War Memorial Research Centre (Canberra, Australia)
MAA: MacArthur Memorial Research Centre Archives (Norfolk, VA, United States)
NAA: National Archives of Australia (Canberra and Melbourne branches)
NLA: National Library of Australia (Canberra)

Introduction: Occupying Japan

1 T.A.G. Hungerford, 'Tourist with Haiku', in *A Knockabout with a Slouch Hat* (Fremantle Arts Centre Press, Fremantle, 1985), pp. 64–65.
2 'Democratising': quoted in Major A.W. John, *Duty Defined; Duty Done: the evolution of a director of army education* (The Gen Publishers, Cheltenham, Vic., 2004), p. 166; on American Tokyo: see Eiji Takemae, *The Allied Occupation of Japan*, trans. Robert Ricketts and Sebastian Swann (2002; Continuum, New York, 2003), p. 73.

3   Figures provided in 'A Brief History of Australia's Participation in the Occupation of Japan', at the BCOF web page: www.bradprint.com.au/bcof. See also Takeshi Chida, 'The British Commonwealth Occupation Forces in Japan and its Association with the Japanese', in Ian Gow and Yoichi Hirama (eds), *The History of Anglo-Japanese Relations 1600–2000*, vol. 3, *The Military Dimension* (Palgrave Macmillan, Basingstoke, 2003), p. 283. Australian Department of Veterans' Affairs estimates in 2004 provide the figure of 'about' 17,000 Australians serving with BCOF (with 77 deaths). See ch. 15, 'British Commonwealth Occupation Forces in Japan', p. 2, Report of the Review of Veterans' Entitlements, Hon John Clarke QC (chair), www.veteransreview.gov.au. On Australia's leadership of BCOF, see Jeffrey Grey, *Australian Brass: the career of Lieutenant General Sir Horace Robertson* (Cambridge University Press, Cambridge, 1992), p. 127.

4   Australian army, air, and naval forces served (under British command) alongside various Commonwealth units in the Malayan emergency in the late 1950s. Fifty-one Australians were killed in the emergency, which eventually ended in July 1960, 15 as a result of military operations.

5   A plethora of books, mainly concentrating on diplomatic and military aspects of the Occupation, has appeared in recent years. Among them are: Peter Bates, *Japan and the British Commonwealth Occupation Force 1946–52* (Brassey's, London, 1993); George Davies, *The Occupation of Japan: the rhetoric and reality of Anglo-Australasian relations 1939–1952* (University of Queensland Press, St Lucia, 2001); Christine de Matos, *Encouraging 'Democracy' in a Cold War Climate: the dual-platform policy approach of Evatt and Labor toward the Allied Occupation of Japan 1945–1949* (Australia–Japan Research Centre, University of Western Sydney, 2001); James Wood, *The Forgotten Force* (Allen & Unwin, Sydney, 1998). See also Carolyne Carter, 'Between War and Peace: the experience of Occupation for members of the British Commonwealth Occupation Force 1945–1952'; PhD thesis (Australian Defence Force Academy, Canberra, 2002).

6   Donald Richie, Preface to *Where Are the Victors?* (1956; Tuttle, Tokyo, 1986), p. 6.

7   Gordon Edwards, audiotaped interview with author, 18 March 2005.

8   Shizuo Inoue, response to Robin Gerster, 'A Cultural Study of the Occupation of Japan' questionnaire, 9 May 2005.

9 Shizuo Inoue, audiotaped interview with author, 23 May 2006.

10 Donald Richie, 'General Robertson Speaks on Japan', with text of Hiroshima speech, *Pacific Stars and Stripes*, c. September 1948.

11 Ibid.

12 See Robertson interview with Frank Clune, in *Ashes of Hiroshima* (Angus & Robertson, Sydney, 1950), p. 149; non-fraternisation edict quoted in full in Davies (2001), pp. 176–77.

13 Complaint: see John Morris, *The Phoenix Cup* (The Cresset Press, London, 1947), pp. 51–52; Japanese press reportage of Australian dislike: a correspondent to the *Nippon Times* in March 1950 wrote that he had recently asked an 'intelligent and pleasant' Australian woman why her husband had refused a good position in Japan early in the Occupation. '"It was my fault," she answered, "I was afraid to go there."' "Afraid of what?" the correspondent asked. '"Oh", she replied, "I couldn't bear the thought of living amongst those horrible little creatures."' See letter to editor, *Nippon Times*, 6 March 1950. Ball dinner anecdote: see Alan Rix, (ed.), *Intermittent Diplomat: the Japan and Batavia diaries of W. Macmahon Ball* (Melbourne University Press, Melbourne, 1988), p. 63.

14 Massey Stanley, 'Our men in Japan can't help fraternising', *Daily Telegraph*, 4 March 1946; J.G. Collins, *The War of the Veterans* (John G.F. Collins, Toowoomba, Qld, 2001), p. 33.

15 Allan S. Clifton, *Time of Fallen Blossoms* (Cassell, London, 1950), p. xiii; Douglas H. Mancktelow, *Atsuko and the Aussie* (DMA Press, Vancouver, 1991), pp. 2–3.

16 Clifton Pugh, letters to mother, Violet Pugh, 3 March 1946; 3 July 1946. NLA MS 9096 Papers of Clifton Pugh, Series 1.

17 T.A.G. Hungerford, *Sowers of the Wind* (Angus & Robertson, Sydney, 1954), pp. 165, 170; 'favours': Robert Bell, Australians at War Film Archive, Australian Government Department of Veterans' Affairs, interview 0953 (2004).

18 Clune (1950), pp. 56, 152.

19 See Hal Porter, *A Handful of Pennies* (1958), in Mary Lord (ed.), *Hal Porter* (University of Queensland Press, St Lucia, 1980), p. 79; Barry Demmler, personal correspondence, 30 October 2004.

20 See Gavan McCormack and Hank Nelson, *The Burma–Thailand Railway: memory and history* (Allen & Unwin, Sydney, 1993), pp. 153–55.

21 In Conrad's novel *An Outcast of the Islands*, set in what was then the Dutch East Indies, an Eastern trader advises a European businessman not to worry about being in a place so remote from his homeland: 'In leaving home one learns life. You travel. Travelling is victory! You shall return with much wisdom.' See *An Outcast of the Islands* (1896; J.M. Dent, London, 1949), p. 131. The military historian Jeffrey Grey has noted that the Occupation was Australia's 'first serious exposure to Japan'. See Jeffrey Grey, 'The Australian Occupation of Japan', *Journal of the Australian War Memorial*, issue 30 (April 1997).

22 Clune (1950), p. 185; I.R. Carter, *Alien Blossom: a Japanese–Australian love story* (Lansdowne, Melbourne, 1965), pp. 10, 12.

23 George Martin, personal correspondence, 10 January 2004.

24 Hungerford (1985), p. 67.

25 Murray Elliott, *Occupational Hazards: a doctor in Japan and elsewhere* (Griffith University, Brisbane, 1995), pp. 80, 91, 93; Betty Page, unpublished diary entry, Bofu, Japan, 27 February 1948; Bruce Fisher, personal correspondence, 6 November 2004.

26 Journalists visit Ball: see Rix (1988), p. 20; Calwell in *Sydney Morning Herald*, 6 March 1950.

27 Poll: see Prue Torney-Parlicki, '"Whatever the Thing May Be Called": the Australian news media and the atomic bombing of Hiroshima and Nagasaki', *Australian Historical Studies*, 31, no. 114 (April 2000), p. 61; Peter Ryan, 'Remembering Hiroshima', *Quadrant* (September 1994), p. 87.

28 Bill Towers diary, 24 February 1946, William Towers Papers, NLA MS 9112/3; Jim Grover, response to questionnaire, 15 January 2005; Gerry Walshe, quoted in http://bcofonline.com/raaf.com.

29 Hal Porter, *The Paper Chase* (Angus & Robertson, Sydney, 1966), pp. 280–81.

1. The Long Road

1 Peter Carey, *Wrong About Japan* (Faber and Faber, London, 2005), pp. 58, 87; 'bedouin encampment': C.B. Liddell, 'Nobuyoshi Araki – Intimate Photography: Tokyo, nostalgia and sex', *Japan Times*, 23 November 2006.

2 *Pacific Stars and Stripes*, 9 May 1946.

3 Message from Commander-in-Chief BCOF to the Acting Prime Minister of Australia, 11 May 1946, AWM 114, 130/1/10.

4 See account of the speech in Herbert P. Bix, *Hirohito and the Making of Modern Japan* (Perennial, New York, 2000), pp. 525–30.

5 Photographs in 'The Price of Freedom: Americans at war' gallery, National Museum of American History, Washington DC; 'front': MacArthur entry in *Australian Dictionary of Biography* www.adb.online.anu.edu.au.

6 See Douglas MacArthur, *Reminiscences* (McGraw-Hill, New York, 1964), p. 271. The precise wording of this famous quip varies slightly from account to account.

7 Major General Courtney Whitney, *MacArthur: his rendezvous with history* (Knopf, New York, 1968), pp. 249–50, 251.

8 Robert L. Eichelberger, *Our Jungle Road to Tokyo* (The Viking Press, New York, 1950), pp. 277, 279.

9 Bowers quoted in Robert Harvey, *American Shogun* (John Murray, London, 2006), p. 15; response to photograph: see Eiji Takemae, *The Allied Occupation of Japan*, trans. Robert Ricketts and Sebastian Swann (2002; Continuum, New York, 2003), p. 236.

10 'Chin' pun: see Edward Seidensticker, *Tokyo Rising* (Harvard University Press, Cambridge, Mass., 1990), p. 172.

11 Coleman letter dated 10 January 1947, MMA, R6-5 B.2 F.6, 'O.C., Jan–Dec 47'.

12 John Dower, *Embracing Defeat: Japan in the aftermath of World War II* (1999; Penguin, Harmondsworth, 2000), p. 23; General Arthur MacArthur: see Stanley Karnow, *In Our Image: America's empire in the Philippines* (Random House, New York, 1989), p. 171, and also 'Military Outlook in the Philippines', *New York Times,* 11 November 1900, p. 1.

13 Max Boot, *The Savage Wars of Peace: small wars and the rise of American power* (Basic Books, New York, 2003), p. 340; E.O. Reischauer, *The United States and Japan* (Harvard University Press, Cambridge, Mass., 1950), p. 40.

14 'Laboratory': see MacArthur, *Reminiscences*, pp. 283–84.

15 MacArthur on 'advanced spirituality': MacArthur quoted in Toshio Nishi, *Unconditional Democracy: education and politics in Occupied Japan 1945–1952* (Hoover Institution Press, Stanford, 1982), pp. 42–43 (bibles, p. 43); 'long stunted': MacArthur quoted in *BCON*, 31 September 1947, p. 1; 'personification': MacArthur quoted in Nishi, p. 46.

16 'Preeminently Christian': MacArthur's speech to the Veterans of the Rainbow (42D) Infantry Division of World War I, 14 July 1935, *Representative Speeches of General of the Army Douglas MacArthur* (U.S. Government Printing Office, Washington DC, 1964), p. 4; 'spiritual repugnance': Nishi, p. 42. See also Lawrence S. Wittner, 'MacArthur and the Missionaries: God and man in Occupied Japan', *Pacific Historical Review*, 40, no. 1 (1971).

17 'Signing of the Surrender Instrument by Japan', USS *Missouri*, Tokyo Bay, 2 September 1945: MacArthur, *Representative Speeches*, p. 9; press code: see Monica Braw, *The Atomic Bomb Suppressed: American censorship in Japan 1945–1949* (Liber Forlag, Tokyo, 1986), p. 42.

18 Wilfred G. Burchett, *Democracy with a Tommygun* (Cheshire, Melbourne, 1946), pp. 273, 275–76; Burchett, *Shadows of Hiroshima* (Verso, London, 1983), p. 32; Burchett dispatch quoted in *Shadows*, pp. 34–36; response to dispatch, see Tom Heenan, *From Traveller to Traitor: the life of Wilfred Burchett* (Melbourne University Publishing, Melbourne, 2006), p. 73.

19 Kurihara quoted in Braw (1986), p. 14.

20 Stimson quoted in Braw (1986), p. 141. The American self-image was at stake, as well as its international good name. While Japanese writers and filmmakers published a flood of previously suppressed narratives and images when the Occupation ended in 1952, film footage remained largely confiscated in the US until the late 1960s. See Lane Fenrich, 'Mass Death in Miniature', in Laura Hein and Mark Selden (eds), *Living with the Bomb: American and Japanese cultural conflicts in the nuclear age* (M.E. Sharpe, New York, 1997), p. 126.

21 Donald Richie, 'The Occupied Arts', Mark Sandler (ed.), *The Confusion Era: art and culture of Japan during the Allied Occupation 1945–1952* (Arthur M. Sackler Gallery, Washington DC, 1988), p. 12.

22 Prue Torney-Parlicki, *Somewhere in Asia: war, journalism and Australia's neighbours: 1941–75* (UNSW Press, Sydney, 2000), p. 59; see Homer, *The Iliad*, translated by Richmond Lattimore (University of Chicago Press, Chicago, 1951), book 20, line 48, p. 405.

23 James Murdoch quoted in David Walker, *Anxious Nation: Australia and the rise of Asia 1850–1939* (University of Queensland Press, St Lucia, 1999), p. 66.

24 Anon., *My Very First Little Book About Other Countries* (Henry Frowde and Hodder and Stoughton, no date), p. 41.

25 Murray Elliott, *Occupational Hazards: a doctor in Japan and elsewhere* (Griffith University, Brisbane, 1995), pp. 1–2.

26 See Frank Clune, *Sky High to Shanghai* (Angus & Robertson, Sydney, 1941), p. 88.

27 Frank Clune, 'Maps of Japanese empire', *Sydney Morning Herald*, 31 May 1938.

28 *Argus*, 13 February 1942; Curtin quoted in Peter Dennis et al, *The Oxford Companion to Australian Military History* (Oxford University Press, Melbourne, 1995), p. 323.

29 Blamey and Slim quoted in John Dower, *War Without Mercy* (Pantheon Books, New York, 1986), pp. 71, 112. Blamey interview, *New York Times*, 9 January 1943.

30 Faubion Bowers, 'Reminiscences', transcription of interview with Beate Gordon (1960), p. 12, no. 394, Oral History Research Office, Butler Library, Columbia University, New York.

31 Violation of corpses: see Mark Johnston, *Fighting the Enemy: Australian soldiers and their adversaries in World War II* (Cambridge University Press, Melbourne, 2000), pp. 87, 80; Lindbergh in Dower (1986), pp. 70–71.

32 See 'Webb Report on Japanese Atrocities', *Sydney Morning Herald*, 11 September 1945.

33 Rohan D. Rivett, *Behind Bamboo* (1946; Penguin, Melbourne, 1991), pp. 378–80; 'War Correspondent Indicts Jap POW Authorities', *Argus*, 15 September 1945; see also 'Appalling Ordeal of Prisoners on "Death Railway"', *Argus*, 13 September 1945; Norman Carter, *G-String Jesters* (Currawong Publishing, Sydney, 1966), p. 18.

34 See William H. Coaldrake (ed.), *Japan From War to Peace* (RoutledgeCurzon, London, 2003), p. 45.

2. Approaching Japan

1 W. Macmahon Ball, 'Australian Policy towards Japan since 1945' (1963), in Ball, *Australia and Japan: documents and readings in Australian history* (Thomas Nelson, Melbourne, 2000), p. 107; Christine de Matos, *Encouraging Democracy in a Cold War Climate* (Australia–Japan Research Centre, University of Western Sydney, 2001), p. 2, *passim*; see also Christine de Matos, 'Diplomacy Interrupted? Macmahon Ball, Evatt and Labor's Policies in Occupied Japan', *Australian Journal of Politics and History*, 52, no. 2 (2006), p. 193.

2 T.B. Millar, 'An Australian's Experiences in BCOF: Kaitaichi and Hiroshima, 1946–7', in Ian Nish (ed.), *The British Commonwealth and its Contribution to the Occupation of Japan, 1945–8* (Suntory-Toyota International Centre, London, 1991), p. 18; Chifley/Atlee negotiations: see George Davies, *The Occupation of Japan* (University of Queensland Press, St Lucia, 2001), pp. 105–06.

3 See Appendix 3, 'The MacArthur/Northcott Agreement', in Davies (2001), pp. 322–29; 'iniquitous document': Robertson, 'Some Reminiscences', Papers of Lt Gen Sir H.C.H. Robertson, AWM PR 87/167, p. 94.

4 MacArthur quoted in Davies (2001), p. 109.

5 Curtin–MacArthur correspondence, MMA, R6-5, Box 107, F-7 'Aust. P.M. Correspondence, Mar 42–Aug 50'; Chifley telegram 15 August 1945, MMA, R6-5 Records of General Headquarters, SCAP, 1945–1951, Folder 4.

6 Herbert Passin, *Encounter with Japan* (Kodansha International, Tokyo, 1982), p. 119; Theodore Cohen, *Remaking Japan: the American Occupation as new deal* (The Free Press, New York, 187), pp. 119, 122.

7 Eiji Takemae, *The Allied Occupation of Japan*, trans. Robert Ricketts and Sebastian Swann (2002; Continuum, New York, 2003), p. 67; Yuki Tanaka, *Japan's Comfort Women* (Routledge, London, 2002), see pp. 116–25; crime figures: p. 118.

8 Tanaka (2002), p. 149.

9 Ray Parkin, *The Sword and the Blossom* (Hogarth, London, 1968), pp. 217, 225.

10 For a discussion of the RAA, see John Dower, *Embracing Defeat: Japan in the aftermath of World War II* (1999; Penguin, London, 2000), pp. 126–30; 'shock absorber': see Takemae (2003), p. 68; 'female floodwall': see Michael S. Molasky, *The American Occupation of Japan and Okinawa* (Routledge, London, 1999), pp. 105, 107; see also Eric Talmadge, 'Coercion seen in brothels for Occupation', *Japan Times*, 27 April 2007.

11 See Tanaka (2002), p. 147; see also Takemae (2003), p. 68.

12 Tokyo prostitution figures: Tanaka (2002), p. 155; on Hiroshima brothels: Tanaka (2002), pp. 136–37; Takeshi Chida, 'The British Commonwealth Occupation Forces in Japan and its Association with the Japanese', in Ian Gow and Yoichi Hirama (eds), *The History of*

Anglo–Japanese Relations 1600–2000, vol. 3, *The Military Dimension* (Palgrave Macmillan, Basingstoke, 2003), p. 286.

13 Northcott quoted in Peter Bates, *Japan and the British Commonwealth Occupation Force 1946–52* (Brassey's, London, 1993) p. 43; Jack Percival, 'Japanese Ask: Why a British Force?' *Sydney Morning Herald*, 12 January 1946.

14 See Jeffrey Grey, *Australian Brass: the career of Lieutenant General Sir Horace Robertson* (Cambridge University Press, Cambridge, 1992), p. 127.

15 See Carolyne Carter, 'Between War and Peace: the experience of Occupation for members of the British Commonwealth Occupation Force 1945–1952', PhD thesis (Australian Defence Force Academy, Canberra, 2002), p. 50. Figures taken from 34 Aust Inf Bde War Diary General Summary, 25 September 1945–31 October 1945, AWM 52, 8/2/33, p. 1.

16 T.A.G. Hungerford, 'Incident in Morotai', in *A Knockabout with a Slouch Hat* (Fremantle Arts Centre Press, Fremantle, 1985), p. 48; see Anne Blair, *Ruxton: a biography* (Allen & Unwin, Sydney, 2004), p. 33.

17 Terry Briscoe, response to Robin Gerster, 'A Cultural Study of the Occupation of Japan' questionnaire, 5 December 2004; Les Semken in *The Forgotten Force*, dir. Raymond Quint (Film Australia, 1993); William Towers, letter 7 April 1946, NAA MS 9112/3.

18 Steve Macaulay, 'The Long Road to Japan', in Larry Lacey, *BCOF: an unofficial history* (Larry Lacey, Yamba, NSW, 1995) p. 113.

19 John Morris, *The Phoenix Cup* (The Cresset Press, London, 1947), p. 56; Les Murray, *The Boys Who Stole the Funeral* (Angus & Robertson, Sydney, 1980), p. 128.

20 Recruiting advertisement: see, for example, *Daily Mirror* (Sydney), 25 March 1946; Bob Christison, correspondence with author, 19 October 2004; Murray Elliott, audiotaped interview with author, 13 July 2006.

21 Steve Macaulay, 'The Long Road to Japan', p. 113; T.B. Millar, 'An Australian's Experiences in BCOF', in Ian Nish (ed.), *The British Commonwealth and its Contribution to the Occupation of Japan* (Suntory–Toyota International Centre, London, 1991), p. 20; Murray Elliott, *Occupational Hazards: a doctor in Japan and elsewhere* (Griffith University, Brisbane, 2005), p. 17.

22 Allan S. Clifton, *Time of Fallen Blossoms* (Cassell, London, 1950), p. xiii.

23 Dan Hart, *Fido and Friends* (Tempe Harvey, Brisbane, 2005), pp. 281–82; also personal correspondence, 13 October 2005.

24 Hungerford (1985), p. 50.

25 See Ron Orwin, *The Signal Continues: a history of the BCOF Signals Regiment* (Ron Orwin, Logan Lea Q'land, 2006), pp. 11–12; James Wood, *The Forgotten Force* (Allen & Unwin, Sydney, 1998), pp. 45–47.

26 James Hingston, *The Australian Abroad* (Sampson, Low, Marston, Searle and Rivington, London, 1879), p. 70; 66 Inf. Bn BCOF War Diary, December 45–February 46, Appendix Q, Summary of Events – 66th Bn's Advance Party', AWM 52 8/3/103; see also Stephen Kelen, 'The Day We Landed in Japan', *Shinbun*, no. 53 (March–April 1993), p. 57.

27 *Taos Digger*, no. 6, 21 February 1946.

3. In the City of the Dead

1 Donald Richie, *The Inland Sea* (1971; Stone Bridge Press, Berkeley, Cal., 2002), pp. 206–09.

2 Northcott's reconnaissance described in Carolyne Carter, 'Between War and Peace: the experience of Occupation for members of the British Commonwealth Occupation Force 1945–1952', PhD thesis (Australian Defence Force Academy, Canberra, 2002), p. 62.

3 Murray Elliott, *Occupational Hazards: a doctor in Japan and elsewhere* (Griffith University, Brisbane, 1995), see pp. 17–19.

4 Reference to 'the City of the Dead' contained in correspondence with Derek Hopper (who served, in Intelligence, with the 2nd Battalion of the Dorsetshire Regiment), 20 November 2004; William H. Coaldrake (ed.), *Japan from War to Peace* (RoutledgeCurzon, London, 2003), p. 325.

5 Hal Porter, *The Paper Chase* (Angus & Robertson, Sydney, 1966), pp. 266, 287.

6 H.K. Wood, 'A soldier from Japan says it's hell at Kure', *Sunday Sun & Guardian*, 11 August 1946.

7 See Brian Rose, personal correspondence, 11 February 2005; Earle Morgan, personal correspondence, 30 November 2004; Clifton Pugh, letter to mother, 24 February 1946, NLA MS 9096 Papers of Clifton

Pugh, Series 1; cast-off clothing: see Stewart Legge, 'Men for Japan Discouraged and Impatient', *Courier Mail,* 15 January 1946.

8   Harry Roskolenko, 'Tokyo Letter', *Meanjin,* 6, no. 1 (Autumn 1947), p. 64.

9   Atcheson quoted in Akio Watanabe, 'From Bitter Enmity to Cold Partnership: Japanese views of the United Kingdom 1945–52', in Ian Nish (ed.), *Anglo–Japanese Alienation 1919–1952* (Cambridge University Press, Cambridge, 1982), p. 249; arguments: see for example the set-to between Atcheson and Derevyanko on the censorship of militaristic Japanese publications, verbatim minutes of Allied Council meeting 24 July 1947, Papers of William Macmahon Ball, NLA MS 7851 Series 13 Folder 3. Evatt's caustic assessment of Ball was communicated to a friend of MacArthur's, the newspaper proprietor Roy Howard, who passed it on to the general. See Roy Howard, 'Personal and Confidential' letter to MacArthur, 31 May 1946, MMA, R6-5.B107.F3, 'Australian Mission Corresp.' Macmahon Ball's resentment at Evatt's apparent double-dealing is expressed in a letter to Sir Frederic Eggleston, 5 August 1947; see Ball Papers Series 13 Folder 16.

10 'Report on Lecture Tour of BCOF in Japan', p. 4, T. Inglis Moore Papers, NLA MS 8130, Series 8B, Folder 3; Willoughby and map: see Peter Bates, *Japan and the British Commonwealth Occupation Force 1946–52* (Brassey's, London, 1993), p. 84.

11 Gascoigne quoted in Jeffrey Grey, *Australian Brass: the career of Lieutenant General Sir Horace Robertson* (Cambridge University Press, Melbourne, 1992), p. 157; Ball's opinion of Robertson in Alan Rix (ed.), *Intermittent Diplomat* (Melbourne University Press, Melbourne, 1988), p. 143; 'Some Reminiscences', Papers of Lt Gen. Sir H.C.H. Robertson, AWM PR 87/167, pp. 82, 103–04.

12 'British Commonwealth Occupation Force: entertainment allowance for Commander-in-Chief, BCOF', NAA 1698/1 Series No A5954/69; *Chicago Tribune,* 20 November 1946, quoted in Grey (1992), p. 142; 'feudal baron': Thwaites in *The Express,* 24 April 1948, quoted in Prue Torney, '"Renegades to their Country": the Australian press and the Allied Occupation of Japan, 1946–1950', *War & Society,* 25, no. 1 (May 2006), p. 101.

13 Robertson profile: *Sun* 'Weekend Magazine', 24 April 1954; Major H.C.H. Robertson, *Defence of Australia* (Smith and Lane Printers,

Sydney, 1934), p. 2, Robertson Papers, AWM PR 87/167; Robertson, 'Some Reminiscences', pp. 36–37.

14 BCOF's role: see George Davies, *The Occupation of Japan* (University of Queensland Press, St Lucia, 2001), p. 173; 'prestige': Patrick Shaw, 'Report by the Head of the Australian Mission on his visit to BCOF Area', dated 17 May 1948, NAA 52/301/273 Series A816, p. 1.

15 Robertson on Gairdner and Gascoigne: 'Some Reminiscences', pp. 53–54, 56.

16 Foreign Office official: see Watanabe, 'From Bitter Enmity to Cold Partnership', p. 263; Robertson's view, 'Some Reminiscences', p. 64; Dening in Grey (1992), p. 154 (see also p. 157); Robertson to Ball: Rix (1988), p. 149.

17 Robertson, 'Some Reminiscences'; on American browbeating: p. 73; trains: p. 6.

18 Ibid., pp. 13–14.

19 Eichelberger quoted in Grey (1992) p. 159; Gascoigne letter to Robertson, 26 August 1952, quoted in Grey (1992), p. 177.

20 Audience with MacArthur: Robertson, 'Some Reminiscences', p. 14.

21 Earle Morgan, personal correspondence, 30 November 2004; Papers of C.R. Stringer, unpub. typescript, p. 4, AWM 749/100/24.

22 Ian A. Wood, 'Diary kept while with the Australian Army of Occupation, Japan 1946', State Library of Victoria, MS 11637; Dorothy Drain, 'Tokio Japs curiously submissive to conquerors', *The Australian Women's Weekly*, 13, no. 51, 1 June 1946, p. 17.

23 H.K. Wood, 'A soldier from Japan says it's hell at Kure', *Sunday Sun & Guardian*, 11 August 1946.

24 'Lost souls': 65 Inf Bn BCOF War Diary February–March 1946, 21 March 1946, AWM52, 8/3/102; tours: 66 Aust. Inf Bn Monthly Intelligence Summary no. 2 for the period ending 31 May 1946, AWM 52 8/3/103.

25 Robertson, 'Some Reminiscences', pp. 49–50; see also David Horner (ed.), *Duty First: the Royal Australian Regiment in war and peace* (Allen & Unwin, Sydney, 1990), p. 39.

26 Hal Porter review in *The Gen*, 7, no. 10 (October 1949).

27 Miles Franklin, letter to Frank Ryland, 14 June 1946, NLA MS 6238; 'Production of BCON Forces Newspaper in Japan', Appendix 'A', NAA Series A 5954, item 1909/2.

28 Robertson to Ball: see Rix (1988), p. 128.

29 Jim Grover, response to Robin Gerster, 'A Cultural Study of the Occupation of Japan' questionnaire, 15 January 2005; golf: see Arthur W. John, *Uneasy Lies the Head that Wears a Crown* (The Gen Publishers, Cheltenham, Vic., 1987), p. 64; picnic: see *Shinbun*, no. 54 (May–June 1993), p. 49.

30 *The Manoora Times*, vol. 1 no. 10, 14 April 1947.

4. Bile, Spit, and Polish

1 See Paul Fussell, *Abroad: British literary traveling between the wars* (Oxford University Press, New York, 1980), p. 39.

2 BCOF Labour Service figures quoted in James Wood, *The Forgotten Force* (Allen & Unwin, Sydney, 1998), p. 135.

3 Jim Grover, response to Robin Gerster, 'A Cultural Study of the Occupation of Japan' questionnaire, 15 January 2005; Brian Rose, personal correspondence, 11 February 2005.

4 'Some Reminiscences', Papers of Lt Gen. Sir H.C.H. Robertson, AWM PR87/167, p. 37.

5 'Troops Rush from Swaying Buildings', *BCON*, 23 December 1946.

6 Alan Queale, 'Japan Diary', *As You Were* (Australian War Memorial, Canberra, 1947), p. 190.

7 Returnees: see table of figures, Carolyne Carter, 'Between War and Peace: the experience of Occupation for members of the British Occupation Force 1945–1952', PhD thesis (Australian Defence Force Academy, Canberra, 2002), p. 203; photograph by Allan George Cuthbert, 27 June 1946, AWM collections, no 131649.

8 Allan S. Clifton, *Time of Fallen Blossoms* (Cassell, London, 1950), pp. 82–83, 86; see Ulrich Strauss, *The Anguish of Surrender: Japanese POWs of World War II* (University of Washington Press, Seattle, 2003), pp. 234–35.

9 See Clifton (1950), pp. 132–33.

10 Ibid., p. 132; Semken: see Wood (1998), pp. 75, 77.

11 Murray Elliott, *Occupational Hazards: a doctor in Japan and elsewhere* (Griffith University, Brisbane, 1995), p. 30.

12 D.D. Hopper, letter to BCOF Veterans Association, dated 1 March 1988, reprinted in *Sukoshi Shimbun*, BCOF Veterans (NSW Branch) newsletter, 1, no. 10 (no year) p. 16.

13 Charles E. Astley, 'Grisly Memories', *Sukoshi Shimbun*, 1, no. 10 (no year), p. 15.

14 'British Force's Inadequate Duties', *The Times*, 5 February 1947; 'C-in-C Opens WLKS, States BCOF Men Efficient', *BCON*, 30 November 1946.

15 Report on Phase I Operation FOXUM – 2 September 1946, BCOF HQ Base, AWM 114, 130/1/41.

16 SCAP Directive 642, 21 January 1946; Clifton (1950), pp. 180–81.

17 HQ BCB, BCOF Monthly Intelligence Summary no. 7, October 1946, p. 3, AWM 114 423/10/17; 'terrible': Eric Lambert, *The Twenty Thousand Thieves* (Newmont, Melbourne, 1951), p. 27.

18 See figures in Wood (1998), p. 142; see also p. 137.

19 Bob Christison, 'Lasting Memories', *BCON* magazine, 2, no. 4 (Oct 2000); Ian A. Wood, *On Patrol with the B.C.O.F. in Japan* (Ian A. Wood, Mudgeeraba, Qld, 1994), p. 30; John Morris, *The Phoenix Cup* (The Cresset Press, London, 1947), p. 49.

20 Frank Clune, *Ashes of Hiroshima* (Angus & Robertson, Sydney, 1950), p. 185.

21 Clune (1950), p. 186; Wood (1994), pp. 50–52.

22 'British Force's Inadequate Duties', *The Times*, 5 February 1947,

23 Peter Russo, 'Then and Now', *BCON*, 25 December 1948.

24 See HQ BCB, BCOF Monthly Intelligence Summary, Appendix A to Summary no. 9 (December 1946), p. 2, AWM 114 423/10/17.

25 Noboru Ota quoted in Takeshi Chida, 'The British Comonwealth Occupation Forces in Japan and its Association with the Japanese', in Ian Gow and Yoichi Hirama (eds), *The History of Anglo–Japanese Relations, 1600–2000*, vol. 3 *The Military Dimension* (Palgrave Macmillan, Basingstoke, 2003) pp. 285–86.

26 'Convicts': Takeshi Chida quoted in Peter Bates, *Japan and the British Commonwealth Occupation Force 1946–1952* (Brassey's, London, 1993), p. 115.

27 Stephen Kelen, *Goshu* (Horwitz, Sydney, 1965), p. 116; Ray Parkin, *The Sword and the Blossom* (Hogarth, London, 1968), p. 220.

28 See Major Jim Hammett, 'We Were Soldiers Once', *Australian Army Journal* (Autumn 2008). An infantry officer who served in Somalia, East Timor, and Iraq, Hammett claims that the Australian infantry's frustrations at being shielded from combat action in Iraq led to some soldiers being ashamed of their uniforms. Hammett's article received widespread publicity at home and abroad, at a time when Australia drastically downsized its military commitments in Iraq.

29 Morris (1947), p. 17; Richard Hughes, *Foreign Devils* (Andre Deutsch, London, 1972), p. 73.

30 Richard Hughes, 'BCOF "Muffs" Opportunity', Melbourne *Herald*, 11 April 1947; see also 'Anzac Display in Japan Cut', Melbourne *Herald*, 9 April 1947.

31 Richard Hughes, 'Tokyo Anzac March Side Street Affair', Melbourne *Herald*, 28 April 1947.

32 Atcheson letter to MacArthur, quoting Ball, 21 May 1947, MMA, R6-5.B.107.F.3 'Australian Mission Corresp.'; Stephen Kelen, 'The Day We Landed in Japan', *Shinbun*, no. 53 (March–April 1993), p. 67; Lt-Col F.J.C. Piggott, 'Occupying Japan', *Army Quarterly*, 54 (April 1947–July 1947), p. 115.

33 See figures in Carter (2002), p. 201.

34 Robertson and the archbishop: see Ball anecdote in Alan Rix (ed.), *Intermittent Diplomat: the Japan and Batavia diaries of W. Macmahon Ball* (Melbourne University Press, Melbourne, 1988), p. 150.

35 Cabinet Agendum, 'Fraternisation Policy of British Commonwealth Occupation Force in Japan', NAA Series MP1049/5 Item 1869/2/52; see Melbourne *Herald*, 29 September 1949.

36 Russo, 'Then and Now'.

37 T.A.G. Hungerford. 'Tourist with Haiku', *A Knockabout with a Slouch Hat* (Fremantle Arts Centre Press, Fremantle, 1985), p. 70.

5. Tabi No Haji Wa Kakisute

1 See Walt Sheldon, *The Honorable Conquerors* (Macmillan, New York, 1965), pp. 143–44.

2 Shizuo Inoue, audiotaped interview with author, 23 May 2006; George Martin, personal correspondence, 10 January 2004.

3 Allan Wells, response to Robin Gerster, 'A Cultural Study of the Occupation of Japan' questionnaire, 12 December 2004.

4 'Example': see 'C-in-C Opens WLKS, States BCOF Men Efficient', *BCON*, 30 November 1946; Stephen Kelen, *Goshu* (Horwitz, Sydney, 1965), p. 34, see also p. 67; age of officers: commanding officer report for Nov 1945, HQ 34th Aust. Inf. Bde War Diary, AWM 52, 8/3/104; quoted in Carolyne Carter, 'Between War and Peace: the experience of Occupation for members of the British Commonwealth Occupation Force 1945–1952', PhD thesis (Australian Defence Force Academy, Canberra, 2002), p. 50.

5   Donald Richie, *Where Are the Victors?* (1956; Tuttle, Tokyo, 1986), pp. 44, 158.

6   Bede Wall, 'In the Army of Occupation 1946–47', unpublished and undated ms, pp. 1, 6; Les Tanner, 1991 interview, in Mary Lord, *Hal Porter: man of many parts* (Random House, Sydney, 1993), p. 50; Allan S. Clifton, *Time of Fallen Blossoms* (Cassell, London, 1950), p. 22.

7   Murray Elliott, *Occupational Hazards: a doctor in Japan and elsewhere* (Griffith University, Brisbane, 1995), pp. 22–23.

8   Wall, 'In the Army of Occupation', p. 14; Steve Macaulay, audiotaped interview with author, 14 September 2005.

9   Jennie Woods, *Which Way Will the Wind Blow?* (Jennie Woods, North Sydney, 1994), p. 64.

10 Hal Porter, *A Handful of Pennies* (1958), in Mary Lord (ed.), *Hal Porter* (University of Queensland Press, 1980), p. 132. (The disgrace of the Nijimura schoolteacher is alluded to in *The Paper Chase*, p. 293).

11 Ibid., pp. 136, 152. There may be some self-exculpation in Porter's handling of the padre's homosexuality, given his own rumoured infatuations with senior male students at Nijimura, and his tendency to deflect or suppress those paedophilic tendencies sensationally revealed by his biographer and friend Mary Lord, who disclosed he had engaged in sexual activity with her own ten-year-old son: see Lord (1993).

12 Wall, 'In the Army of Occupation', p. 13; T.A.G. Hungerford, *Sowers of the Wind* (Angus & Robertson, Sydney, 1954), p. 164.

13 L.H. Evers, *Pattern of Conquest* (Currawong, Sydney, 1954), pp. 27–29, 62.

14 Hal Porter, letter to Margery Sullivan, 2 August 1977, in author's possession; Pugh, letter to mother, 27 August 1946, NLA MS 9096, Papers of Clifton Pugh, Series 1.

6. Crimes and Misdemeanours

1   123 Aust. Transport Platoon War Diary, June–September 1947, AWM 52 10/4/128; 66 Inf Bn BCOF War Diary, October–December 1947, Routine Orders Part 1, 15 October 1947, AWM52 8/3/103/17.

2   123 Transport Platoon War Diary January–May 1947, AWM 52 10/4/128.

3   *Gloom* ('Being a detailed account of the carryings-on at Eta Jima'), 'Mark 7', illustrated typescript, undated.

4   Deputy Assistant Marshal HQ BCOF, January–December 1948, AWM 52 18/1/10.

5   History of BCOF Provost Services – Work of SIB Sections, Appendix A, 2 April 1948, AWM 114 803/5/1.

6   Provost Monthly Résumé of Serious Incidents in BCOF area during month ending 31 May 1948, Deputy Assistant Marshal HQ BCOF, 1948 AWM 52 18/1/10; Provost Monthly Résumé, period ending 28 January 1949, AWM 52 18/1/10; Provost Monthly Résumé, period ending 28 Febuary 1951, AWM 52 18/1/10.

7   'Incidents Involving the Occupation Forces', HQ BCB Kure, 23 July 1946, AWM 52 1/8/52 Part 1.

8   Carolyne Carter, 'Between War and Peace: the experience of Occupation for members of the British Occupation Force 1945–1952', PhD thesis (Australian Defence Force Academy, Canberra, 2002), p. 213; crime statistics: tabled pp. 287, 289.

9   See reports in *Chugoku Shimbun*, 30 September 1952; *Chugoku Nippo*, 1 May 1953; for example, *Chugoku Shimbun*, 11 November 1952; *Asahi Shimbun*, 6 June 1953. See Australia–Japan Research Project Database, Australian War Memorial, www.awm.gov.au.

10 *Chicago Tribune*, 20 November 1946; quoted in Jeffrey Grey, *Australian Brass: the career of Lieutenant General Sir Horace Robertson* (Cambridge University Press, Cambridge, 1992), p. 142.

11 Yuki Tanaka, *Rape and War* (Monash University Papers of the Japanese Studies Centre, Clayton, Vic., 1995), p. 41; *Hidden Horrors: Japanese war crimes in World War II* (Westview Press, Boulder, Col., 1996), p. 104.

12 Allan S. Clifton, *Time of Fallen Blossoms* (Cassell, London, 1950), pp. 142, 144–45, 147.

13 Ibid., pp. 141, 143.

14 'Conduct of BCOF Troops – Allegations by Allan Clifton – Statement by Capt. T.B. Millar', 13 March 1951, NAA MP 742/1 85/1/109. My italics.

15 Bruce Ruxton quoted in 'RSL Denies Mass Rape in Occupied Japan', *The Australian*, 24 September 1993; letter writer: *The Australian*, 18 October 1993; Carroll's support: *The Age*, 25 September 1993.

16 Les Oates, taped interview with author, 26 July 2006; Clifton in Tanaka (1996), p. 104.

17 Clifton (1950), pp. 143–44.

18 HQ BCB Monthly Intelligence Summary no. 12; Japanese Attitude to the Civil Police, Appendix A, 12 April 1947, AWM 114, 423/10/64; quoted in Carter (2002), p. 192; sentences: see Carter (2002), p. 294.

19 Hugh Cortazzi, 'Britain and the Occupation of Japan', in Ian Nish (ed.) *The British Commonwealth and its Contribution to the Occupation of Japan* (Suntory–Toyota International Centre, London, 1991), p. 43.

20 Provost Monthly Résumé of Serious Incidents in BCOF Area during month ending 31 May 1948, Deputy Assistant Marshal HQ BCOF, AWM 52 18/1/10; 'Some Reminiscences', Papers of Lt Gen. Sir H.C.H. Robertson, AWM PR 87/167, p. 41.

21 Letters of Flight Lt James H. Hawes, RAAF, BCOF 1946–1947, AWM PR 85/044. Letters dated 3, 6 May 1946.

22 'Riot at Hiro 30th August 1947 Concerning Indian and Australian Personnel' NAA A5954 1883/6; see also account in Colin Funch, *Linguists in Uniform* (Japanese Studies Centre, Clayton, Vic., 2003), p. 249.

23 Eiji Takemae, *The Allied Occupation of Japan*, trans. Robert Ricketts and Sebastian Swann (2002; Continuum, New York, 2003), p. 135.

24 *Daily Telegraph* report and Army Cipher Message, 13 October 1947, Classified 'Secret' from BCOF to Defence Department, in 'Riot at Hiro' documentation NAA A5954 1883/6.

7. Anything Goes

1 A.B. Facey, *A Fortunate Life* (Penguin, Harmondsworth, 1981), p. 252.

2 Allan S. Clifton, *Time of Fallen Blossoms* (Cassell, London, 1950), pp. 144–45.

3 Herbert Passin, *Encounter with Japan* (Kodansha International, Tokyo, 1982), pp. 125–26; HQ BCB, BCOF Monthly Intelligence Summary, no. 11 (for the month of February 1947), p. 1, AWM 114 423/10/17. 'Drink causes some horrible strife here,' Allan Chick wrote home from Japan in November 1947. See letter dated 4 November 1947, Allan Chick Papers, AWM PR 52 85/189.

4 T.B. Millar, 'An Australian's Experiences in BCOF', in Ian Nish (ed.), *The British Commonwealth and its Contribution to the Occupation of Japan* (Suntory–Toyota International Centre, London, 1991), pp. 20, 31; Lt Gen. John Northcott, Foreword to *Know Japan* (The Rodney Press, South Yarra, Vic., 1946), p. 3.

5 *Know Japan*, pp. 40–42, 87.

6 BCOF Intelligence Summary no. 11; T.A.G. Hungerford, *Sowers of the Wind* (Angus & Robertson, Sydney, 1954), pp. 164–65.

7 Skillicorn's objections: see *Sukoshi Shimbun*, 1, no. 1 (January–February 1995), p. 4.

8 Clifton (1950), p. 148; Gordon Leed, unpublished and undated manuscript entitled 'Sailing without a Chart', in author's possession, p. 152.

9 'Safeguarding British Commonwealth Occupation Force Stores', Report by the Joint Administrative Planning Committee, 11 May 1948, NAA A 5799 55/1948; 'Résumé of Serious Incidents During Week Ending 25 July 1946', AWM 52 1/8/52, Appendix A, Part 1.

10 Clifton (1950), p. 52.

11 'Marketo', in *Gloom*, Mark 7, undated.

12 Pugh letters to mother, 24 February, 17 April 1946, NLA MS 9096, Papers of Clifton Pugh, Series 1.

13 Hugh Cortazzi, 'Britain and the Occupation of Japan', in Ian Nish (ed.), *The British Commonwealth and its Contribution to the Occupation of Japan* (Suntory–Toyota International Centre, London, 1991), p. 38. See Carolyne Carter, 'Between War and Peace: the experience of Occupation for members of the British Commonwealth Occupation Force 1945–1952', PhD thesis (Australian Defence Force Academy, Canberra, 2002), p. 184, on punishments for black market offences.

14 Murray Elliott, audiotaped interview with author, 13 July 2006; Hungerford (1954), p. 192; Dan Hart, audiotaped interview with author, 13 July 2006.

15 Hungerford (1954), pp. 164, 198; T.A.G. Hungerford, 'Tourist with Haiku', *A Knockabout with a Slouch Hat* (Fremantle Arts Centre Press, Fremantle, 1985), p. 72.

16 L.H. Evers, *Pattern of Conquest* (Currawong, Sydney, 1954), p. 268.

17 Brian Rose, personal correspondence, 11 February 2005.

8. Home Affront

1 See *Reveille*, 1 March 1930, p. 48.

2 Allan S. Clifton, *Time of Fallen Blossoms* (Cassell, London, 1950), p. xiv; Michael Crouch, *The Literary Larrikin: a critical biography of T.A.G. Hungerford* (University of Western Australia Press, Perth, 2005), p. 131; L.H. Evers, *Pattern of Conquest* (Currawong, Sydney, 1954), p. 267.

3 Stewart Legge, 'Men for Japan Discouraged and Impatient', *Courier Mail*, 15 January 1946; T.A.G. Hungerford, 'Incident at Morotai', *A*

Knockabout with a Slouch Hat (Fremantle Arts Centre Press, Fremantle, 1985), p. 50.

4   H.K. Wood, 'A soldier from Japan says it's hell at Kure', *Sunday Sun & Guardian*, 11 August 1946.

5   See 'How Long Must this Be Endured?' *Smith's Weekly*, 5 October 1946.

6   'Australian Sufferings in Kure', *Sunday Telegraph*, 15 August 1946.

7   A Smaller Force in Japan', *The Age*, 16 April 1948.

8   VD advertisement: *Sydney Morning Herald*, 4 January 1946; 'whoremongers': Dr William Regan, response to Robin Gerster, 'A Cultural Study of the Occupation of Japan' questionnaire, 20 April 2005.

9   Peter Bates, *Japan and the British Commonwealth Occupation Force 1946–52* (Brassey's, London, 1993), p. 104; 'High incidence of venereal disease within BCOF', appendix to JCOSA agendum 61, 30 August 1946, quoted in Jeffrey Grey, *Australian Brass: the career of Lieutenant General Sir Horace Robertson* (Cambridge University Press, Cambridge, 1992), p. 139.

10 Bruce Ruxton quoted in *The Australian*, 24 September 1993; JCOSA report in Grey (1992), p. 139.

11 '"Moral rot" among BCOF men', *Daily Telegraph*, 13 January 1948; 'Hiroshima Orphans', *Sydney Morning Herald*, 26 April 1948; Thwaites: 'Charges By Ex-officer from Japan', *Sydney Morning Herald*, 5 April 1948. Prue Torney, '"Renegades to their Country": the Australian press and the Allied Occupation of Japan 1946–1950', *War & Society*, 25, no. 1 (May 2006), provides an excellent account of the press controversies surrounding BCOF.

12 'Dentist': 'Some Reminiscences', Papers of Lt Gen. Sir H.C.H. Robertson, AWM 87/167, p. 107; Les Oates, 'The Australian experience of the occupation, 1946 to 1952', in Paul Jones and Pam Oliver, *Changing Histories: Australia and Japan* (Monash Asia Institute, Clayton, Vic., 2001), p. 81; 'B.C.O.F. Men "Defamed"', *Sydney Morning Herald*, 20 May 1947; reports quoted in Torney (2006), p. 103; see also pp. 99–100, 102.

13 They remain so. As late as 1993, Heylen's speech was comprehensively quoted in the BCOF veterans' magazine *Shinbun*. See 'Remember This?', *Shinbun*, no. 54 (May–June 1993), pp. 33–36.

14 See Torney (2006), p. 104.

15 Chambers letter to prime minister Chifley, 17 January 1947, Appendix A, p. 3, NAA 19/307/388 Series A 816; Major-General S.R. Burston, 'Report of a visit to the British Commonwealth Occupation Forces in Japan', AWM 114 130/1/45, pp. 17–18.

16 Robertson letter to Chifley, 2 July 1946, NAA A5954/1 1886.

17 See Roma Donnelly, 'The Forgotten Women: women in the British Commonwealth Occupation Force in Japan, 1946–1952', in Paul Jones and Vera Mackie (eds), *Relationships: Japan and Australia 1870s–1950s* (History Department, University of Melbourne, 2001), p. 204; Robertson in *Australian Women's Weekly*, 15, no. 33, 24 January 1948, p. 19, quoted in Roma Donnelly, 'A Civilising Influence? Women in the British Commonwealth Occupation Force in Japan 1946–1952', MA thesis (Swinburne, Melbourne, 1994), p. 139. See Rosa Donnelly Papers, AWM MSS 1555.

18 Mary Bleechmore quoted in Donnelly, 'The Forgotten Women', p. 208; Paddy Power, audiotaped interview with author, 31 August 2005.

19 *Smith's Weekly*, 5 October 1946.

20 See 'Police Guard Troopship', *Sydney Morning Herald*, 14 September 1946; psychiatric evacuees: see Major A.W. John, *Duty Defined; Duty Done* (The Gen Publishers, Cheltenham, Vic., 2004), p. 210; problems: Carolyne Carter, 'Between War and Peace: the experience of Occupation for members of the British Commonwealth Occupation Force 1945–1952', PhD thesis (Australian Defence Force Academy, Canberra, 2002), p. 298.

21 'Psychiatric Report for the Quarter Ending 30 Sept 1947', 92nd Indian General Hospital (Combined) Statistical Section Quarterly Report, AWM 114 130/1/16; Burston report, pp. 6, 7.

22 Death statistics cited in Senate *Official Hansard* (Canberra), Wednesday 27 August 1997, in answer given by Senator Newman, the minister representing the Minister for Defence, Industry, Science, and Personnel, to question (no. 625) concerning BCOF pension entitlements.

23 Colin Funch, *Linguists in Uniform* (Japanese Studies Centre, Clayton, Vic., 2003), p. 247; Dan Hart, audiotaped interview with author, 13 July 2006.

24 Daniel Hart, *Fido & Friends* (Tempe Harvey, Brisbane, 2005), p. 288.

9. At the Kawana Hotel

1 'Complaints about Australian "Whites Only" Policy and Discrimination', NAA A5104 8/2/1 Part 2; see Peter Kalischer, 'Racial Bar Put up by BCOF Rest Hotels', *Nippon Times*, 18 September 1949.

2 See letter to Chifley, 2 November 1949, 'Complaints', NAA A5104 8/2/1 Part 2; Faubion Bowers, 'Reminiscences', transcription of interview with Beate Gordon (1960), p. 11, no. 394, Oral History Research Office, Butler Library, Columbia University, New York.

3 The prohibition on Aborigines and Torres Strait Islanders did not apply to those already serving in the AIF. See Richard A. Hall, *The Black Diggers* (Allen & Unwin, Sydney, 1989), p. 193; Chambers' denial: see 'Statement by the Minister for the Army', 16 November 1949; 'Copy of BCOF Signal' 1315001; see also Shaw Memorandum to the Secretary, Department of External Affairs, 21 October 1949, 'Complaints', NAA A5104 8/2/1, Part 2.

4 E.M. Forster, *A Passage to India* (1924; Penguin, London, 1979), pp. 23, 291–92. My italics.

5 Mark Gayn, *Japan Diary* (1948; Tuttle, Rutland, Vt., 1981), p. 300; Bowers, 'Reminiscences', p. 32.

6 Alan Rix (ed.), *Intermittent Diplomat: the Japan and Batavia diaries of W. Macmahon Ball* (Melbourne University Press, Melbourne, 1988), p. 75.

7 Ibid., pp. 21, 86.

8 Ibid., pp. 171, 175–76.

10. A Passage to Japan

1 Faubion Bowers in Thomas W. Burkman (ed.), *The Occupation of Japan: arts and culture* (The General Douglas MacArthur Foundation, Norfolk, Virginia, 1988), p. 204; Donald Richie, *The Japan Journals 1947–2004*, ed. Leza Lowitz (Stone Bridge Press, Berkeley, Cal., 2004), pp. 27–28; Donald Richie, *Where Are the Victors?* (1956; Tuttle, Tokyo, 1986), p. 41.

2 Richie (1986), p. 72.

3 Lorraine Stumm, *I Saw Too Much: a woman correspondent at war* (Write-On Group, Coopernook, NSW, 2000), pp. 128, 133, 135, 137.

4 Annetta Chisholm, AWM PR 85/292. Letters dated, in chronological

order, 18 November 1947; 16 December 1947; 20 December 1948; 29 December 1948; 16 June 1949.

5　Frank Clune, *Ashes of Hiroshima* (Angus & Robertson, Sydney, 1950), pp. 56, 60, 152.

6　See, for example, Pte. M.D. Guppy, 'A Japanese diary' (c.1948), AWM MSS 1618, p. 27.

7　Pat McKinnon, 'Families come home from Japan', *Woman's Day and Home*, 16 October 1950, p. 19; Paddy Power, audiotaped interview with author, 31 August 2005; Jennie Woods, *Which Way Will the Wind Blow?* (Jennie Woods, North Sydney, 1994), pp. 67–68; Joan Haigh, *With the "Y" and B.C.O.F. in Japan and Germany* (Joan Haigh, Australia, 1995), p. 84.

8　Rosa Donnelly, 'A Civilising Influence?', MA thesis (Swinburne, Melbourne, 1994), p. 111.

9　*BCOF Bound: for the women and children of the British Commonwealth Force in Japan* (BCOF, Hiroshima, 1946), pp. 12, 22, 24.

10　Ibid., pp. 1, 5, 7.

11　See 'Wives for Japan', *The Sun* (Melbourne), 1 May 1947.

12　'Canberra': Noreen McAllister, response to Roma Donnelly dated 21 May 1991, Roma Donnelly AWM MSS 1555; see Donnelly, 'A Civilising Influence?', pp. 117–18.

13　Hal Porter, *The Paper Chase* (Angus & Robertson, Sydney, 1966), p. 292; Walt Sheldon, *The Honorable Conquerors* (Macmillan, New York, 1965), p. 258.

14　Heather Arthur, personal correspondence, 3 May 2006.

15　See Alice Jackson, 'Australian Families Are Enjoying Life in Japan', *The Australian Women's Weekly*, 6 December 1947, pp. 20–21; Gladys Cory, letter dated 25 June 1947, provided by her son, Douglas. Excerpts from the letter were published in the Bellingen newspaper, the *Courier Sun* in July 1947.

16　Japan letters and diary of Mrs Elsie Boyd (photocopies provided by her daughter, Jennifer Collier).

17　Paddy Power, audiotaped interview with author, 31 August 2005; Betty Comeadow, audiotaped interview 18 December 2005 (Betty Comeadow died in early 2007); Olga Stubbe, 'Reminiscences of a year spent in occupied Japan 1947–1948', State Library of Victoria, MS 10429.

18　Letters and diary of Mrs Betty Page.

19 Letter to Rosa Donnelly 1 July 1991, in Rosa Donnelly papers AWM MSS 1555; see also Donnelly, 'A Civilising Influence?', pp. 115–16.

20 Clune (1950), p. 152; Hal Porter, *The Extra* (Angus & Robertson, Sydney, 1975), p. 21; Rosemary Jeanneret, response to Robin Gerster, 'A Cultural Study of the Occupation of Japan' questionnaire, 28 October 2004.

21 Geoff Ockerby, response to questionnaire, 15 January 2005; Jennifer Collier, response to questionnaire, 5 February 2005.

22 Geoff Ockerby, response to questionnaire, 15 January 2005; Lyn Thompson, response to questionnaire, 12 November 2004; 'wonderful time': Prudence Keys, audiotaped interview with author, 23 June 2005; 'idyllic': Judith Fisher, *B.C.O.F. Kids: collected memories of Japan 1947–2007* (J. Fisher, Geelong West, 2006), p. 49; 'artificial': Dorelle Ashford, response to questionnaire, 28 October 2004; Mrs D.J. Cory 'An Australian's Impressions of Japan', published in the Bellingen *Courier Sun*, 25 July 1947; extracts provided by her son, Douglas Cory.

23 See George and Max Bazzica in Fisher (2006), p. 26; see also Wendy Barry, response to questionnaire, 24 July 2006.

24 Reunions: see Adelle Makepeace, response to questionnaire, 7 November 2004; Elaine Ladyga, 'Memories of BCOF in Japan 1947 to 1952', unpublished pamphlet, 11 November 2004, p. 3.

25 Wendy Barry, in Fisher (2006), p. 23 and response to questionnaire, 24 July 2006; on visit to Mikimoto pearl farm, see Prudence Keys, audiotaped interview; see also Brenda Berry, in Fisher (2006), p. 32; Ockerby, response to questionnaire.

26 Wendy Barry in Fisher (2006), p. 23 and response to questionnaire; John Coghlan, response to questionnaire 16 November 2004.

27 Lyn Thompson, response to questionnaire; Norman Hogg, response to questionnaire, 1 November 2004. A schoolteacher in his working life, Norman Hogg taught the author geography and history at Burwood High School in suburban Melbourne in the late 1960s.

28 John Coghlan, response to questionnaire; Barry Demmler, response to questionnaire, 30 October 2004; Bruce Fisher, response to questionnaire; Brenda Berry, response to questionnaire, 1 December 2004; Margery Sullivan, response to questionnaire, 13 January 2005.

29 Margery Sullivan, letter to Hal Porter 19 July 1977; Porter (1966), p. 278; Rosemary Jeanneret, response to questionnaire, 28 October 2004.

30 George and Max Bazzica in Fisher (2006), p. 29.

31 John Hearnden, audiotaped interview with author, 17 August 2005.

32 See Brenda Berry, response to questionnaire, 1 December 2004; also Fisher (2006), pp. 32–33.

33 See Rosemary Jeanneret, response to questionnaire, 28 October 2004.

11. Honoured Tourists

1 John Morris, *The Phoenix Cup* (The Cresset Press, London, 1947), p. 44; Allan S. Clifton, *Time of Fallen Blossoms* (Cassell, London, 1950) p. 31.

2 Rosemary Jeanneret, response to Robin Gerster, 'A Cultural Study of the Occupation of Japan' questionnaire, 28 October 2004; see 'Summary of Major Investigations by BCOF S.I.B. Sections', Appendix A, History of B.C.O.F. Provost Service, AWM 114, 803/5/1; Hal Porter, *A Handful of Pennies* (1958); in Mary Lord (ed.), *Hal Porter* (University of Queensland Press, St Lucia, 1979), see pp. 161–62. The Iwakuni bridge was faithfully reconstructed, again without the use of a single nail, but with steel reinforcing, in 1953.

3 See Chris Coney, 'Hal Porter's Japans', *Ritsumeikan Journal of Asia Pacific Studies*, 11 (March 2003), see esp. pp. 106–07. Porter references: *The Watcher on the Cast-Iron Balcony* (Faber & Faber, London, 1963), p. 87; *The Actors* (Angus & Robertson, Sydney, 1968), p. 8; *The Paper Chase* (Angus & Robertson, Sydney, 1966), pp. 245, 262–63.

4 Porter (1968), p. 6; Arthur John, letter to author, 29 October 2004.

5 Pugh, letter to mother, 24 February 1946, NLA MS 9096, Papers of Clifton Pugh, Series 1; Clifton (1950), p. 157; Morris, p. 35; James Havelock Hawes, letter, 3 May 1946, AWM PR85/044.

6 L.H. Evers, *Pattern of Conquest* (Currawong, Sydney, 1954), p. 228; Clifton, p. 204; see 'Like the Circus', *Time* magazine, 29 October 1945.

7 Laurie Brocklebank, *Jayforce: New Zealand and the Occupation of Japan 1945–48* (Auckland, Oxford University Press, 1997), p. 110.

8 See Clement N. Govett, *The Story of the B.C.O.F. Tourist Club* (The Club, Hiroshima, 1950), p. 31.

9 Ibid. p. 38; Fuji trek: see Arthur John, *Uneasy Lies the Head that Wears a Crown* (The Gen Publishers, Cheltenham, Vic., 1987), pp. 102–03; William H. Coaldrake (ed.), *Japan from War to Peace* (RoutledgeCurzon, London, 2003), p. 299.

10 Norman ('Bluey') White, *How Bluey and Friends Occupied Japan 1946–1947* (Norman Stanley White, Wentworth Falls, NSW, 1991), pp. 54–55.

11 Phillip M. Green, *Memories of Occupied Japan* (Phillip Maxwell Green, Blackheath, NSW, 1987), pp. 119, 128, 134.

12 Clifton (1950), p. 7; Pte M.D. Guppy, 'A Japanese diary', AWM MSS 1618, pp. 38, 25; Pugh, letter to mother, 27 August 1946.

13 Alan Rix (ed.), *Intermittent Diplomat: the Japan and Batavia diaries of W. Macmahon Ball* (Melbourne University Press, Melbourne, 1988), p. 176.

14 Coaldrake (2003), pp. 308, 199, 201.

15 Porter (1968), pp. 195, 45.

16 Porter (1966), pp. 264–65.

17 Morris (1947), p. 60.

12. By Ground Zero

1 T. B. Millar, 'An Australian's Experiences of BCOF', in Ian Nish (ed.), *The British Commonwealth and its Contribution to the Occupation of Japan* (Suntory–Toyota International Centre, London, 1991), p. 21.

2 John Morris, *The Phoenix Cup* (The Cresset Press, London, 1947), p. 58.

3 See Yoshiteru Kosakai, *Hiroshima Peace Reader* (Hiroshima Peace Culture Foundation, Hiroshima, 13th edition, 2007), pp. 46–48.

4 See Carola Hein et al, *Rebuilding Urban Japan After 1945* (Penguin, Macmillan, New York, 2003), p. 96. See also www.arch-hiroshima. net.

5 MMA, R6.5 Box Z.F.5 "O.C., Aug–Dec. 46". Memos dated 20, 22 August 1946.

6 Lisa Yoneyama, *Hiroshima Traces* (University of California Press, Berkeley, Cal., 1999), p. 20.

7 Australian observer quoted in Herbert P. Bix, *Hirohito and the Making of Modern Japan* (Perennial, New York, 2001), p. 629; interview with Yoko Ota: see Robert Jay Lifton, *Death in Life: survivors of Hiroshima* (Simon and Schuster, New York, 1967), pp. 262–63.

8 See Kosakai (2007), pp. 20–21; Frank Clune, *Ashes of Hiroshima* (Angus & Robertson, Sydney, 1950), pp. 64, 86, 108.

9 William John Coffman, 'Impressions', *Scoshi Shinbun*, BCOF Association of NSW small newsletter (December 1992), p. 8.

10 Shirley Hazzard, *The Great Fire* (Virago, London, 2003) p. 8; Hazzard, 'A Writer's Reflections on the Nuclear Age', *Boston Review* (December 1981), http://bostonreview.net/BR06.6/hazzard.html.

11 Major A.W. John, *Duty Defined; Duty Done* (The Gen Publishers, Cheltenham, Vic., 2004), pp. 223–27.

12 HQ BCB, BCOF Monthly Intelligence Summary, no. 11 (for the month of February 1947), Appendix A, Attitude of BCOF Troops to the Japanese, p. 2, AWM 114 423/10/17.

13 R.C. Adkins, response to Robin Gerster, 'A Cultural Study of the Occupation of Japan' questionnaire, 21 November 2004.

14 C.G. Jones, response to questionnaire, 2 November 2004; Maurice Anderson, response to questionnaire, 21 January 2005; Allan S. Clifton, *Time of Fallen Blossoms* (Cassell, London, 1950), p. 158.

15 Paul Fussell, *Thank God for the Atom Bomb and Other Essays* (Summit Books, New York, 1990), pp. 25, 28, 39–41.

16 Don Nancarrow, response to questionnaire, 14 December 2004; Hazzard, 'A Writer's Reflections on the Nuclear Age'.

17 BCOF Intelligence Summary, no. 11; John C. Allen, response to questionnaire, 8 December 2004; Clune, pp. 89–90, 116–118.

18 Kenneth Harrison, *Road to Hiroshima* (Rigby, Adelaide, 1983), pp. 15, 265–66, 267.

19 Albert Tucker, 'Hiroshima 1947', Australian War Memorial collection 29483.

20 Kurihara quoted in John Whittier Treat, *Writing Ground Zero: Japanese literature and the atomic bomb* (University of Chicago Press, Chicago, 1995), pp. 42–43; Kenzaburo Oe, *Hiroshima Notes* (1965; Grove Press, New York, 1981), pp. 66–67. SCAP was still strenuously denying that survivors were dying of bomb-related disease in February 1946: see *Pacific Stars and Stripes*, 9 February 1946.

21 Eric Thornton, 'Atom Bomb Ruin Staggers Australians in Japan', the *Argus*, 10 February 1946; Lorraine Stumm, *I Saw Too Much* (Write-On Group, Coopernook, NSW, 2000), p. 140; Frank Hayter, response to questionnaire, 17 October 2004.

22 Albert Tucker, interview with Robin Hughes, ABC Radio National programme 'Verbatim', 14 February 1994. Full interview transcript www.australianbiography.gov.au/tucker/intertext3.html; Norm Craig, 'The Ashes of Hiroshima', and response to questionnaire, 12 March 2005.

23 G.M. Hollis, 'Reverie in Hiroshima', in *As You Were* (Australian War Memorial, Canberra, 1948), p. 153; see 'Clamavi Ad Te', *The Gen*, 1, no. 1 (19 August 1946), p. 3.

24 Christine Cheetham, response to questionnaire, 8 November 2004.

25 Mary Bros, response to questionnaire, 12 August 2005; Rosemary Jeanerret, response to questionnaire, 28 October 2004; Margery Sullivan, response to questionnaire, 13 January 2005.

26 Clune (1950), p. 103; also pp. 106–08; Stephen Kelen, *I Remember Hiroshima* (Hale & Iremonger, Sydney, 1983), pp. 52–54.

27 On Hiroshima tourism, see: Hal Porter, *A Handful of Pennies* (1958), in Mary Lord (ed.), *Hal Porter* (University of Queensland Press, St Lucia, 1980), pp. 161–62; Annetta Chisholm AWM PR85/292, letter, 23 August 1948; Harrison (1983), p. 266; Murray Elliott, *Occupational Hazards: a doctor in Japan and elsewhere* (Griffith University, Brisbane, 1995), p. 24.

28 Gordon Leed, personal correspondence, 25 November 2004; Leed, 'Sailing without a Chart', unpublished and undated manuscript, p. 157.

13. Sleeping with the Enemy

1 *Sir Richard Burton Personal Narrative of a Pilgrimage to Al-Madinah and Meccah*, vol. 1 (Longman, London, 1857), p. 85.

2 Allan S. Clifton, *Time of Fallen Blossoms* (Cassell, London, 1950), pp. 21–22.

3 Bede Wall, 'In the Army of Occupation: Japan 1946–47', unpublished and undated manuscript, p. 9; Wall, response to Robin Gerster, 'A Cultural Study of the Occupation of Japan' questionnaire, 8 October 2005.

4 Wall, 'In the Army of Occupation', pp. 10, 13; Pugh, letter to mother, 25 July 1946, NLA MS 9096, Papers of Clifton Pugh, Series 1; Pte M.D. Guppy 'A Japanese diary', AWM MSS 1618, p. 39; Arthur W. John, *Uneasy Lies the Head that Wears a Crown* (The Gen Publishers, Cheltenham, Vic., 1987), p. 106. See also Frank Lees, 'The Long Weekend', *Shimbun*, no. 118 (Spring 2005), p. 25.

5 James Hingston, *The Australian Abroad* (Sampson, Low, Marston, Searle, and Rivington, London, 1879), p. 62; George Ernest Morrison, *An Australian in China* (Horace Cox, London, 1985), p. 14; Hal Porter, 'House Girl', the *Bulletin*, 1 September 1954, p. 21; Alan Queale,

'Japan Diary', *As You Were* (Australian War Memorial, Canberra, 1947), pp. 189, 195; Pugh, letter to mother, 25 July 1946.

6 Murray Elliott, *Occupational Hazards: a doctor in Japan and elsewhere* (Griffith University, Brisbane, 1995), pp. 63–64; Guppy, p. 36; Les Denton, 'The Occupation', *Shinbun*, no. 71 (January–February 1996), pp. 27–29.

7 Lt Gen. John Northcott, *Know Japan* (The Rodney Press, South Yarra, Vic., 1946), p. 61.

8 See Elliott (1995), p. 68.

9 Major A.W. John, *Duty Defined; Duty Done* (The Gen Publishers, Cheltenham, Vic., 2004), p. 211; harassed house girls: see Jennie Woods, *Which Way Will the Wind Blow?* (Jennie Woods, North Sydney, 1994), p. 67.

10 'Butterflying around': see Eiji Takemae, *The Allied Occupation of Japan*, trans. Robert Ricketts and Sebastian Swann (2002; Continuum, New York, 2003), p. 79; on the 'six inch rule': see Donald Richie, 'The Occupied Arts', Mark Sandler (ed.), *The Confusion Era: art and culture of Japan during the Allied Occupation 1945–1952* (Arthur M. Sackler Gallery, Washington DC, 1988) p. 15.

11 John (2004), p. 270; *The Church Chronicle*, 1, no. 3 (November 1946).

12 Wall, 'In the Army of Occupation', p. 12.

14. Brides of Japan

1 W.E. Griffis, *The Mikado's Empire* (1876, Harper, New York, 1883), pp. 559–60.

2 James A. Michener, *Sayonara* (1954; Corgi Books, London, 1968), p. 127.

3 John Dower, *Embracing Defeat: Japan in the aftermath of World War II* (1999; Penguin, London, 2000), p. 134.

4 Keiko Tamura, *Michi's Memories: the story of a Japanese war bride* (Pandanus Books, Canberra, 2001), pp. 24, 26; L.H. Evers, *Pattern of Conquest* (Currawong, Sydney, 1954), p. 165.

5 *BCOF Bound* (BCOF, Hiroshima, 1946), p. 12; Douglas Mancktelow, *Atsuko and the Aussie* (DMA Press, Vancouver, 1991), p. 16.

6 HQ BCB, BCOF Monthly Intelligence Summary no. 11 (for the month of February 1947), p. 2, AWM 114, 423/10/17; Steve Macaulay, 'Our House Girl', in Larry Lacey, *BCOF: an unofficial history* (Larry

Lacey, Yamba, NSW, 1995), p. 83; Hisako letter contained in the Hawes papers, AWM PR85/044.

7   Mary Lord, *Hal Porter: man of many parts* (Random House, Sydney, 1993), p. 50; Hal Porter, *The Paper Chase* (Angus & Robertson, Sydney, 1950), pp. 269, 296–97, 303–4; Hal Porter, 'House Girl', the *Bulletin*, 1 September 1954, p. 22.

8   T.A.G. Hungerford, *Sowers of the Wind* (Angus & Robertson, Sydney, 1954), pp. 159, 198; T.A.G. Hungerford, 'Tourist with Haiku', in *A Knockabout with a Slouch Hat* (Fremantle Arts Centre Press, Fremantle, 1985), pp. 71–72; Michael Crouch, *The Literary Larrikin: a critical biography of T.A.G. Hungerford* (University of Western Australia Press, Perth, 2005), p. 117.

9   Hungerford (1954), p. 199; Evers (1954), p. 81; Hal Porter, *A Handful of Pennies* (1958), in Mary Lord (ed.), *Hal Porter* (University of Queensland Press, St Lucia, 1980), pp. 50, 66, 155.

10 'Pinkerton-like': see Hungerford (1985), p. 112; yellow progeny: Hungerford (1954), pp. 277, 199.

11 'The Scourge', in Lacey (1995), p. 142; Carlton Dawe, *A Bride of Japan* (Hutchinson, London, 1898), pp. 9, 62–4, 122, 158.

12 T.B. Millar, 'An Australian's Experiences in BCOF', in Ian Nish (ed.), *The British Commonwealth and Its Contribution to the Occupation of Japan* (Suntory–Toyota International Centre, London, 1991), p. 26.

13 See Yukiko Koshiro, *Trans-Pacific Racisms and the U.S. Occupation of Japan* (Columbia University Press, New York, 1999), pp. 159, 161, 163–64.

14 Australian fathered children: see Major A.W. John, *Duty Defined; Duty Done* (The Gen Publishers, Cheltenham, Vic., 2004), p. 322; Tamura (2001), p. 14; Walter Hamilton, transcript of ABC television broadcast, 'Foreign Correspondent' programme, 'Japan – Kure Kids', 9 August 2005. www.abc.net.au/foreign/content/2005/s1435277.htm.

15 Joan Haigh, *With the "Y" and B.C.O.F. in Japan and Germany* (Joan Haigh, Australia, 1995), pp. 26–27; Menzies govt.: see Rosa Donnelly, 'A Civilising Influence?' MA thesis (Swinburne, Melbourne, 1994), p. 23; the Ferguson Fund: see Tamura (2001), p. 96.

16 See Tamura (2001), pp. 24–27.

17 Immigration of Japanese women: Calwell's edict quoted in Routine Orders Part 1, 123 Transport Platoon War Diary April–May 1948, AWM 10/4/128.

18 Letter from Lt-Col Gordon King to Major Arthur John, 8 September 1987, quoted in John (2004), p. 328. See also Ron Orwin, *The Signal Continues* (Orwin, Logan Lea, Qld, 2006), p. 86.

19 Photographs of arrivals from Britain: *Sydney Morning Herald*, 9 March 1948; see Calwell, 'The Long Range Threat We Face', the *Argus*, 6 March 1948; 'public indecency': Calwell quoted in *Sydney Morning Herald*, 10 March 1948.

20 Henderson wife anecdote told in Orwin (2006), p. 87.

21 See John (2004), p. 323.

22 Mancktelow (1991), p. 20; Provost Monthly Résumé of Serious Incidents in the BCOF Area During Month Ending 31 May 1948, Deputy Assistant Marshal HQ BCOF, AWM 52 18/1/10.

23 See Hal Porter, *Mr Butterfry and Other Tales of the New Japan* (Angus & Robertson, Sydney, 1970); Gregory Clark, 'Across the Cultural Chasm', *The Australian*, 24 February 1973.

24 Reg Clancy, unpublished and untitled ms (2005), in author's possession. See also *Australia Society Review*, no. 2, (April–September 1958), p. 2.

15. Coming to Terms

1 T.A.G. Hungerford, *Sowers of the Wind* (Angus & Robertson, Sydney, 1954), p. 165; letter to the editor, *The Australian*, 18 October 1993, p. 10; Peter V. Russo, 'What is the Geisha Really Like?', *Argus* Week-End Magazine, 13 March 1948; T.A.G. Hungerford, 'Tourist with Haiku', in *A Knockabout with a Slouch Hat* (Fremantle Arts Centre Press, Fremantle, 1985), pp. 71–72.

2 Allan S. Clifton, *Time of Fallen Blossoms* (Cassell, London, 1950), p. 22; Douglas Mancktelow, *Atsuko and the Aussie* (DMA Press, Vancouver, 1991), p. 23; Keiko Tamura, *Michi's Memories* (Pandanus Books, Canberra, 2001), p. 69; Clifton (1950), pp. 75–76.

3 Les Oates, audiotaped interview with author, 26 July 2006; Beard: see Gregory Clark, 'Across the Cultural Chasm', *The Australian*, 24 February 1973.

4 On BCOF and the Japanese language: see Dan Hart, *Fido & Friends* (Tempe Harvey, Brisbane, 2005), p. 291; *BCOF Education News Sheet*, no. 22, 22 March 1946; Clifton (1950), p. 76, also Colin Funch, *Linguists in Uniform* (Japanese Studies Centre, Clayton, Vic., 2003), p. 243; HQ BCB, BCOF Monthly Intelligence Summary no. 11, for the month of February 1947, Appendix A, Attitude of BCOF Troops

to the Japanese, AWM 114 423/10/17; Les Oates, 'The Australian Experience of the Occupation, 1946 to 1952', in Paul Jones and Pam Oliver (eds), *Changing Histories: Australia and Japan* (Monash Asia Institute, Clayton, Vic., 2001), p. 81.

5 Major A.W. John, *Duty Defined; Duty Done* (The Gen Publishers, Cheltenham, Vic., 2004), p. 178.

6 See Funch (2003), pp. 243–44.

7 Ibid., pp. 244–45; Alex Weaver, response to Robin Gerster, 'A Cultural Study of the Occupation of Japan' questionnaire, 9 January 2006. Weaver anecdotes appear on www.bcofonline.com; Ralph Perrott, response to questionnaire, undated.

8 Stephen Kelen, 'New Australians – From Japan', *Sydney Morning Herald*, 12 April 1952.

9 Keith Lobb, response to questionnaire, 20 January 2005.

10 Christine de Matos, '"For Good or for Evil": Australia, labour reform and the military occupation of Japan', Conference Proceedings of the 15th Biennial Asian Studies Association of Australia, Canberra, 2004, esp. pp. 12–13. http://coombs.anu.edu.au/SpecialProj/ASAA/biennial-conference/2004/DeMatos-C-ASAA2004.pdf; B.L. Robinson, response to questionnaire, 19 November 2004.

11 Halton Stewart, response to questionnaire, 10 April 2005; Semken quoted in James Wood, *The Forgotten Force* (Allen & Unwin, Sydney, 1998), pp. 96–97, and interviewed in the documentary film *The Forgotten Force*, dir. Raymond Quint (Film Australia, 1993); Keith Reeves, response to questionnaire, 16 November 2004.

12 Richard A. Hines, personal correspondence, 1 November 2004.

13 William H. Coaldrake (ed.), *Japan From War to Peace* (RoutledgeCurzon, London, 2003), p. 157. See also 'Report on a Tour to Japan and the Philippines Dec 30th 1947 to March 11th 1948', p. 5, T. Inglis Moore Papers, NLA MS 8130 Series 8B, Folder 3.

14 Foster Barton, personal correspondence, 8 September 2005.

15 Veterans quoted in Larry Lacey, *BCOF: an unofficial history* (Larry Lacey, Yamba NSW, 1995), pp. 88–89; see also p. 81.

16 Pte M.D. Guppy, 'A Japanese diary', AWM MSS 1618, pp. 8–9; Hart (2005), pp. 290–91.

17 Geoffrey Collings, cinematographer, *Watch Over Japan*, AWM, FO1309.

18 Translation of the copperplate inscription monument provided by

Shizuo Inoue.

19 See Eric Saxon's BCOF story in www.australiansatwar.gov.au; C.F. Jarrett, response to questionnaire, 3 March 2005.

20 See John (2004), pp. 244–48.

21 Ibid., pp. 233–34.

22 See Stephen Kelen, 'Memories of Hiroshima' (1999), *Reveille*, Souvenir Collectors Edition 2003, p. 77.

23 Letters and other correspondence held by Bruce Fisher; letter from Teiko Yamashita to Frank Fisher, 24 November 1952; letter from Shigeko Akiyama to Frank Fisher, 28 May 1952.

16. Cultural Penetrations

1 Alison Broinowski, *The Yellow Lady: Australian impressions of Asia* (Oxford University Press, Melbourne, 1990), pp. 66–67.

2 See Les Murray, review of C. J. Koch, *The Year of Living Dangerously*, *Sydney Morning Herald*, 21 October 1978; Barbara Hogg, audiotaped interview with author, 24 June 2005.

3 Peter Russo, 'Australia and Japan', *Argus*, 27 July 1940; Pugh, letter to mother, dated 13 September 1946, NLA MS 9096, Papers of Clifton Pugh, Series 1; Stephen Kelen, 'The Day We Landed in Japan', *Shinbun*, no.54 (May–June 1993), p. 44.

4 Allan S. Clifton, *Time of Fallen Blossoms* (Cassell, London, 1950), pp. 202, 204; Louise Allen and Jean Wilson (eds), *Lafcadio Hearn: Japan's Great Interpreter: a new anthology* (Japan Library Ltd., Sandgate, UK, 1992), p. 195. Tony Clifton related to me the story of his father's cremation at a symposium on the Occupation held at the University of Wollongong, NSW, in November 2007.

5 Clifton (1950), pp. 145, 118–19, 175.

6 See HQ BCB, BCOF Monthly Intelligence Summary, no. 11 (for the month of February 1947), Appendix A, Attitude of BCOF Troops to the Japanese, AWM 114 423/10/17; Major A.W. John, *Duty Defined; Duty Done* (The Gen Publishers, Cheltenham, Vic., 2004), p. 180.

7 *The Gen*, 'Know Japan' articles quoted – on the women: 5, no. 1 (2 June 1947); 'brutality': 2, no. 8 (16 December 1946); 'revelation': 5, no. 2 (9 June 1947).

8 See John (2004), pp. 230, 351–52, 289–90.

9 Joan Haigh, *With the "Y" and B.C.O.F. in Japan and Germany* (Joan Haigh, Australia, 1995), pp. 46–47; Jean Westmore, audiotaped

interview with author, 9 March 2005.

10 Jean Westmore, interview and response to Robin Gerster, 'A Cultural Study of the Occupation of Japan' questionnaire, 31 October 2004.

11 See Anne Blair, *Ruxton: a biography* (Allen & Unwin, Sydney, 2004), p. 37; Norman (Bluey) White, *How Bluey and Friends Occupied Japan* (Norman White, Wentworth Falls, NSW, 1991), pp. 111.

12 White (1991), pp. 35–36.

13 Dan Hart, *Fido & Friends* (Tempe Harvey, Brisbane, 2005), p. 284.

14 See Kelen obituary, *Shimbun*, no. 114 (Sept. 2004), pp. 46–47; also Ian Stennard, 'The Way It Was …' www.sttta.org.au/the_way_it_was_.htm.

15 Stephen Kelen articles: 'Japan's Cult of Death', *Sydney Morning Herald*, 3 January 1942; 'What Sort of Person Is the Japanese Soldier?', the *Argus Weekend Magazine*, 24 January 1942; 'Japs Differ from Us in Many Little Things', the *Argus Weekend Magazine*, 6 June 1942.

16 Stephen Kelen, *I Remember Hiroshima* (Hale & Iremonger, Sydney, 1983), p. 30.

17 Ibid., p. 32.

18 See Sydney *Daily Telegraph*, 3 September 1945.

Conclusion: Remembering the Occupation

1 See for example, 'President Bush Discusses Iraq Policy at Whitehall Palace in London', 19 November 2003. http://www.state.gov/p/eur/rls/rm/2003/26360.htm. (US Department of State web site). John W. Dower, among others, has convincingly refuted glib comparisons between the two occupations. See 'History in the Remaking', *Los Angeles Times*, 8 December 2003; see also Dower, 'Occupations and Empires: why Iraq is not Japan', *Mercury News*, 9 May 2003.

2 'Some Reminiscences', Papers of Lt Gen. Sir H.C.H. Robertson, AWM PR87/167, p. 5.

3 W. Macmahon Ball, 'Australian Policy towards Japan since 1945' (1963), in Ball, *Australia and Japan: documents and readings in Australian history* (Thomas Nelson, Melbourne, 2000), p. 113.

4 On the 'depurge': see John Dower, *Embracing Defeat: Japan in the aftermath of World War II* (1999; Penguin, London, 2000), p. 272; Mark Gayn, *Japan Diary* (1948; Tuttle, Rutland, Vt, 1981) p. 303.

5 Women in Japan: see report in *Japan Times*, 23 November 2006; Bibles, Christians: see Toshio Nishi, *Unconditional Democracy* (Hoover Institution Press, Stanford, 1982), p. 43.

6 'Memos confirm secret Okinawa pact', *Japan Times*, 8 October 2007; see Gavan McCormack, *Client State: Japan in the American embrace* (Verso, London, 2007), pp. 122–23; on Japanese subsidisation of the US military, see McCormack (2007), p. 83.

7 David McNeill, 'In the Shadow of Hiroshima', *Japan Focus*, 25 March 2007, p. 2.

8 MacArthur's message as contained in cablegram from the Australian Mission in Japan to the Department of External Affairs in Canberra, 29 May 1950. NAA A 5104/2 8/2/1 Pt 2. Quoted in MacArthur, *Reminiscences* (McGraw Hill, New York, 1964), p. 323; state of BCOF in mid-1950: see David Horner, *Duty First: the Royal Australian Regiment in war and peace* (Allen & Unwin, Sydney, 1990), p. 57.

9 Patrick Knowles in Larry Lacey, *BCOF: an unofficial history* (Larry Lacey, Yamba, NSW, 1995), pp. 164–65; *Australian Society Review* (April–September 1958), p. 3.

10 Howard Schuler, audiotaped interview with author, 7 June 2006.

11 Paul Kelly, 'Security pact to deepen Japan ties', and Peter Nicholson cartoon, *The Weekend Australian*, 12–13 August 2006; letter writer: *The Age*, 15 March 2007.

12 Laurie Edwards, response to Robin Gerster, 'A Cultural Study of the Occupation of Japan' questionnaire, 20 November 2004; 'disappearing coastline': Maurice Anderson, response to questionnaire, 21 January 2005.

13 Allan Chick, letter, 23 July 1946, AWM 52 85/189.

14 Calwell in *Sydney Morning Herald*, 10 March 1948.

15 R.T. Foster, 'Our Soldiers Like the Japanese', *The Sunday Herald* (Sydney), 20 January 1952; Allan Chick, letter dated 2 June 1952, AWM PR52 85/189; Colin Simpson, *The Country Upstairs* (Angus & Robertson, Sydney, 1956), pp. 5–6.

16 Brian Rose, report on RSL National Executive Visit to Japan 19–30 November 2003, (in author's possession); Norm White, audiotaped interview with author, 25 September 2006.

17 Christine de Matos, 'Aussies who aren't Aussies', *The Australian*, 29 January 2008.

18 On suppressing the experience, see Judith Fisher, *B.C.O.F. Kids: collected memories of Japan 1947–2007* (J. Fisher, Geelong West, 2006), pp. 3, 50. Gail Young, response to questionnaire, 19 October 2004; Kerry Seipolt, response to questionnaire, 26 October 2004; Margery

Sullivan, personal correspondence, 13 January 2005; Wendy Barry, personal correspondence, 24 July 2006.

19 Dean Wells, response to questionnaire, 2 November 2004.

20 Glenda Gauci obituary: Philippa Brear, 'Pioneering diplomat bridged cultural divides', *The Age*, 7 September 2006; numbers of war brides: see Keiko Tamura, 'Home Away from Home: the entry of Japanese war brides into Australia', in Vera Mackie and Paul Jones, *Relationships* (University of Melbourne, Parkville, Vic., 2001), pp. 258–59.

21 Frank Akhurst, personal correspondence, 25 November 2004; removal of colour patches: see Peter Bates, *Japan and the British Commonwealth Occupation Force 1946–52* (Brassey's, London, 1993), p. 178.

22 Veteran quoted: Halton Stewart, personal correspondence to author, 10 April 2005. On the issue of official indifference to BCOF illnesses, see Alan Ramsey, 'Old soldier gets the mushroom treatment again', *Sydney Morning Herald*, 25–26 August 2007; Larry Lacey on BCOF cancers, *Shinbun*, no. 71 (January–February 1996), p. 31.

23 Murray Elliott, *Occupational Hazards: a doctor in Japan and elsewhere* (Griffith University, Brisbane, 1995), p. 24; Rosemary Jeanneret, response to questionnaire, 28 October 2004; Frank Clune, *Ashes of Hiroshima* (Angus & Robertson, Sydney, 1950), pp. 95–96.

24 Scepticism: see Ryann Connell, 'Hibakusha: Occupation's Aussie atomic veterans still fighting for recognition', *Mainichi Daily News*, 9 August 2007; BCOF lament: see Lacey, (1995), p. 4.

25 J.G. Collins, *The War of the Veterans* (John G.F. Collins, Toowoomba, Qld, 2001), p. vii; see also p. 38.

26 Dower (2000), p. 73.

27 Macdonald Hull, *Snow on the Pine* (Hammond Hammond, London, 1956), pp. 77–78.

28 Bob Christison, personal correspondence, 19 October 2004; 'best disciplined': see Lacey (1995), p. 3.

29 Beverley Waldie, personal correspondence, 15 November 2004.

Afterword

1 Ian Buruma. *The Wages of Guilt: memories of war in Germany and Japan* (Meridian, New York, 1995), p. 94.

2 Carrington Clarke, 'Australia and Japan reverse tourism relationship', ABC News, 16 January 2018, http://www.abc.net.au/news/2018-01-16/australia-and-japan-reverse-tourism-relationship/9332518

Accessed 1 Jan 2019. Julia Baird, 'Australian tourists risk turning Japan into another Bali', *Sydney Morning Herald*, 19 October 2018, http://www.smh.com.au/world/asia/australian-tourists-risk-turning-japan-into-another-bali-20181019-p50aph.html Accessed 19 October 2018.

3   John Whittier Treat, *Writing Ground Zero: Japanese literature and the atomic bomb* (Chicago: The University of Chicago Press, 1995), p. 9.

4   Peter Ryan, 'Saved by the atom bomb', *The Australian*, 16 August 2008, https://www.theaustralian.com.au/news/inquirer.saved-by-the-atom-bomb/news-story/2c189cc7467878de7bc875d767df31c9 Accessed 24 December 2018.

5   See, for example, Tim Colebatch, 'Epiphany at Hiroshima for deeply moved Rudd', *Sydney Morning Herald*, 10 June 2008, https://www.smh.com.au/national/epiphany-at-hiroshima-for-deeply-moved-rudd-20080609-2nzg.html Accessed 17 December 2018.

6   Harry Roskolenko, 'Tokyo Letter', *Meanjin*, 6 no. 1 (autumn 1947), p. 64.

7   Agnieszka Sobocinska, *Visiting the Neighbours: Australians in Asia* (NewSouth Publishing, Sydney, 2014), p. 77.

8   See Christine De Matos, *Imposing Peace and Prosperity: Australia, social justice and labour reform in occupied Japan* (Australian Scholarly Publishing, North Melbourne, 2008).

9   'Introduction', Ian Nish (ed.), *The British Commonwealth and the Allied occupation of Japan, 1945–1952: personal encounters and government assessments* (Global Oriental, Leiden, 2013), p. 16.

10 'Menzies Pleads: "Hate the Japs No Longer"', *The Argus*, 18 March 1954, p. 1.

11 'Kishi Offers Apology for Japanese War', *Canberra Times*, 5 December 1957, p. 1.

12 See account of meeting of Prime Ministers Abbott and Abe in Canberra in July 2014: 'Putting meat on the bones of a 1957 agreement', *The Australian*, 21 July 2014, p. 10. See also 'Tony Abbott says Japan is Australia's "closest friend in Asia"', *The Australian*, 9 October 2013, p.1. See also Melisa Miles and Robin Gerster, *Pacific Exposures: Photography and the Australia-Japan Relationship* (ANU Press, Acton ACT, 2018), p.168.

13 Natsume Soseki, *And Then* (1909), trans. Norma Moore Field, (Louisiana State University Press, Baton Rouge, 1978), n. 11, p.120.

14 Eiji Takemae, *The Allied Occupation of Japan*, trans. Robert Ricketts

and Sebastian Swann (2002; Continuum, New York, 2003), p. 135.

15 Neil C. Smith, *Disarming the Menace: Australian soldiers with the British Commonwealth Occupation Forces Japan 1946–1952* (Mostly Unsung Military History, 2012), pp. 4, 9.

16 See, for example, Oscar Wills, 'Commonwealth Occupation Force veterans continue to fight for recognition for work in post-WWII Japan', ABC News, 31 October 2018, https://www.abc.net.au/2018-10-31/commonwealth-occupation-force-veterans-continue-fight/10433398 Accessed 17 December 2018.

Index